The McGraw-Hill

HANDBOOK OF BUSINESS LETTERS

The McGraw-Hill
HANDBOOK OF BUSINESS LETTERS

Roy W. Poe

McGRAW-HILL BOOK COMPANY

New York   St. Louis   San Francisco   Auckland
Bogotá   Hamburg   Johannesburg   London   Madrid
Mexico   Montreal   New Delhi   Panama   Paris
São Paulo   Singapore   Sydney   Tokyo   Toronto

Library of Congress Cataloging in Publication Data

Poe, Roy W., date.
   The McGraw-Hill handbook of business letters.

   Includes index.
   1. Commercial correspondence—Handbooks, manuals,
etc.   I. Title.   II. Title: Handbook of business
letters.
HF5726.P55 1983   808′.066651021   82-18017
ISBN 0-07-050367-2

567890   HAL/HAL   898765

ISBN 0-07-050367-2

The editors for this book were William A. Sabin and Christine
Ulwick, the design supervisor was Mark E. Safran, the designer
was Dennis Sharkey, and the production supervisor was Thomas
G. Kowalczyk. It was set in ITC Bookman Light by University
Graphics, Inc.
Printed and bound by Halliday Lithograph.
Layout by Small Kaps Associates, Inc.

CONTENTS

**PART 5
LETTERS TO
CUSTOMERS**

**Section 15   Letters of Appreciation and
Congratulation   135**

**Section 16   Apologizing for Delays and
Errors   141**

**Section 17   Handling Misunderstandings With
Customers   147**

CONTENTS

ABOUT THIS HANDBOOK

Nearly everyone with writing responsibilities occasionally faces a problem of composing "just the right letter" in a situation that he or she has not met up with before. This statement can be verified by librarians, bookstore proprietors, communication specialists, and others who frequently receive requests for a certain model that will guide the writer in framing the appropriate letter.

Over the years I have conducted letter-writing clinics in various companies and at several universities for front-line supervisors, department managers, business owners, and others with a wide variety of managerial responsibilities. Some came with virtually no letter-writing experience; others were veteran communicators who felt the need for refresher training. Because such programs rarely extended beyond 24 classroom hours, I was forced to concentrate on basic principles and hope that the students could apply them successfully to any problem they faced on the job. And, generally speaking, they could. Yet I learned that a surprising number of situations arose when these people were really stuck; they needed to *see* an actual model—not necessarily to copy but to trigger ideas.

That, in short, is the reason why this handbook was written. In it you'll find the answer to the question, How do I go about writing a letter to:

- "Congratulate" an individual who is retiring from the company involuntarily because of age or health?
- Respond to an irate and thoroughly abusive critic of my company's policy or stance on a particular issue (employment, service, prices, advertising, etc.)?

- Explain to good customers that when returned merchandise is unsalable, it cannot be accepted for credit?
- Express grave concern to a usually reliable supplier who botched the same order four times in a row?
- Answer a request for information about a former employee who was fired for incompetence?
- Resign from a position because a promise of promotion was not kept?
- Request special favors from people who have little, if anything, to gain by granting them?
- Warn a valuable employee of termination because of indiscretions in dealing with company secrets?
- Deny a request for information that the company considers confidential?
- Prepare an impressive job résumé and an accompanying application letter when I need or want to change jobs?

And so on. All these situations—plus more than 150 others covered in this handbook—were selected because they are the ones you are most likely to encounter, no matter where you work or what you do.

WHY THIS HANDBOOK?

Letter-writing handbooks have been around for a very long time, so the idea is not new. Most of those in paperback seem to be written for people outside the business arena and concentrate heavily on "bread-and-butter" notes and other social communications. (Some even have models of love letters.) Those published for business people deal almost exclusively with sales and promotion letters, with a hefty swipe at collection letters. Besides being highly specialized, the handbooks that I know about are too antiquated in language, style, and tone to be really useful to today's business letter writer.

In preparing this handbook, I chose those letter-writing situations that are commonly faced by all people in business, independent of their job title or job function. I deliberately avoided highly specialized situations. In the first place, it would be impossible in one volume to thoroughly cover the job-specific situations that would be encountered by a controller, personnel or PR director, purchasing executive, manufacturing manager, marketing director, company attorney, credit manager, and so on. Moreover, many organizations have their own policies and manuals to guide their personnel in writing letters of a specialized nature. For example, food and beverage distributors know exactly what to say to people who write to them complaining about impurities found in their products;

utility companies have form letters to answer the thousands who criticize them for poor service and exhorbitant rates; airlines have developed models for dealing with complaints from passengers whose luggage has been irretrievably lost or who choked from cigarette smoke during a trip; and so on. Such communications are handled by highly trained personnel (often with the aid of the company attorney). Therefore, I chose only those models that will be of the greatest help to the greatest number.

FOUR UNIQUE FEATURES

Four features of *The McGraw-Hill Handbook of Business Letters* make it a unique reference:

1. A wide variety of letter-writing situations are covered—from asking for special favors to saying no with the least possible offense to terminating an employee by mail.
2. The situation that precedes each model tells the reader why the letter is written and what the writer hopes to achieve in composing it.
3. The analysis that runs alongside each communication explains its organization, style, tone, and underlying psychology.
4. The number and title of each communication make it easy to locate the precise model that you're looking for.

Although this is primarily a reference book, I strongly encourage you to give careful attention at the outset to the general discussions—all of Part One and the kick-off material for each of the remaining parts and sections. It is here that the basic principles of good letter writing are emphasized. These principles will provide you with a solid foundation for communicating effectively and help you create your own letters with greater confidence and independence.

A FINAL WORD

No two people will or should approach a letter situation in the same way. The letter that is actually written will depend on who the writer is, who the reader is and what relationship he or she has to the writer, what the problem (if any) is, and what the writer expects to accomplish. There are as many different ways of writing a good letter as there are letter-writing problems. My principal objective in this handbook is to stimulate your thinking and, based on the models given, help you to write letters that accomplish what you want to accomplish.

Roy W. Poe

PART 1

THE LETTER-WRITER'S CRAFT

Over the years, a lot of fuss has been made over the high cost of business letters. And with justification. When you think about such elements as stationery and postage, the writer's time, the secretary's time, and overhead expenses—the cost of a single letter can boggle the mind. Each time a new study is made by cost-conscious executives, there's usually a mad scramble to trim this expense. It seems impossible that an average letter might cost $5, $10, or even $15 to put in the mail, so when one of these figures is arrived at, out goes the pronouncement: Write fewer letters! Write shorter letters! Use form letters more often! And so on.

We are frank to admit that letter-writing costs are much too high in many companies. A few people do write too many letters. Many, many individuals write letters that are a good deal longer than they need to be. And form letters, in some instances, can save money without tarnishing the organization's image.

But let's be realistic. The dollars *spent* to put a letter in the mail can be inconsequential when compared to the dollars *lost* by writing a bad letter (or no letter at all). A terse, quickly tossed-off message to a highly valued customer may delight the cost accountant with its economy, but could result in a diminution or total loss of that customer's business. Thus it could be an incredibly expensive "inexpensive" letter.

Letters are not merely mediums of communication. They are effective substitutes for face-to-face visits, making and keeping friends, attracting and holding customers, and building a favorable image for your company.

In this part, we offer several suggestions on how you can make your letters do all these things, with emphasis on triggering greater profits by writing effective messages.

1

WHAT A GOOD BUSINESS LETTER IS—AND IS NOT

If you have ever taken a course in business letter writing, chances are you learned that a good letter is brief, friendly, conversational, tactful, unfailingly courteous, clear, and interesting. You were probably also told that every letter you write is a sales letter; that is, you're always selling something—a product, a service, a company image, yourself, or simply an idea. And you were cautioned to handle responses to all communications promptly, meaning within a day or two.

It's hard to quarrel with these rules because most of them make good sense for most letters. But watch that phrase, *for most letters.*

It's easy to make lists of rules for doing things, and anybody can do it. Rules for writing good letters are no exception. Many large companies publish manuals for letter writers that are essentially rulebooks. Unfortunately, the rules supplied don't always work. The reason is that they are usually established to fit ideal conditions, and unfortunately communication situations are not always ideal. If you're answering an inquiry from a potential customer who is genuinely interested in your company's products, you can simply grab your list of rules and you're off and running. Your letter is friendly, tactful, personal, courteous, sales-structured, and the rest. But what if you're a credit manager and you have to write a fifth letter to a dealer who appears to have no intention of paying the $2500 that is now sixteen months past due? What happens to your warmth, friendliness, tact, courtesy, and so on? Here you can close your rule book. Nothing in it is going to work; you've used up all the "good" rules in the first four letters. Now you're going to have to write an "or-else" letter that will sound about as friendly as a wounded grizzly.

One more example why rules don't work. You've been told since you were 3 years old that you never cross the street against a red light. That seems like a good, safe rule for everyone. But now you're a lot older. You are in a big city trying desperately to get a cab to take you to an important meeting. It's pouring rain. Finally, the driver of an empty taxi across the street sees you, but notes that you have a red light and is about to move on. We won't say what *you* would do, but we're willing to bet that you will glance quickly at the traffic picture, and if it's okay you'll sprint. Goodbye rules!

WHAT IS A GOOD LETTER?

Maybe you think we've started off this discussion negatively, talking about the unpleasant side of letter writing. Certainly we don't want to give the impression that letter writers are Simon Legrees at heart. But we're just as anxious that you don't get the impression that good letters are always tidings of great joy. Many excellent letters are not brief or friendly or interesting or salesy or even courteous. Letters are simply human contacts on paper. You know that, in your daily dealings with people, there are sometimes strong differences of opinion, that some individuals are cranky and urereasonable, that tempers flare when stupid mistakes generate agonizing crises. The true utopia is not likely to be found in any organization where there are pressures for performance, profits, or productivity. So why should it exist *between* organizations?

On the other hand, most employees are intelligent enough to know that it's a lot more fun to work in a place where there is harmony and an atmosphere of good cheer, that surliness and bickering affect not only attitudes, but productivity. So, thank goodness, most workers bring their "company manners" (learned at home) to the workplace.

Thus it is with business letters. Those who write them should display their "company" behavior, striving very hard to make or keep friends, generate goodwill, and enhance sales opportunities.

Maybe now we're ready for an informal definition of a good business letter. *A good business letter is one that obtains the results the writer hoped for.* To make this definition work, we have to assume that the writer wants what is best for (1) the organization he or she works for and (2) the individual to whom the letter is addressed.

READER-WRITER RELATIONSHIPS

The definition we've just given you sounds simple and workable. But don't be misled; a good letter can be very difficult to write. One reason is that people are so different.

Let's say you were several days late getting a contract in the mail (it was accidentally filed instead of mailed), and you wrote something like this to John Doe in response to his inquiry about the contract:

WHAT A GOOD BUSINESS LETTER IS—AND IS NOT

It's too bad you were inconvenienced by our delay in mailing the service contract to you . . .

Doe may be happy with your apology and accept it with appreciation.

However, Richard Roe might view your response in an entirely different light. Perhaps he thinks that your statement "It's too bad . . ." is simply a crocodile tear, that you're being a smart-aleck. It's hard to know how a person will react to something you've said. How can you predict a reader's reaction? You really can't. You just have to try to avoid, if you can, statements that would offend anybody—a big order indeed. Miss Crump, the first-floor receptionist, may beam ecstatically when told "That new hair style makes you look ten years younger," and think about it pleasantly all day. Miss Dooley on the second floor may thank you sweetly for the same compliment, then brood the rest of the day about how old she must have looked before the trip to the hair stylist!

Not only people, but circumstances, can affect the reaction you receive. Let's say you wrote a beautifully apologetic letter to Customer A explaining why for the fourth time in two months the wrong merchandise was shipped, and the response you received was something like this:

That's understandable; we make our share of mistakes, too. Think nothing of it.

"Wow," you think, "that was some letter I wrote!" And justifiably so. The reaction you got was exactly what you'd hoped for.

But Customer B got the same elegant explanation for four similar boners, and the response you got from her was:

I'm fed up. No matter what you say, I can't ignore the shabby way you've handled my four orders. I've lost a lot of business because of you, and I want nothing more to do with you.

How is it possible to win and lose with the same letter? The two readers and/or their circumstances may be entirely different. Customer A may have had plenty of stock in the warehouse and was not inconvenienced much by getting the wrong merchandise. Or he may be a long-time satisfied customer and have many personal friends in the company. Or he may owe you a favor for some special service. Perhaps he's a person who doesn't rile easily.

On the other hand, Customer B may own a small business with a limited inventory, and any delay in getting the right merchandise could be disastrous. Or she may be a new customer who has placed only four orders with your company, all of which were fouled up. Or she may simply have a short fuse, not uncommon among harried business owners.

Except for mass-produced letters (such as sales-promotion letters that are sent to thousands of people), nearly every letter-writing situation is different. Let's look at another example. As credit manager, you know that Eleanor Brown, an important customer for twenty years, is slow in paying her bills. Sometimes several months go by without your receiving any money from her, but she always settles up eventually, and you'd hate to lose her as a customer. Her account balance is now $5660, and she has paid nothing for six months, though you've sent her several gentle reminders. The tone of your letter is friendly, as it should be:

Dear Mrs. Brown:

I'm getting ready to prepare our semiannual schedule of long overdue accounts, and I'd like to leave your name off the list. Your check for $5660 will do the trick.

Thank you, and best personal wishes.

Sincerely,

Robert J. Smith is a new customer. Five months ago he placed an order in the amount of $1320 on terms of sixty days. He has bought nothing since and has ignored six follow-ups, each progressively more somber in tone. You've begun to think that Smith has no intention of paying.

Are you likely to write the same letter to Smith that you wrote to Brown? If you're a good credit manager, you won't. Here the risk is great that you will lose money, and it seems obvious that Smith is not the kind of loyal customer you'll turn handsprings to save. Following is the letter you are apt to write.

Dear Mr. Smith:

I've had no response to my six requests for payment of the amount you owe—$1320—not even an explanation. Unless I hear from you by April 12—one week from today—your account will be placed in the hands of our collection agency.

Very truly yours,

Perhaps the two letters above prove that people and circumstances often determine the kinds of letters you write. Though the two letters could hardly be more different, each is good if it results in full payment of the money owed. We'd like to assume that Mrs. Brown sent her check in a not-unhappy mood and will continue to buy from you. It won't be very important, however, what Smith's mood is!

So to be a good letter writer, you have to know as much as possible about the person or persons who will read the correspondence. For some people this is fairly easy. A lot of writers know their readers simply because they deal with them so often. Others have to depend mainly on their imagination, since most of the individuals they write to are strangers. But even here there are often clues—the company they work for, their importance as revealed by their job title, something about their personality as indicated by *what* they do, and so on. Even the person who writes a promotional letter to 50,000 people (names obtained from a mailing list) to persuade them to subscribe to, say, *Digest of Current Books* will usually have some information about their educational level, approximate income, primary interests, size of family, and so on. Certainly the writer promoting renewal subscriptions to *Progressive Farmer* or *Sports Afield* or *Car and Driver* will have a fairly accurate bead on the readers.

Although there are very few hard-and-fast rules for good letter writing, most people will respond favorably to your letters if you observe the following guidelines when possible:

- *Don't waste words.*
- *Keep the language lively and simple.*
- *Personalize your letters.*
- *Emphasize the positive.*
- *Use correct letter form.*

SECTION 2
DON'T WASTE WORDS

The writer who takes 200 words to say what might have been said just as well in 40 is a nuisance, a time-waster. It has been estimated that about one-third of the words in the typical business letter are wasted words.

Don't get the idea, though, that you should always write in a telegraphic style. Sometimes you may want to include words that aren't really necessary, but that do add warmth and friendliness, and this results in a two-page letter. That's fine. The wasted words we refer to are those that clutter your message without adding anything to it—indeed, that detract from your message.

CLUTTER WORDS AND PHRASES

If you want to be an effective letter writer, start now to edit your writing to eliminate nonsense words and phrases, repetition, and redundancies. For example:

ORIGINAL (UNEDITED)

With reference to your request for an extension on your note under date of March 20, we have considered the matter carefully and are pleased to tell you that we will be willing to allow you an additional ninety days to make payment on your note.

ORIGINAL (EDITED)

With reference to your request for an extension on your note under date of March 20, we have considered the matter carefully and are pleased to tell you that we will be willing to allow you an additional ninety days to make payment on your note, dated March 20.

The edited version now reads as follows:

We are pleased to allow you an additional ninety days to pay your note dated March 20.

Note that the original paragraph contains forty-six words; the revision, seventeen. As you can see, there was no sacrifice in clarity by eliminating the clutter words and phrases; indeed, the message has been strengthened by this surgery.

Other examples follow on the next page.

ORIGINAL (56 WORDS)

With reference to your recent request for fifty reprints of "How Good Are Sales Aptitude Tests?" in the May issue of *Modern Marketing Management*, these copies are enclosed for your convenience.

With appreciation for your kind remarks about this article and trusting you will find it very useful in your recruitment seminar in October, I remain,

Yours very truly,

EDITED (31 WORDS)

Here are your fifty reprints of "How Good Are Sales Aptitude Tests?" I'm pleased you like the article and hope it will be exactly what you need for your recruitment seminar.

Sincerely yours,

ORIGINAL (115 WORDS)

In looking at your current catalog, I notice that the emergency couch on page 50 (No. 273-1960) is shown in the illustration in the color of blue. However, in the description provided under the illustration, the colors listed as being available are black, ivory, green, and red. Does this mean that the color of the couch in the illustration is not available at this time?

If I could obtain the blue vinyl, which would match our decor, I would place an order in the near future for four at the price of $118.50 each. But I do not wish to order any of the other colors that you list in your description in the catalog.

Very cordially yours,

EDITED (39 WORDS)

Is the emergency couch on page 50 of your catalog available in the blue vinyl illustrated? The colors listed as available do not include blue.

If the blue vinyl couch is available, I will place an order for four.

Very cordially yours,

Compare the following.

Unedited	Edited
your check in the amount of $360	your check for $360
keep in mind the fact that	remember that
engaged in making a salary study	making a salary study
held a meeting to discuss	met to discuss
during the course of our research, we learned that	our research revealed that

until such time as you are in a position to	when you are able to
at this point in time	at this time
an extremely important element in building employee morale is the matter of recognition	recognition is extremely important in building employee morale
in the event that	if
a large segment of the employees are of the opinion that	many employees believe that
the size of the report is 112 pages in length	the report contains 112 pages
I hope you will be able to put in a brief appearance	I hope you can drop in for a few minutes
it is the recommendation of the operations committee that	the operations committee recommends that
the treasurer made the announcement that	the treasurer announced that
there was only one objection to your proposal, and that was the matter of timing	the only objection to your proposal was timing
the manufacturing costs were quite a bit lower than any of us thought they would be	the manufacturing costs were much lower than expected
I hope you will be in a position to make a decision within a short time	I hope you can decide soon
the difficulty with the present stock control system is that it cannot be depended on	the present stock control system is not dependable
upon completion, please mail the application in the envelope that is being enclosed	please mail the completed application in the envelope enclosed
these tractors are being sold at a price of $2995	these tractors are priced at $2995

REPETITION

A common fault of some letter writers is repeating themselves. Following are examples.

Repetitive

1. Most industrial relations specialists recommend that *employees participate* in job evaluation, although many employers think that *employee participation* is not desirable.

2. Although it is our policy to *accept returned merchandise* that is in good condition, *returned merchandise* that is not salable cannot be *accepted.*

3. When we print your *form letters,* your customers will not recognize them as *form letters.* The *letters* will appear to be individually typewritten.

4. It is *possible,* of course, that the damage occurred because of faulty packing. An even greater *possibility* is that the *shipper* was careless in storing the merchandise for safe *shipment.* In any event, we'll do everything *possible* to *ship* a replacement this week.

Edited

1. Most industrial relations specialists recommend that employees participate in job evaluation, although many employers do not share this point of view.

2. We accept only merchandise that can be resold.

3. When we print your form letters, your customers will think they were individually typewritten.

4. It is possible, of course, that the damage was the result of faulty packing. More likely, however, the carton was stored improperly by the shipper. In any event, we'll try to send a replacement this week.

Another form of repetition—redundancy—is illustrated in the following.

Redundant

meets Thursday mornings at 10:00 o'clock a.m.

first and foremost

prompt and speedy

assemble together

consensus of opinion

baffling and puzzling

invisible to the eye

Edited

meets Thursday mornings at ten (or 10:00)

first *or* foremost

prompt *or* speedy

assemble

consensus

baffling *or* puzzling

invisible

Redundant	Edited
the only other alternative	the only alternative
repeat again	repeat
the new procedure will begin to be initiated	the new procedure will begin (or take effect)
contractual agreement	contract *or* agreement
fiscal financial year	fiscal year
agree and concur	agree *or* concur
free gratis	free *or* gratis
massively large	massive
true facts	facts
vitally essential	vital *or* essential
and etc.	etc.
endorse on the back	endorse
revert back	revert
new beginner	beginner

WASTED WORDS VERSUS BREVITY

In spite of our earlier admonition, you may by now have the idea that brevity is a cardinal virtue in business letters. Not so! Brevity can be a curse if you leave something important out of your letters or wind up with a message that has no life.

More often than not, your relationship to your reader will determine the length of your letters. Let's say you recently attended a training directors' convention in Duluth where you heard a speaker describe a new series of sales motivation films her company is distributing. As a training director, you're interested in the films and decide to write for information. (You did not meet the speaker personally, so she will not remember you.) Here is what you might write.

Dear Mrs. Ashforth:

I thoroughly enjoyed your talk at the AATD convention in Duluth and was especially interested in the new series of sales motivation films your company is about to release.

Would you please send me complete details? If I could borrow one of the films temporarily, I will see that it is returned within a week.

Sincerely yours,

That's a good letter—no wasted words, but specific and friendly. But suppose that the speaker you heard in Duluth turned out to be an old college friend whom you haven't seen for two or three years. You had no chance to chat with her, but you want more information on the films she spoke about.

Dear Carla:

It was great seeing you at AATD in Duluth—what a pleasant surprise! I thought your talk was super, and the rest of the audience was obviously equally impressed.

As training director here at Rothmere's, I'm always searching for new things. We're not happy with our sales training materials, and I'm intrigued by your new series of motivation films.

Would you send me complete details? What are the chances of my borrowing one of the films for viewing by several people here? I promise to take good care of it and get it back within a week.

I'm sorry we didn't have a chance to visit in Duluth, but you were mobbed as soon as the meeting broke up, and I had to dash for a plane. If you ever get to Cincinnati or I to Monterey, we've got a lot of catching up to do! Did you know that Tim Grubbs is now the new assistant manager of the Singapore Hilton?

                              Cheers,

In very routine situations, the length of your letters is a matter of personal preference. Suppose, for example, you saw an advertisement in a financial magazine inviting readers to write the senior vice president for a copy of the company's latest annual report. Here is the letter you might write:

Dear Mr. Weber:

Please send me your latest annual report.

                              Sincerely yours,

Mr. Weber, or perhaps a subordinate who takes care of such matters, will know what you want and, assuming you write on your company's letterhead, where to send it.

Another person might write quite a different letter.

Dear Mr. Weber:

Please send me the latest annual report of Bardex, Inc., referred to in your ad in the June issue of *Financial Monthly*.

I have been following with great interest the growth of Bardex in recent years and am eager to learn more about its increasing involvement in energy conservation.

                              Sincerely yours,

Is the second letter better? Not necessarily. It is likely to elicit the same response as the first one in this particular instance because the chances are good that neither Weber nor anyone else of importance will see the letter. So the choice boils down to what *you* think you ought to say.

KEEP THE LANGUAGE
LIVELY AND SIMPLE

Too many writers have the notion that big words are signs of literacy and high intelligence. We harped on "big-wordism" earlier, but this malady deserves a fuller treatment. No matter how many communication experts warn against pretentious speaking and writing—bombast—government leaders, sociologists, educators, business executives, and others merrily continue to communicate in an unknown tongue. It would seem to be a game in which the winners are those who can speak and write the foggiest prose.

We do not discount the importance of a rich vocabulary. There are many useful big words for which there is no satisfactory substitute. As long as you use them correctly and are certain that your readers or listeners are not baffled by them, go right ahead. They can add spice to your writing.

But in letters that you write to employees, customers, and the general public, put away your lexicon (a fancy word for dictionary) and choose the word that you know is familiar to most people. Nearly everybody responds more warmly to the word *home* than to *abode* or *domicile*. Only a few people in a crowded theater will rush to the exit if someone yells "Conflagration!" But watch them make tracks when they hear the word "Fire!" It is said that P. T. Barnum had a hard time getting crowds to leave his sideshows once they paid to get in. To make room for other customers waiting in line, he erected the sign "THIS WAY TO THE EGRESS." Thinking this was another gigantic attraction, lingering visitors made their way to the sign only to find themselves outside the tent. *Egress*, of course, is a fancy word for *exit*.

When you're writing a letter, express yourself pretty much as you would if you were facing your reader. Would you say to your boss: "My analytical evaluation of the incentive plan that has been instituted revealed myriad discrepancies and inconsistencies, with the inevitable result that serious inequities prevail among personnel"? Of course you wouldn't! Here is probably what you would say: "I've studied our present incentive plan carefully, and I think some changes are in order.

What bothers me most about it is that the plan is very fair to some, but not at all fair to others."

Stuffy, overblown language has become so common that a name has been coined for it: *federalese*. This is because federal government writers have a special fondness for abstruse expressions (*abstruse* is a federalese word that means *hard to understand*). But they're not alone. Sociologists, educators, psychologists, scientists, engineers, and business executives also often seem intent on hiding meaning rather than speaking plain English.

Even when you know that the person you are writing to is highly literate, it's still a good idea to choose the simple word over the showy word—not because the reader won't understand you, but because conversational writing is livelier and more interesting. Following is a short list that illustrates what we mean.

Somewhat Showy	Conversational
cogitate upon	think about
be cognizant of	know that
comprehend	see, understand
comprised	made up of
conjecture	think, believe
consummate	wind up, agree to
corroborate	confirm, make sure
deliberate upon	think about
disbursements	payments
increment	increase, raise
maximal	fullest
initial	first
nominal	small, little
obviate	make unnecessary
origination	beginning
proclivity	leaning, tendency
predicated	based
ratify	approve, confirm
rationale	basis, reason
remunerate	pay
scrutinize	read, examine, inspect, look at
transpire	happen, take place
ultimate	final

Now let's look at examples of federalese writing.

Federalese	Natural Style
1. The contract enclosed herewith requires your signature before it can be executed and should be directed to the undersigned.	1. Please sign the contract enclosed and return it to me.
2. Due to a low inventory situation, we are reluctantly compelled to transmit a partial shipment of five Crescent motors in lieu of the twelve that were requested. We anticipate shipment of the remainder subsequently.	2. I'm sending five Crescent motors today. The remaining seven will go out to you just as soon as we get a new shipment— probably next week.
3. The expeditious manner in which you executed our high-priority order for maple seedlings is hereby gratefully acknowledged.	3. The maple seedlings arrived this morning, and I can't thank you enough for this fast service.
4. Commensurate with standard practice in the industry, as a wholesale enterprise our organization must decline direct distribution to consumers. Undoubtedly you can satisfy your requirements at a local retail establishment in the Atlanta area.	4. As wholesalers, we sell only to retail stores and other distributors. However, you can buy Oneida appliances in several Atlanta stores. Most are listed in the Yellow Pages.
5. Your recalcitrance in expediting payment of your obligations obviates consideration of further extension of credit privileges, and we foresee no viable alternative than cancellation of aforesaid privileges.	5. I'm sorry, Mr. Baxter, that we are not able to offer you additional credit. I'm sure you know the reason: You still owe us money that we haven't been able to collect.

KEEP THE LANGUAGE LIVELY AND SIMPLE

COINING NEW WORDS

An executive who wanted employees to give priority in their planning to cost control issued the directive that "the matter must be prioritized." People understood what *prioritized* meant, although they had never seen the word before. They had simply become accustomed to strange terms that people think up to "save time."

Ize words, as in *prioritize*, are favorites for federalese writers. Did you ever see the word *definitize?* Someone thought it up as a substitute for make definite. And more and more we see such terms as *legitimize, politicize, factionalize, strategize, accessorize, finalize, maximize, circularize,* and so on. Of course, there are many *ize* words that are perfectly acceptable—*standardize, visualize, jeopardize, economize, pressurize,* for example. But let a good dictionary guide you when you are tempted to tack on *ize* indiscriminately. (Or, should we say, when you are tempted to oversyllabize?)

There's also a growing tendency to tack on *wise* whenever possible: *policywise, procedurewise, weightwise, personnelwise,* and the classic *sizewise* (!). *Wise* endings make ugly words; people probably use them simply to prove that they are not strangers to the "in" jargon of officialdom.

Here are a few examples of "wise-itis" and their plain-talk equivalents.

"Wise-itis"	Plain Talk
1. *Newscaster:* "Weatherwise, it looks like a damp, humid weekend."	1. *Newscaster:* "Sorry, folks, but the weekend is going to be damp and humid."
2. This appears to be the right thing to do profitwise.	2. I think the new plan will result in bigger profits.
3. Costwise, it is inadvisable for sales representatives to concentrate on sparsely populated areas.	3. We can cut our costs by working only those territories where we can expect volume sales.
4. Distancewise, it's a toss-up between Colfax and Denton as a new-plant location.	4. Colfax and Denton are about the same distance away, so mileage is not a factor in picking one over the other.
5. I can see no effect moralewise on personnel under this new policy.	5. I doubt that employee morale will be affected by this new policy.

Finally are the folks who have an uncontrollable urge to add *uate* to certain words to indicate action. There are hundreds of good *uate* words—*perpetuate, evaluate, fluctuate,* and *evacuate,* for example—but among these are not *actuate, effectuate, eventuate,* and others of that ilk. Don't, for example, say, "We expect to actuate the revised retirement plan early next year." This is better: "The revised retirement plan goes into effect early next year." And *not:* "It is our hope that the results of the study will eventuate in substantial savings." *But:* "We hope our study will result in substantial savings."

VOGUE WORDS

Like teenage fads, words come and go. It would seem that the minute some government official throws out a sophisticated-sounding word at a press conference, every respectable bureaucrat immediately picks it up as his or her own. Several years ago, the word *parameter* mysteriously appeared in print as a synonym for *perimeter* or boundary, and hundreds of thousands of speakers and writers picked it up. Today it is a vogue word. Unfortunately, *parameter* does not mean the same thing as *perimeter,* which is an indication of how gullible we are when it comes to word selection.

Today, there seem to be no alternatives but *viable* ones; people who have a personal appeal are *charismatic* (or have *charisma*); when positions of people conflict or contrast on a particular issue, there is *polarization;* when we struggle to make a decision, we *interface* with the problem; when we offer an opinion, we take a *posture* or *stance;* and when different groups disagree on something, there is a *dichotomy.* And so on.

Just as serious is the tendency to use verbs as nouns, as in "How will the move impact on turnover" (instead of "What impact will the move have on turnover?") and "Please critique the attached report" (instead of "Please let me have your critique [or assessment] of the attached report."

If you are one of those who believe there is nothing wrong with going along with the crowd in using federalese language, that's up to you. We urge you, however, to use plain English in your letters, for it is the simple word, the natural word, the conversational word, the everyday word that will do the most to make your writing readable, interesting, and persuasive.

STEREOTYPED WRITING

Almost as bad as federalese is writing that is lifeless and stale. In the days of celluloid collars and spats, almost every letter began with "Yours of the fifth inst. and contents duly noted," which really meant, "I read with interest your letter of June 5." And the same letter usually ended something like this: "Begging your kind indulgence, I remain, sir, your most obedient servant." Probably you've never seen such phrases and wonder why we even call attention to them. It's because letter writers tend to fall into a rut, using the same words and phrases over and over without thinking. Even today, if you could examine one day's worth of correspondence that emanates from a typical large company, you'll find stereotyped writing such as the following.

Stereotyped: *I am in receipt of your letter of the 15th.* (This is a throat-clearing phrase that says absolutely nothing, the slow windup before the pitch.)

Lively: The 25,000 mailing labels you asked about in your letter of May 15 left here yesterday.

Stereotyped: The terms of the contract are not clear to me. *Please advise.*

Lively: Please explain paragraph 7 on page 2 of the contract.

Stereotyped: *As per your instructions,* the hood ornaments are being sent air express.

Lively: I've sent the hood ornaments by air express, and you should have them by now.

Stereotyped: Please let me hear from you *at your earliest convenience.*

Lively: I really need this information by May 16— please.

Stereotyped: *Attached herewith* is the information you requested on Marple Brothers.

Lively: Here is the information you requested on Marple Brothers.

Stereotyped: I hope you will *avail yourself of the opportunity* to save 20 percent on all your cardboard containers.

Lively: I think you'll agree that a 20 percent saving on your cardboard containers represents big money. Why not order now?

Stereotyped: *Hoping for your concurrence in this matter, I remain . . .*

Lively: I hope you will agree that this is a good arrangement.

Stereotyped:	*Due to the fact* that we've had trouble getting the parts . . .
Lively:	We've had trouble getting parts. Therefore . . .
Stereotyped:	*According to our records,* there is an *outstanding balance* of $322.76 in your account.
Lively:	Your check for $322.76 will clear your account.
Stereotyped:	*Kindly* let me know if this date *meets with your approval.*
Lively:	Is December 14 a good time for us to meet?

Other stereotyped expressions include the following:

along this line
at hand (your letter)
attached (or enclosed) please find
I wish to state
I hereby advise
I solicit your kind indulgence
in due course
your order has gone forward
under separate cover
up to this writing
with your kind permission
pursuant to your request
this is to inform you that
we wish to call your attention to
above-mentioned (person, invoice, letter, etc.)
we are writing to tell you that

PERSONALIZE YOUR LETTERS

Letters are written by people to people. Even though you use a company letterhead and represent that organization when you write letters, it's still you who deliver the message. Generally, you will have complete freedom to write as you please.

We hope this means that you will treat people as live human beings and not as "to whom it may concerns." Earlier we mentioned that people are different and that, when possible, these differences should be taken into account. On the other hand, people are very much alike in certain respects. Most are reasonable, civilized, thoughtful, and friendly. All have an ego, which means they like to be treated as though they have better-than-average intelligence and are important to the company they work for.

Knowing these things about people, how could a sales manager dictate this message to a new customer whose business the company has sought for many months?

Dear Sir:

This will acknowledge your order for sixteen Multi-Craft belt sanders and eight disc grinders. This order will be shipped promptly. Thank you for your business.

Yours truly,

It's not a bad letter. All the "necessary" ingredients are there: order acknowledged, shipment will go forth promptly, and thank you. But there's something missing: the from-me-to-you personal touch. Depending on the circumstances, several different, friendlier approaches might be used. In the following, we've focused on the sales representative who calls on this customer.

Dear Mr. Rosetti:

Just last month Hal Milsap and I were talking about how we might persuade you to carry our Multi-Craft line of power tools at Four Corners Building Supplies. Then this morning Hal strode in and handed me your order for sixteen belt sanders and eight disc grinders. I didn't get to keep it very long because Hal grabbed it, saying something about "getting these items on the truck this afternoon."

We're mighty happy, Mr. Rosetti, that a reputable store like yours has chosen Multi-Craft tools. I admit prejudice when I say that they're in a class by themselves, but I'm predicting that you'll have such success with them that you'll think I've been modest!

Hal will be in touch with you soon to see how he can help you with your display and promotion. And if I can do anything, just pick up the phone and call me.

Thank you—and good luck!

Sincerely yours,

The second letter should leave no doubt in Mr. Rosetti's mind that he is not looked upon as just another new customer, but a person who is somewhat special. Note that we've used Mr. Rosetti's name in the body of the letter, which adds a personal touch. This is a good idea for many, if not most, of your letters; just be careful not to overdo it.

Following is another example of a to-whom-it-may-concern letter. It was written by a town tax supervisor in response to a property owner's note that her property tax was paid twice.

Madam:

The enclosed check for $378.88 is due you because of the duplicate payment of taxes on your property.

Yours truly,

The letter above will not make the taxpayer cranky. She wanted a refund and she got it. But why treat her as just another anonymous taxpayer? Why not something like this?

Dear Mrs. Guilford:

You're entirely right—there was a duplication of payment of your property taxes. Both you and Oakdale Savings and Loan sent checks, and the enclosed $378.88 is your refund.

This situation arises every now and then, Mrs. Guilford. Eventually, we discover the duplicate payment and mail a refund, but you speeded things up by calling the matter to our attention.

Sincerely yours,

FORM LETTERS

Certainly, the second letter illustrated takes a little more time to write, and this is the excuse many people give for not exerting extra effort in answering routine letters. But in many instances, the time problem can be solved by writing a model letter for each frequently recurring situation, then adapting it slightly to fit the circumstances.

For example, let's say you are a personnel supervisor, and you receive dozens of applications for positions for which there are no vacancies. Your model letter might look something like this:

Dear _____ :

I appreciate your letter in which you inquire about a position in our _____ department.

Unfortunately, (name), we have no vacancies in this department now, and I cannot predict when there will be one. Certainly, I will be pleased to hold your application and get in touch with you if the situation changes. However, I suggest that you continue your search for a position in other companies, rather than wait to hear from me.

I'm very grateful for your interest in Hutchinson-McGee, and I wish I could be more optimistic about employment opportunities. In any event, I hope you are successful in locating precisely the job you want in the _____ field.

Sincerely yours,

You might wind up with a dozen or more model letters, in which case you can instruct the typist on the incoming letter, "Send #5." Or, "Send #5 with this P.S.: 'The latest issue of our employee magazine, which you requested, is being mailed separately.'"

ADDITIONAL EXAMPLES OF PERSONALIZED AND NONPERSONALIZED LETTERS

On the following pages are six additional examples of personalized and nonpersonalized letters.

EXAMPLE 1

NONPERSONALIZED

Dear Friend:

We have your request for a trial copy of *Cooking With the Experts,* which we recently published.

We regret to say that this book is temporarily out of stock. A copy will, however, go forward promptly when a new supply is available. This should be approximately April 10.

DIAMOND PUBLISHERS

PERSONALIZED

Dear Mrs. Morley:

Thanks a lot for your interest in *Cooking With the Experts.*

It seems that this exciting new book is attracting a good deal more attention than we predicted, and at the moment there isn't a single copy left. Naturally, we ordered a new printing before we ran out, and we expect to receive copies by April 10. To speed delivery, I'm having your book sent directly from the printer, so you should have it by the time (or before) we get ours.

Bon appetit!

Sincerely,

Martha Mallon

Martha Mallon
Editor in Chief

EXAMPLE 2

NONPERSONALIZED

Dear Sir:

Regrettably, this organization is no longer supplying free tote bags to business show visitors, although Scribe ballpoint pens are still being made available for such events.

Upon receipt of an estimate of your requirements, shipment will be made.

Yours truly,

PERSONALIZED

Dear Mr. Dunn:

I wish we could supply tote bags for your visitors to the Phoenix Business Show. However, we discontinued this practice a few months ago because the demand dropped to a trickle, leading us to believe that so many other organizations were supplying bags that ours weren't needed.

I'm pleased to say, however, that Scribe ballpoint pens are still being distributed without cost for affairs such as yours. If you'll let me know about how many you need, Mr. Dunn, I'll get them to you well before your opening on October 9.

I have hopes of attending the Phoenix Business Show; certainly, several of our people will be there. In any event, I hope it's the best ever.

Sincerely,

EXAMPLE 3

NONPERSONALIZED

Dear Madam:

Your request for a home demonstration of the ElectraVac has been received and forwarded to the district office in Tallahassee who, we are sure, will accord your request immediate attention.

Very truly yours,

PERSONALIZED

Dear Mrs. DeGroat:

I'm delighted that you want a demonstration of the new ElectraVac in your home.

The office nearest you is in Tallahassee, and I've written the general manager, Olivia Cayman, asking her to get in touch with you at once. I'm confident you'll hear from her within a day or so after you receive this letter.

I think you've made a very intelligent decision, Mrs. DeGroat. As we say in our ads, "The best place to see how a vacuum cleaner really performs is in your own home."

Thank you for writing.

Yours very cordially.

EXAMPLE 4

NONPERSONALIZED

Dear Sir:

Your request for dealer terms on Rasmussen sonar instruments has been received. The enclosed booklet provides complete information.

Yours truly,

PERSONALIZED

Dear Mr. Claiborne:

I'm pleased to learn that you are interested in carrying the Rasmussen line of sonar instruments at Candlewood Marina. We have no dealers in Fairfield County, and I very much hope that you will be the first.

Enclosed is our latest catalog. You'll find a description of our complete line and, on page 32, our dealer terms. I'm sending our Connecticut representative, Rene Berenson, a copy of this letter, asking him to get in touch with you to help in any way he can.

In the meantime, if I can supply additional information, just drop me a line or call me collect at (415) 622-7180.

Sincerely yours,

EXAMPLE 5

NONPERSONALIZED   Dear Ms. Osberg:

The button-tufted swivel chair (Naugahyde with chrome base) you inquired about is not available in sunset yellow, and it is regretted that your preference cannot be satisfied.

Yours truly,

PERSONALIZED   Dear Ms. Osberg:

Thank you for your interest in our button-tufted swivel chair in Naugahyde with chrome base.

Although we do not have this chair in sunset yellow, there are four other colors that you might choose from: chestnut brown, black, moss green, and gold. I'm enclosing the sheet from our catalog on which all these colors are shown.

I'm hoping, Ms. Osberg, that the gold Naugahyde is near enough to sunset yellow to please you. Incidentally, the most popular color with our customers is black—very smart-looking in any office environment.

Please let me know if I can supply you with one of the colors mentioned. The price is $169.95, with a discount of 10 percent on cash orders.

Sincerely,

EXAMPLE 6

NONPERSONALIZED   Sirs:

Please return the Merlin compact copier that you claim arrived in a damaged condition. All shipping charges will be paid by us.

The damaged copier is being replaced by another one.

Very truly yours,

PERSONALIZED   Gentlemen:

This afternoon I sent you a replacement of the Merlin copier by UPS, and you should have it by the time you receive this letter. I'm sorry the first shipment was damaged.

One of our representatives will drop by in a day or two to pick up the first copier you received. Thanks for your patience.

Yours very sincerely,

"I" AND "YOU" BUSINESS LETTERS

Somewhere along the line you may have had instructions to avoid the pronoun *I* in business letters and, wherever possible, use the pronoun *you*. Scores of textbooks emphasize that good writers should always employ the "you approach," which means playing down *I* (the writer) and playing up *you* (the reader). Some authors harp especially on the sin of starting a paragraph with *I*.

These rules are sheer nonsense. Nothing in a letter is more personal than *I*, and you should use it just as naturally as though you were carrying on a conversation with a friend. *You* is also a good word that should show up frequently in your letters, but if you force its use, you can sound patronizing. For example:

"You" approach: You will be pleased to learn that your application for credit has been approved.

Natural: I'm pleased to tell you that your application for credit has been approved.

We think the "you" approach is a bit condescending (lucky you; our great company has approved you for credit). "I'm pleased to tell you" gives the message an entirely different meaning (we're glad to have you as a credit customer).

Compare:

1. Your presentation at the workshop was very enjoyable, provocative, and valuable.
2. I certainly enjoyed your presentation at the workshop. I found it very provocative and valuable.

Compare:

1. You are to be congratulated on your promotion to product manager.
2. I'm delighted to learn about your promotion to product manager. Congratulations!

The point is that you should not struggle for ways to use *you* and avoid *I*. Use both prorouns, along with *your*, *me*, and *my*, when it seems natural to do so.

"WE" AND "I"

It is sometimes difficult to choose between *I* and *we* in letters concerning business matters. In a few companies, *we* is often preferred on the theory that the writer speaks for the company and not just for himself or herself. In most cases, however, the choice is left up to the individual. Our advice is this: Use *I*, *me*, and *my* when you want your letters to have a from-me-to-you flavor; use *we*, *us*, and *our* when you want your reader to feel that others share the message you are conveying. For example:

1. I very much enjoyed your visit to my office last Tuesday. Enclosed are the materials I promised to send you.
2. Thank you for calling this situation to our attention, Mr. Culver. We appreciate your patience with us.

Often, you will use both *I* and *we* in the same letter.

Dear Mr. Rambeau:

All of us at Lazarus Brothers have been highly pleased with the excellent service you gave us during the trucking strike. The situation called for great inventiveness on your part to see that we got the materials we needed. I really believe that we were the only contractors in this area who didn't have to shut down because of lack of materials.

For the whole crew here, I want to express sincere thanks for your performance during this difficult period. Thank you!

Sincerely yours,

Here is another.

Dear Professor Strachan:

I enjoyed immensely your talk on supplemental benefit plans at AMA's Symposium on Life Insurance in San Francisco last week.

We are in the process of evaluating our voluntary benefits program here at Beckwith Corporation, and I know our group would find your ideas not only stimulating, but extremely helpful in our planning. Is a copy of your paper available? If so, may we borrow it and reproduce it for distribution here? We'd be extremely grateful. We will, of course. return your paper just as soon as we have made a half-dozen copies.

Sincerely,

SECTION 5

EMPHASIZE THE POSITIVE

We've said it several times before, but it's worth repeating: most of the letters you write will have a sales flavor. You don't have to be selling a product—a relatively small percentage of business letters are written for this specific purpose. But if you're an effective writer, you try to make or keep friends and customers, persuade readers to accept an idea (whether it's an apology or a proposal), or build a favorable image for you and your company. Call it what you will—tact, warmth, friendliness, enthusiasm—any method you use to persuade people to think well of you is still salesmanship.

The first thing a salesperson learns is to be positive. You wouldn't make many sales if you approached each prospect like this: "You wouldn't like to join our Books-on-Tape Club, would you, Mrs. Wimple?" You've made it too easy for her to say, "You're certainly right; I wouldn't like to join your Books-on-Tape Club. Good day!"

You'll have a lot better chance making a sale if you say something like this: "I expect that, like most people, Mrs. Wimple, you love to read but simply can't find the time . . ." Then, when Mrs. Wimple nods in agreement, you proceed to show how your Books-on-Tape Club can solve her problem.

You can emphasize the positive in your letters in several ways, four of which are:

---

1. *Stress what you* can *do—not what you can't.*
2. *Stay away from negative words and phrases.*
3. *Do more than you have to.*
4. *Time your letters for best results.*

STRESSING WHAT YOU CAN DO

Some people just naturally think negatively. Following are two examples.

Example 1: In a national magazine, a mail-order firm advertised a flight bag for $24.95 in colors of brown, tan, *and black. The black bags were quickly sold out, but a new shipment is expected within ten days. What response should be given to those who order black flight bags?*

NEGATIVE

Dear Mr. Dillon:

I'm sorry that we are presently out of stock of black Nova flight bags and will be unable to fill your order at this time.

An order has been placed with the manufacturer in the color you want, but it will be at least ten days before we will receive shipment.

I trust this delay will not inconvenience you.

Yours very sincerely,

Observe the negative words and phrases in the example above: "I'm sorry" (a poor beginning for almost any letter), "unable," "will be at least ten days," "delay," and "inconvenience."

POSITIVE

Dear Mr. Dillon:

Thank you for ordering a black Nova flight bag.

The color you chose proved to be very popular, and we quickly sold all we had in stock. However, we've placed a rush order for more and are promised delivery within ten days. Yours will be shipped the same day our new supply arrives.

I know you'll be delighted with this unique carry-on flight bag, Mr. Dillon. It's not only very handsome, but incredibly rugged.

Yours very sincerely,

Example 2: A well-known university president has been invited to give the keynote address at the annual Delaware Education Association convention in Dover on April 11. The theme is "The Impact of New Technologies on Education." The president can't accept the invitation since he will be in Europe at that time. He suggests another speaker from the university staff.

NEGATIVE

Dear Professor Kinkaid:

I regret that I will be unable to accept your invitation to speak at the Delaware Education Association convention on April 11. Unfortunately, I will be in Europe at that time.

If you would be willing to accept a substitute, I'm quite certain that Dr. Adele Josephson, vice president of administration, would be available. If this proves to be an unsuitable recommendation, I'm sorry.

Cordially yours,

Dear Professor Kinkaid:

Nothing would please me more than to give the keynote address at the Delaware Education Association convention on April 11. Not only are educators my favorite audience, but your theme is of special interest to me.

Several months ago, however, I made arrangements to attend the International Education Congress in Stockholm and will be out of the country the first two weeks in April.

May I suggest an alternate? Dr. Adele Josephson, our vice president of administration, is not only a well-known authority on new educational technologies (you may have seen her recent series of articles on this subject in the *Journal of Higher Education*) but an excellent speaker as well. I have discussed this assignment with her, and she showed much enthusiasm for it. You may write her directly if you wish.

In any event, I wish for you the best convention the DEA has ever had. I'm really sorry to miss it.

Cordially yours,

STAY AWAY FROM NEGATIVES

Be especially careful in your letters not to attach labels to people or intentions or actions that will be offensive to them. Following are examples.

Negative: In your October 3 order, you *neglected* to specify the color of vinyl sheeting you require.

Better: Just let me know the color of vinyl sheeting you prefer, and I'll send the materials immediately.

Negative: Your *complaint* about the quality of paper used in the forms we supplied you is regrettable.

Better: I'm sorry that the quality of paper in the forms we supplied you was not up to your expectations.

Negative: You *claim* that you did not understand our discount terms.

Better: The terms of sale are described on the invoice we sent you, and perhaps you overlooked them.

Negative: You *obviously ignored* the assembly instructions accompanying the equipment.

Better: The assembly instructions accompanying the equipment are very specific about proper installation. Did you not receive them?

Negative: *Quite frankly, I am surprised at your insinuation.*

Better: Of course, I can't claim that we're infallible, but let me explain how this problem came about.

Negative: Your *alibi* for *skipping* the March payment on your promissory note . . .

Better: Thank you for explaining why you did not make payment in March on your promissory note . . .

Negative: *I dispute your assertion* that the merchandise we sent is *inferior.*

Better: Please look at the specifications on page 321 of our catalog. I think you'll agree that the shirts you received match them.

Negative: *Surely you don't expect us* to violate company policy by extending six-month credit terms to you.

Better: You will remember that we allowed you four months to pay for your October 23 order, which is the maximum permitted under our standard policy.

Negative: *You should know by now* that we need at least two weeks' lead time in filling orders for imported articles.

Better: As indicated in our catalog, we need at least two weeks' lead time in filling orders for imported articles.

Negative: *If you had read our advertisement carefully,* you would have seen that at least a year's field experience is required for sales representatives.

Better: As noted in our ad, at least a year's field experience is necessary for sales representatives.

Negative: You *failed* to enclose the check you referred to in your letter of May 10. *Obviously,* we can't credit your account until we receive payment.

Better: By the time you receive this, you will probably have discovered that the check you meant to enclose in your letter of May 10 was missing. No doubt, you have already placed it in the mail.

DOING MORE THAN YOU HAVE TO

It costs very little to do a bit more than you actually have to when answering letters. Not only will this extra effort make friends, it will make you feel better. The following illustrate what we mean.

Example 1: *The Creighton Academy of Art is a private art museum. Because its name suggests a school, many young people write asking for information about the curriculum, tuition, and so on.*

GRUDGING   Dear Miss Douglass:

The Creighton Academy of Art is not a school—it is a private art museum. Therefore, I'm afraid we can't help you.

Sincerely yours,

HELPFUL   Dear Miss Douglass:

I appreciate your letter asking about art education at the Creighton Academy of Art.

Although our name does suggest that we offer art education courses, we are actually a private art museum. There are, however, several reputable art schools in the Philadelphia area that are accredited by the state. A photocopy of the art schools section from the state directory is enclosed.

Sincerely yours,

Example 2:   Robert Rheinhold, 70, is retiring as an engineer in a firm where he worked for forty-eight years. During this time, he often spoke about a book of mathematical tables he used in college and to which he referred frequently later on the job. Unfortunately, it was lost, and he failed to try to replace it, even though he often talked about doing so. His friends want to try to find a copy to present at the retirement party, but no one is sure (not even Rheinhold) of the exact name of the author (Schultz?), the date of publication (about 1920?), or the publisher. One of Rheinhold's friends writes a dealer in rare and out-of-print books. Following are two responses.

GRUDGING   Dear Ms. Lomax:

I am sorry we cannot identify the book about which you wrote and therefore cannot help you. Certainly we have nothing that fits your sketchy description.

Yours sincerely,

HELPFUL   Dear Ms. Lomax:

I have scoured our lists of out-of-print books very carefully, and I think I have a clue to the identity of the one you asked for. A book entitled *Practical Handbook of Mathematical Tables*, by J. W. Shurz, was published in 1919 by Eureka Publishing Company. It went out of print in 1932, and the publisher is no longer in business. At one time we had a few copies, but unfortunately have had none for several years.

There are many dealers throughout the country who specialize in rare books, and you may wish to write some of them. I suggest that you visit a good library and ask for such publications as *Harper's*, *The Atlantic*, and *Publisher's Weekly*, all of which often contain back-of-the-book ads of rare book dealers.

Good luck!

Yours sincerely,

TIMING FOR POSITIVE REACTION

Promptness in attending to your correspondence nearly always reveals a positive attitude. It shows you're eager to be of service, you respect your correspondents' time, and you want them to be impressed with your level of efficiency. Certainly a lot of friends have been lost by writers who are too slow in answering their mail.

When you receive a letter to which you cannot respond fully in less than a week or so, acknowledge it immediately and say when you will have the information asked for. Here is an example.

Dear Mr. Ireland:

Thanks for sending the sample cartons we are so eager to make a decision on.

Three of my colleagues who must see the samples before a final decision can be reached are attending a materials-handling seminar in Aspen this week. Then they plan to spend a couple of days at our Denver subsidiary.

I expect them back by November 14, and I hope we can get a decision that same day. I'll relay it to you by phone—I know you're just as eager to have this thing settled as we are.

Sincerely,

And another.

Dear Ms. Rosmund:

Your proposal of Stroud as a site for our new Tulsa area distribution center caught me in the midst of a series of long-range planning meetings which will require my participation for the next several days—perhaps as long as two weeks.

Just as soon as I have a chance to study your proposal and share it with others here, I will write you.

Sincerely yours,

Yet, there are times when promptness in answering letters may not be wise, even though you are prepared to make a full

EMPHASIZE THE POSITIVE

response immediately. Let's say you've received a proposal from a new ad agency that wants to represent you, or a manufacturer who offers you an exclusive dealership in a new product, or a designer who submits what she thinks is an ingenious packaging idea for your product. In each case, you know the answer is "no." So you could dictate a response at once and put it in the mail. Those who write might be impressed with your fast answer, but they are very likely to think you gave them short shrift—that your mind was closed (as it was).

When you have to say "no" to people who offer what you can't use or ask for a hefty favor you can't grant, it's usually best to let the correspondence age a bit before responding. If you want to, you can write a quick note something like this: "Thanks for your letter about . . . . This matter deserves careful study, and I will be in touch with you about it later." Then after a decent interval—perhaps a week—you can dictate your "no" response.

Overpromptness is especially dangerous if you're dealing with long-time customers who ask for special favors that you are not in a position to grant. Letting the incoming letter age a bit—but not too long—is likely to lead the customer to believe that you're at least considering the request.

The same is true when you're dealing with job applicants. A same-day "no" to qualified applicants may tell them that you didn't think enough of them to even look at their résumés, and it won't hurt to delay a reply for a couple of days. But not much longer, since turned-down applicants will want to get letters out to other companies quickly.

One more thing about timing: don't be too quick about putting letters in the mail that deal with matters of extraordinary importance and are often quite lengthy. (See Letter 24-6 on page 206.) Prepare a rough draft and let it age for a spell, returning to it from time to time to make sure you have written exactly what is appropriate under the circumstances. It is not unusual for executives to rewrite an important letter three or four times before they are ready to release it.

USE CORRECT LETTER FORM

Readers get their first impression of a business letter even before they read it. The quality of paper, letterhead design, placement of the message on the page, and letter style all have something to say about an organization. A weakness in any of these elements can detract from the effectiveness of the message, even though it is expertly written.

PAPER

Quality

Paper quality is based on weight and what the paper is made of. In many companies, letterhead paper that most correspondents use is a 20-pound bond with a 25 percent cotton-fiber (rag) content. In others, a 16-pound bond of the same rag content is standard. Top executives often choose a 24-pound bond with from 50 to 100 percent rag content for personal and social correspondence. A few firms to whom very high quality is enormously important choose this more expensive paper for all their correspondence.

Bond paper comes in a wide variety of finishes—smooth, fluorescent, ripple, and many others. You can select one of the standard finishes available, or you can have paper made with your own watermark.

The least expensive stationery is made of sulfite, and a 16- or 20-pound weight is commonly used for mass mailings, routine announcements (a price change, for example), and for interoffice memoranda.

Of course, envelopes and second sheets should always match the letterhead in quality and finish.

Color

White is by far the most widely used color of stationery, but light tints—gray, blue, antique ivory, green, and so on—are also popular. Organizations whose customers are primarily women may choose such tints as pink, peach, lavender, and aqua.

Size

The standard size of letterhead paper is 8½ by 11 inches. For personal and social use, however, some managers and executives often choose a smaller size, such as Monarch (7¼ by 10½ inches) or Baronial (5½ by 8½ inches). Envelopes should, of course, be chosen expressly for the size of letterhead used. The envelope ordinarily used for the standard letterhead is 4⅛ by 9½ inches (called a No. 10).

THE LETTERHEAD

Letterhead design has become increasingly important over the years. At one time, many companies simply asked a local printer for a book of letterhead models and matched the one they felt most suitable for their needs. Some still do. But in many organizations that sell products and services nationally, letterhead design is taken much more seriously. Indeed, management is apt to think not just in terms of a letterhead, but of an overall corporate image based on a distinctive logo (type and perhaps a symbol) that appears on every visual presentation, whether a letterhead, a magazine ad, a shipping carton, a television commercial, or the product itself. Nearly everyone recognizes the distinctive logos of such organizations as John Hancock Mutual Life Insurance Company, IBM, International Harvester, Gulf Oil Corporation, RCA, Hilton Hotels, and Hertz, but few know the planning and the investment that went into those symbols and lettering. It is not uncommon for a national corporation to engage a firm that specializes in creating image through display, spending hundreds of thousands of dollars to capture its ''soul.''

We mention this simply because the answer to the question, What is a good letterhead? is almost impossible to state categorically. Generally, we can say that a good letterhead is simple, contains only the basic elements (company name and address), looks modern, and employs typefaces that are complementary. That's not a bad set of guidelines, but unfortunately it is simplistic. For example, a company that has spent many years and millions of dollars promoting a name and symbol that is instantly recognized (Coca-Cola, for example) is not likely to change it merely to be modern. A traditional ''no-no'' in letterhead design is cluttering it up with more information than most people have any interest in. Yet, to some companies, it's important to list their senior officers, display their slogan (at the top or bottom), supply addresses of major domestic and foreign offices, show the cable address, perhaps even include their affiliation with various organizations. Perhaps they feel this data impresses their readers. If they're right, who's to argue? Certain types of organizations choose a letterhead design that looks quite outdated by modern standards. They cling to it because they believe it says, ''We've been around a long time; we're stable and dependable.''

The point is this: designing an effective letterhead for a major company is not merely selecting a striking typeface, devising a pictorial gimmick, and putting everything in the right place. A lot of psychology goes into letterhead design, and even the individual who is an expert on typefaces (and few executives are) can fail miserably. The job may look slick and professional, but if the end result does not capture the spirit of the organization, it's not going to enhance that image we spoke about.

If you're in a small company that simply wants something attractive in a letterhead and doesn't want to invest heavily in design, by all means talk to a good printer and look at the models available. With little or no adaptation, you might get exactly what you want. But if you happen to be in on the planning of a new letterhead for a national corporation, get expert help. You'll pay for the service, but the cost is very likely to be worth the investment.

LETTER STYLE

You can choose from a half dozen letter styles (by style, we mean general layout). A few companies select a style and insist that everyone use it, but in most cases the choice is up to the writer. The three most popular styles are illustrated on pages 38, 39, and 40.

Semiblocked Style

In the semiblocked style, the dateline starts at the middle of the page, as does the complimentary close. Each paragraph is indented five spaces. (See Figure 6-1.)

Blocked Style

The only difference between the semiblocked style and the blocked style is that in the block style the paragraphs are not indented. (See Figure 6-2.)

Full-Blocked Style

Here, everything in the message is placed flush with the left margin: dateline, inside address, salutation, paragraph openings, complimentary close, writer's name, and so on. (See Figure 6-3.)

Comparison

Each style has its own devotees, and we won't point out the advantages or disadvantages of each. They are all good-looking, assuming the letter has good balance, as do those illustrated.

Stateport Chamber of Commerce

Crystal Beach Road, Stateport, North Carolina 28461

February 19, 19--

Mr. Charles A. Greenlund
1806 Devon Drive
Clarinda, Iowa 51632

Dear Mr. Greenlund:

I'm delighted to learn that you and your family are thinking about spending your vacation this summer in Stateport.

Located at the southeastern tip of North Carolina, Stateport is the northern-
most subtropical region on the East Coast--"where the pines meet the palms." Its
stately live oaks and scenic waterfront give Stateport a small-town charm
rarely to be found these days.

You won't find high-rise hotels or neon amusements here, but you will find
opportunities galore to enjoy yourself. The town itself is right in the lap of
the historic Cape Fear River and the Intracoastal Waterway, and just down the
road a piece is the beautiful Atlantic with 14 miles of wide, sandy beaches
that are never crowded--a great place for swimming, surfing, collecting seashells,
or just basking.

There are oceanside golf and tennis courts, and the fishing is unsurpassed--
whether you prefer the surf, pier fishing, or angling from your own boat or one
of the many charter boats for hire. And there are protected waters for sailing,
fishing, and water skiing. Bike trails, miniature golf, water slides, and a
dozen other fun things to keep the youngsters amused; and for the less adventuresome, there are historic sites and beautiful gardens nearby and museums only a
short ferry ride away.

You'll find many places to stay in and around Stateport--from beach-front
cottages to apartments to mobile homes in the piney woods. A directory is
enclosed.

Really, the only way to truly appreciate what Stateport has to offer the
vacationer is to come see for yourself. You'll receive a warm welcome!

Sincerely yours,

Ross T. Jessup

Ross T. Jessup
Executive Director

fcd
Enclosure

Figure 6-1 Semiblocked style.

Stateport Chamber of Commerce
Crystal Beach Road, Stateport, North Carolina 28461

February 19, 19--

Mr. Charles A. Greenlund
1806 Devon Drive
Clarinda, Iowa 51632

Dear Mr. Greenlund:

I'm delighted to learn that you and your family are thinking about spending your vacation this summer in Stateport.

Located at the southeastern tip of North Carolina, Stateport is the northern-most subtropical region on the East Coast--"where the pines meet the palms." Its stately live oaks and scenic waterfront give Stateport a small-town charm rarely to be found these days.

You won't find high-rise hotels or neon amusements here, but you will find opportunities galore to enjoy yourself. The town itself is right in the lap of the historic Cape Fear River and the Intracoastal Waterway, and just down the road a piece is the beautiful Atlantic with 14 miles of wide, sandy beaches that are never crowded--a great place for swimming, surfing, collecting sea-shells, or just basking.

There are oceanside golf and tennis courts, and the fishing is unsurpassed--whether you prefer the surf, pier fishing, or angling from your own boat or one of the many charter boats for hire. And there are protected waters for sailing, fishing, and water skiing. Bike trails, miniature golf, water slides, and a dozen other fun things to keep the youngsters amused; and for the less adventuresome, there are historic sites and beautiful gardens nearby and museums only a short ferry ride away.

You'll find many places to stay in and around Stateport--from beach-front cottages to apartments to mobile homes in the piney woods. A directory is enclosed.

Really, the only way to truly appreciate what Stateport has to offer the vacationer is to come see for yourself. You'll receive a warm welcome!

Sincerely yours,

Ross T. Jessup

Ross T. Jessup
Executive Director

fcd
Enclosure

Figure 6-2 Blocked style.

Stateport Chamber of Commerce

Crystal Beach Road, Stateport, North Carolina 28461

February 19, 19--

Mr. Charles A. Greenlund
1806 Devon Drive
Clarinda, Iowa 51632

Dear Mr. Greenlund:

I'm delighted to learn that you and your family are thinking about spending your vacation this summer in Stateport.

Located at the southeastern tip of North Carolina, Stateport is the northern-most subtropical region on the East Coast--"where the pines meet the palms." Its stately live oaks and scenic waterfront give Stateport a small-town charm rarely to be found these days.

You won't find high-rise hotels or neon amusements here, but you will find opportunities galore to enjoy yourself. The town itself is right in the lap of the historic Cape Fear River and the Intracoastal Waterway, and just down the road a piece is the beautiful Atlantic with 14 miles of wide, sandy beaches that are never crowded--a great place for swimming, surfing, collecting sea-shells, or just basking.

There are oceanside golf and tennis courts, and the fishing is unsurpassed whether you prefer the surf, pier fishing, or angling from your own boat or one of the many charter boats for hire. And there are protected waters for sailing, fishing, and water skiing. Bike trails, miniature golf, water slides, and a dozen other fun things to keep the youngsters amused; and for the less adventuresome, there are historic sites and beautiful gardens nearby and museums only a short ferry ride away.

You'll find many places to stay in and around Stateport--from beach-front cottages to apartments to mobile homes in the piney woods. A directory is enclosed.

Really, the only way to truly appreciate what Stateport has to offer the vacationer is to come see for yourself. You'll receive a warm welcome!

Sincerely yours,

Ross T. Jessup
Ross T. Jessup
Executive Director

fcd
Enclosure

Figure 6-3 Full-blocked style.

MARGINS AND PLACEMENT

There should be at least a 1-inch margin at the left side of the letter (that's what we've used in the models illustrated), and the right margin should be roughly the same (some say a little wider). If the letter is short, say, half the length of the ones illustrated, you can increase your side margins to 2 inches or more.

The margin at the bottom of the page is usually at least one and one-half times that of the side margins; the same is true of the top margin when you are using plain paper instead of a letterhead. (When you are using a letterhead, of course, the top margin is established for you.)

As to placement, secretarial reference manuals provide formulas for centering a letter on the page. Most experienced secretaries, however, can tell from the quantity of their shorthand notes how to place the transcribed message so that it has the desired symmetry—like a picture in a frame.

SPACING

Most business letters are single-spaced, as shown in the models. However, there is one blank line between paragraphs, between the inside address and the salutation ("Dear Mr. Greenlund"), and between the salutation and the first line of the message. The complimentary close ("Sincerely yours") is two spaces below the last line of the letter. Four spaces are generally allowed for the signature (see one of the models), although some people think three is enough.

For relatively short letters, say, a couple of brief paragraphs, you can achieve good effect by double-spacing the entire message (though not the inside address). In this case, there is no additional space between paragraphs.

THE SALUTATION

When writing to individuals, always use their name if you know it.

Dear Andy: (personal friend or close business associate)
Dear Mrs. Gibbs:
Dear Dr. Breedlove:
Dear Professor Quinlan:
Dear Miss Diaz:
Dear Ms. Williams: (when you are addressing a woman whose marital status is not known or when you think this is her preference)

If you are addressing an individual whose name you do not know—the purchasing manager, director of personnel, president, and so on—use the following:

Director of Personnel
Leverett Products Corporation
1112 N.W. Lovejoy
Portland, Oregon 97209

Dear Sir or Madam:

When you are writing to an organization rather than to an individual, the following is appropriate.

Windsor Knitting Mills Inc.
295 Magnolia Avenue
Spartanburg, South Carolina 29301

Gentlemen:

Note: This salutation has been widely used for many years. Today, however, it is considered sexist by some, and there is a growing tendency to use "Ladies and Gentlemen."

THE COMPLIMENTARY CLOSE

A complimentary close is nearly always used in business letters. The wording you choose depends on you.

PERSONAL

| Sincerely, | Sincerely yours, | Very sincerely yours, |
| Cordially, | Cordially yours, | Very cordially yours, |

FORMAL

Yours very truly,
Very truly yours,
Respectfully yours, (to one whose stature is awesome)

HIGHLY INFORMAL

| Best wishes, | Cheers! |
| Warmest regards, | See you in Phoenix! |

For the typical business letter, our preferences are "Sincerely yours" and "Cordially yours."

WRITING ON PLAIN PAPER

If you are writing a personal letter on plain paper, you will include your address and the date at the top of the letter. For a semiblocked or blocked style, this information will begin at the center of the page. For example:

708 West Pine Street
Midland, Texas 79701
June 30, 19—

Dear Mr. Newton:

If you're using the full-blocked style, this information is flush with the left margin, thus:

Cambridge Court, Apt. 9-B
4719 McPherson Avenue
St. Louis, Missouri 63108
February 16, 19—

Dear Ms. Young:

OTHER ELEMENTS
The Attention Line

Some people prefer to address the company rather than an individual so that if the person addressed is not the one who would handle the letter or has left the company, the company feels free to open the letter and send it to the appropriate person. (This practice is not as common as it once was. Unless a letter to a former employee is marked "Personal," it is assumed to pertain to company business and is opened without hesitation.)
Following is the placement of a typical attention line.

Plymouth Rock Manufacturing Company
412 Atlantic Avenue
Boston, Massachusetts 02110

Attention: J. P. Scovill, Chief Engineer

Gentlemen:

Note that the salutation is "Gentlemen" (not "Dear Mr. Scovill"), since the letter is addressed to the company.

The Subject Line

To speed up handling of mail, it is sometimes wise to indicate the subject of the letter. The following are typical:

Ms. Olivia Moreno, Claims Supervisor
Pacific Marine Insurance Company
643 Powell Street
San Francisco, California 94108

Dear Ms. Moreno:

Subject: Claim No. MA-457972

I have just received your report concerning the . . .

Dr. Eric G. Hanrahan, Editor
<u>Journal of Neurosurgery</u>
128 South Wabash Avenue
Chicago, Illinois 60603

Dear Dr. Hanrahan:

IN RE: "Carpal Tunnel Tendon Release Without Surgery,"
by Dr. Rosalind B. Nance

You asked for my critique of Dr. Nance's article prior to . . .

Signatures   Unless a man's given name might be confused with that of a woman, he need only sign his name without a title. Compare:

Cordially yours,   Cordially yours,

Daniel A. Speaker   *(Mr.) Loyce O'Donohue*

Daniel A. Speaker   Loyce O'Donohue

Incidentally, many people sign letters with initials only or fail to indicate a courtesy title when their name could be either masculine or feminine. This presents a special problem when you respond to these individuals. The following are recommended:

M. G. Kroeger   Loyce O'Donohue
XYZ Corporation   ABC Company
etc.   etc.

Dear M. G. Kroeger: Dear Loyce O'Donohue:

A woman may sign her name in a variety of ways:

1. If she wants to indicate that she is unmarried:

Sincerely,   Sincerely,

(Miss) Melanie C. Prudhomme   *Melanie C. Prudhomme*

Melanie C. Prudhomme   Miss Melanie C. Prudhomme

2. A woman who does not wish to reveal her marital status may use one of the following:

Very sincerely yours,   Very sincerely yours,

(Ms) Judith Moscowitz   *Judith Moscowitz*

Judith Moscowitz   Ms. Judith Moscowitz

3. A married woman or widow who wants to be addressed as *Mrs.* may use one of the following:

Yours very cordially,   Yours very cordially,

(Mrs.) Sadie Watts Browne   *Sadie Watts Browne*

Sadie Watts Browne   Mrs. Sadie Watts Browne

4. The following signature for a married woman is appropriate for social correspondence; however, it is rarely used in business:

Sincerely,

Norma Wall Harris
Mrs. Vernon O. Harris

PART 2

REQUEST LETTERS

Among the most frequent letters people write are those that ask for something. Sometimes, a request may represent a definite sales opportunity for the recipient, who may have invited readers, viewers, or listeners to send for free samples or descriptive literature or whose advertisements simply have provoked enough interest to trigger an inquiry. Sales-opportunity requests are covered in Section 7.

Other requests may benefit the person who makes them more than the person who receives them—for example, asking for an appointment, for permission to reproduce materials, for a speaker, or for favors. These are referred to as "special-request letters," and they are presented in Section 8.

Other requests, such as for credit information, for money owed, for job interviews, and so on are covered in the parts that deal with those topics.

SECTION 7

SALES-OPPORTUNITY REQUEST LETTERS

Sales-opportunity request letters are those written to obtain materials or information from people who really should welcome the request because they stand to gain from granting it. Any alert business house that gets inquiries that could lead to a sale will (and should) turn handsprings to respond quickly and favorably. For this reason, these are probably the easiest of all letters to write. You don't need to use persuasion, except in very special circumstances; often, all the recipient really wants to know is what you want and where to send it.

REQUESTS TRIGGERED BY ADVERTISING

Advertisements often encourage people to send for a free catalog or other materials and information. Because most of these ads were written expressly to solicit inquiries, responding to them represents little challenge to the writer. Often, all you have to do is fill out a coupon and return it in an envelope that needs no postage.

If you are writing a request letter triggered by advertising, here are three guidelines to follow:

---

1. *Be as brief as you can unless you have your own reasons for supplying details or commentary.*
2. *Be specific about what you want.*
3. *For courtesy's sake:*
   a. *Say "please" or "I would appreciate" or "thank you."*
   b. *Give the source that you used as the basis of your request (the name of a magazine, for example).*

In this section, two examples are given for each request letter illustrated, both entirely suitable for mailing. The purpose is to demonstrate that there is more than one way to write an effective message.

7-1 ASKING FOR FREE MATERIALS

Situation

To attract investors, a company places an ad in *Byte* magazine, inviting readers to write for its latest annual report. You want a copy.

Analysis of Letter A

1. *Be brief—no explanation is required.*

2. *Be courteous. Say "please" and give the source that triggered the request.*

3. *Presumably, you will write on your company letterhead, so usually no further information is required as to where the report is to be sent. If there is, add a "P.S. Address me at . . . ."*

Letter A

Gentlemen:

Please send me a copy of your latest annual report (as advertised in the December issue of <u>Byte</u>).

Yours very truly,

Letter A above is fine. There will be no doubt about what you want or where you learned about it. However, Letter B, which follows, is equally effective, although a little longer.

Analysis of Letter B

1. *Say immediately what you want and where you learned about it.*

2. *The second paragraph is, of course, gratuitous. But if you feel like complimenting the company on its innovations, why not? These aren't really wasted words—they'll be read with interest.*

3. *The final "thank you" is not necessary either, but it doesn't cost anything.*

Letter B

Gentlemen:

I'd like a copy of your latest annual report as advertised in the December issue of <u>Byte</u>.

I have followed with great interest your innovations in computer-assisted instruction, particularly in the fields of science and foreign language. It seems incredible that in my own state there are nearly 3000 computer terminals in the public schools.

Thank you.

Yours very truly,

7-2 TAKING ADVANTAGE OF A TRIAL OFFER

Situation

A publisher writes a letter inviting readers to send for an examination copy of *Handbook of Effective Credit Management*. The letter explains that the book may be kept for a ten-day examination and returned without charge if readers don't want to buy it. You want to take advantage of the offer. A postcard was enclosed, but you misplaced it.

Analysis of Letter A

1. Tactfully ask for what you want, mentioning your source.

2. Restate briefly the terms of the trial offer. The publisher obviously knows the terms offered, but there's no harm in repeating them.

Letter A

Dear Ms. Shuster:

Please send me an examination copy of <u>Handbook of Effective Credit Management</u> referred to in your recent letter.

I understand that I may keep the book for ten days and return it, without cost, if I do not wish to purchase it.

Yours sincerely,

Letter A says it all, but Letter B, which is a bit more detailed, is equally satisfactory. Much depends, of course, on what *you* want to say.

Analysis of Letter B

1. Express interest in the book; then request it.

2. The fact that you lost the card is of no special importance, but it's all right to mention it.

3. Mention the scarcity of new publications in credit management and your anticipation on receiving this one—unnecessary, to be sure, but this statement, plus the "thank you," are highly appropriate if you want to add a little spice to your message.

Letter B

Dear Ms. Shuster:

I am very much interested in your new publication, <u>Handbook of Credit Management</u>, which you described in a recent letter. (I lost the reply card that accompanied the letter.) Please send me the book for examination on your ten-day approval plan.

New publications in the field of credit management are somewhat rare, and I am looking forward to seeing this one. It sounds very much like what I have been searching for.

Thank you.

Yours sincerely,

7-3   REQUESTING THE NAME OF A DEALER

Situation

An ad in *Board Room* magazine announces a new corporate helicopter. The advertiser has a California address, and you want to find out the name of a dealer near Minneapolis, if there is one.

Analysis of Letter A

Here, say only what you want to know—the name and location of a dealer near Minneapolis—and refer to the Board Room *ad.*

Letter A

Ladies and Gentlemen:

Please send me the name and location of a dealer near Minneapolis, where I can see the Luxury XII helicopter, which was advertised in Board Room.

Cordially yours,

Letter A is the soul of brevity, yet the people who receive it need nothing more. The same request is given in Letter B, which has a little more detail. Both are good letters; take your pick.

Analysis of Letter B

1. *Mention the ad and your favorable impression of it, a compliment to the reader.*

2. *Provide a little background as to why you're interested, which may or may not evoke special interest in your request. Then inquire about a nearby dealer.*

3. *Wind up with a "thank you."*

Letter B

Ladies and Gentlemen:

Your ad for the Luxury XII helicopter in the May 16 issue of Board Room is exciting.

Our company is thinking about adding a helicopter to its corporate fleet, and the Luxury XII is very appealing. Is there a dealer near Minneapolis? I and a couple of my associates would like to see this helicopter and experience first-hand its maneuverability and other features.

Thank you.

Cordially yours,

REQUESTING MORE DETAILED INFORMATION ABOUT AN ADVERTISED PRODUCT

Situation

Ads in recent issues of *Business Week* invite readers to join a publisher's Executive Book Club. You are interested in learning how well your field of personnel administration is represented or whether there is a special club for personnel executives.

Analysis of Letter A

1. Ask immediately the questions you want answered, referring to the magazine ads.

2. Express appreciation for help.

Letter A

Ladies and Gentlemen:

I have two questions about the Executive Book Club that you are advertising in <u>Business Week</u>:

1. What proportion of the books published by the club are in the personnel field?

2. Do you have book clubs specifically for those in personnel administration?

Thank you for your help.

Very sincerely yours,

Again, Letter A leaves nothing unsaid that the people at the Executive Book Club need to know. It's brief and courteous—a satisfactory letter. Letter B, which follows, provides a little more background. This doesn't necessarily make it a better letter; it's simply a different way of making the request.

Analysis of Letter B

1. Give the source of your knowledge and your purpose in writing.

2. Describe your specific interest (personnel) and ask about it.

3. Express your gratitude for the information requested.

Letter B

Ladies and Gentlemen:

I notice that the Executive Book Club advertisements in <u>Business Week</u> feature books over a wide spectrum of management. I am considering joining the club, but I'd like some information.

My area of special interest and responsibility is personnel administration. Generally, what proportion of the books that members may choose from is in the personnel field? Or do you perhaps have other book clubs in specific management disciplines, including personnel administration?

I would be very grateful for answers to these questions and any other information you can provide.

Very sincerely yours,

Situation

The sponsor of a TV public affairs program (an airline) invites listeners to send for free guides that have been published for exporters. European and African countries are mentioned specifically, but you want to know whether there are also guides for South American countries.

Analysis of Letter A

1. *Immediately ask for what you want, referring to the source of your information.*

2. *Tactfully ask to be put on the mailing list in case guides not now available will be later. (This should save you a follow-up letter later.)*

Letter A

Gentlemen:

Please send me, if available, export guides for Colombia, Argentina, Brazil, and Venezuela (I learned about the guides on "National Perspectives").

If the guides are not available now but will be in the future, I would appreciate your placing me on the mailing list to receive them upon publication.

Yours very cordially,

Letter A is succinct but clear. It will no doubt get as much favorable attention as Letter B, which follows. Again, neither is better than the other. Although, some may think A is superior because it takes so little time to read, others will prefer B because it supplies more background information and a salute to the quality of the TV program. The choice is yours.

Analysis of Letter B

1. *First, tell who you are and mention your plans briefly. (Another way to start is to ask about the guides first, then tell who you are, etc.)*

2. *Then, refer to the television program and ask about the guides.*

3. *In the last paragraph, compliment the recipient on the quality of "National Perspectives," adding a personal note about your own community.*

Letter B

Gentlemen:

As a manufacturer of farm equipment, our company is making plans to market our products in Colombia, Argentina, Brazil, and Venezuela.

Recently, I learned (from "National Perspectives") that you have export guides to several European and African countries. Are they also available for the countries mentioned above? If so, I would appreciate having them. If not and you have plans for them, would you please send them to me when they are released.

I thoroughly enjoy "National Perspectives," especially the environmental segments. This happens to be a controversial subject in our community right now, and I really wonder whether the problem can be solved to everyone's satisfaction.

Yours very cordially,

REQUESTING INFORMATION ABOUT USES OF AN ADVERTISED PRODUCT

Situation

An advertisement in *Office Administration* features a duplicating paper that is suitable for "nearly all" duplicating methods and invites readers to send for samples. You want clarification of "nearly all" and to receive samples.

Analysis of Letter A

1. *Start with a specific question, referring to the ad and listing your equipment.*

2. *Courteously request samples.*

Letter A

Dear Mr. Keller:

Is your Lancaster paper, which was advertised in the October issue of <u>Office Administration</u>, suitable for the photocopier, stencil (mimeograph), spirit duplicator (Ditto), and offset? These are the four machines we use here at Sterling Distributors.

If your answer is yes, I'd be grateful for samples.

Yours very sincerely,

Letter A is entirely satisfactory for the purpose. It says everything just about as briefly as possible. On the other hand, you might prefer Letter B, which uses a little different approach.

Analysis of Lettter B

1. *Refer first to the ad and the puzzling term "nearly all."*

2. *Then, proceed to list the machines you use.*

3. *Next, ask for the answer to your specific question, followed by a request for samples.*

4. *Express your appreciation.*

Letter B

Dear Mr. Keller:

Your ad in the October issue of <u>Office Administration</u> mentions that your Lancaster brand paper can be used successfully on "nearly all" duplicators. In our business, we make constant use of four—the photocopier, stencil (mimeograph), spirit (Ditto), and offset.

Is the Lancaster brand suitable for all these machines? If so, please send samples in the available colors. I'd appreciate it.

Yours very sincerely,

REQUESTS FOR SALES INFORMATION

You may have seen or heard about products or services, but want more information—about prices and discounts, colors and styles, and other details that are important to you. Because you don't have an ad to refer to, you have to provide a little more background in your requests than if you were responding to an ad.

Here are six guidelines for writing general sales-opportunity requests:

---

1. *Tell where you learned about the company or its products (if appropriate).*
2. *Supply information about your specific needs.*
3. *Make the request, emphasizing the value of the information to you. Its value can be enhanced by saying something complimentary to your reader, if you can do so truthfully. This may strengthen your chances of getting what you want—or even more.*
4. *Ask for specific answers to questions you have, if any.*
5. *Even though the letter may be written to a stranger, personalize it. This makes the letter more interesting and builds rapport with your reader.*
6. *Be courteous and tactful.*

7-7 INQUIRING ABOUT TRAINING MATERIALS

Situation

As training director of a large company, you have been asked to arrange a series of communication seminars (on listening, writing, and speaking) for top executives. At a recent professional meeting, you heard a speaker refer favorably to a new multimedia program on listening. You decide to write the publisher (specifically, the editor in chief) for information on the listening program and to find out whether other communication materials are also available.

Analysis of the Letter

1. *Tell where you learned about the materials— not absolutely essential but certainly interesting and perhaps helpful to the recipient.*

The Letter

Dear Sir or Madam:

Our speaker at this month's Society for the Advancement of Management meeting mentioned that you have developed some excellent programs of instruction on listening.

2. *Provide the setting in which the materials will be used; then, ask specifically for information on the listening program as well as the two other areas you're interested in.*

3. *Finally, emphasize the importance of a fast response and end with a statement of gratitude.*

I am arranging a series of communication seminars for our top executives, which will include instruction in writing, speaking, and listening. I am especially irterested in your materials on listening, but would welcome information about programs you may have on writing and speaking as well.

The seminars will begin October 16, so I don't have a lot of time to choose the materials. Would you therefore rush this information to me? I would be very grateful.

Sincerely yours,

7-8   INQUIRING ABOUT PERFORMANCE AWARDS

Situation

The executive committee of an organization is looking for an appropriate award to employees for meritorious performance (wall plaques have been used in the past, but no one is happy with them). As a member of the committee, you have recently seen a desk set that seems appropriate, and decide to write the manufacturer for information, including prices, styles, and colors.

Analysis of the Letter

1. *It's a good idea to tell how you learned about the product.*

2. *Mention the use you expect to make of the desk set; then, ask for information about it.*

3. *Ask about the logo to be sure there will be no problem matching it.*

4. *A "thank you" is not necessary, but it adds a little warmth.*

The Letter

Gentlemen:

I have just seen your Viceroy desk set that includes the corporate logo, a nameplate, and a brief message. The owner (a Data Control executive) said it had been awarded by his company for outstanding management performance.

I'm interested in the Viceroy desk set for a similar purpose and would like full details about it, including prices, styles, and colors available. Our logo appears above, and we would want it reproduced exactly as shown.

Thanks for your help.

Yours sincerely,

Situation

DataComp, which specializes in computer services, is planning a long-range planning conference in October, and a suitable meeting place is under discussion. Arlington Manor, a resort hotel that specializes in group meetings, has been recommended, but specific information about accommodations is required. You are asked to write for specific details concerning rates, facilities, services, and so on.

Analysis of the Letter

1. *Start the letter on a pleasant note. This is not a must, but the statement is true and provides a good introduction.*

2. *Ask for details concerning matters of special importance, backing up your request with specific information about your needs. Supplying fairly detailed data will help to accomplish the following:*
   a. *Enable Pollock to determine whether sufficient space is available on the dates indicated.*
   b. *Make it easy for her to be specific about your requirements.*

3. *Make no commitment at this time, simply say you'll be in touch after you receive the required information.*

4. *Give the date by which you need the information if time is getting short.*

The Letter

Dear Mrs. Pollock:

Several people have recommended Arlington Manor as a place with first-rate accommodations for our long-range planning conference in October.

Would you please send me full details on rates, meeting rooms, recreational facilities, food services, and so on. The following information will help you.

Date and time: October 22 (evening) to October 27—five nights and five days.

Number: Forty men, double occupancy
Eight men, single occupancy
Sixteen women, double occupancy
Nine women, single occupancy

Food services: Three group luncheons with speaker—seventy-five people

Meeting rooms: One room large enough to accommodate eighty people

Three rooms, each to accommodate thirty to forty people

Equipment: One 16mm film projector, screen, one overhead projector, four chalkboards, four easels

I will also want information on recreational facilities, travel (airport, courtesy limousines, etc.), and any special activities such as entertainment, tours, and so on.

Shortly after I receive this general information, I will be in touch with you. May I hear from you no later than February 7?

Sincerely yours,

7-10

INQUIRING ABOUT DISCOUNTS ON QUANTITY ORDERS

Situation

You have been asked to teach a series of seminars on supervision for your company and have been searching for a textbook. You purchased a copy of *Dynamic Supervision* at a local bookstore, priced at $27.95, which you think would be very satisfactory as a textbook. You decide to write the publisher asking whether a discount is offered on quantity orders. You need the information promptly.

Analysis of the Letter

1. *Identify the book and the author.*

2. *Describe how the book would be used.*

3. *Ask about a discount for quantity purchases, saying about how many you would purchase now and in the future.*

4. *Request prompt attention, since you are pressed for time.*

The Letter

Ladies and Gentlemen:

I have just bought a copy of <u>Dynamic Supervision</u>, by H. L. LaForge, Jr., at a local bookstore. It is excellent.

Our company is planning a series of seminars for supervisors, which I am to teach, and I'm considering using <u>Dynamic Supervision</u> as the textbook. Do you offer a discount for quantity purchases? (I paid $27.95 plus tax at the book store.) Our initial order would be for sixty copies, and if the book proves to meet our needs, I'll probably continue to order in similar quantities three times a year.

The first seminar begins October 9, and I would appreciate hearing from you promptly.

Sincerely,

7-11

ASKING ABOUT DISCOUNTS AND FOR OTHER INFORMATION

Situation

As sales manager for a company that does door-to-door selling, you want to provide each sales representative with an eight-digit electronic calculator. You saw one that you like and want to know about discounts on large orders, and other details.

Analysis of the Letter

1. *Indicate why you're interested in the calculator and how you learned about it. (The latter is optional, but of interest to the manufacturer.)*

2. *Let Wolfenberger know that you've heard what the Wizard retails for; then ask about discounts in the quantities you require.*

3. *Request other information that is important to you. Hinting that your decision will be based on the answers you receive may encourage the manufacturer to sharpen his pencil as well as respond promptly.*

The Letter

Dear Mr. Wolfenberger:

We are considering providing each of our sales representatives with an eight-digit electronic calculator. Last week I saw a demonstration of your Model GH Wizard at the Omaha Business Show, and I think it would fill our needs very nicely.

I understand that the Wizard retails for $33.95. Is there a trade discount for companies that buy in fairly large quantities? Our initial order would be for about 800 units and reorders in perhaps lots of 50.

Not only do I need price information, but I also want complete details about service, warranties, carrying case—any information you think will assist me in making a decision.

Cordially,

Special-request letters include those that may or may not represent a sales opportunity for the recipients. Often they do—for example, when requesting appointments with suppliers to see and talk about their products or services, or when inviting professional speakers (who receive a fee for their services) to appear on a program, or when asking for permission to reproduce materials for which a sizable fee must be paid. Other special-request letters redound almost solely to the benefit of the writer, although they may represent opportunities to develop good public relations.

REQUESTS FOR APPOINTMENTS

Generally, when you want to visit an out-of-town person or business to obtain information that you need, it is usually wise to ask for an appointment in writing, even though it may be of as much or more benefit to the host as it is to you. Often, it is hard to see who and what you want to see if you simply pop in without advance warning. Besides, asking for a specific appointment gives your host a chance to make appropriate arrangements for your visit, saving time for both of you. Follow these guidelines:

1. *If you're unknown to the recipient of your request, tell who you are and the purpose of your visit.*
2. *If you're the primary beneficiary of the meeting, try to convince the recipient that your mission is worthy.*
3. *Suggest a specific date and time, but leave the matter open in case the recipient wants another date.*
4. *Be courteous, no matter what the situation is.*

8-1 REQUESTING INFORMATION—FOR POSSIBLE MUTUAL BENEFIT

Situation

The accounting firm you work for has as one of its clients a chain of six pharmacy stores. You are alarmed at the increasing costs of record keeping in operating a pharmacy business and are looking for ways of reducing them. A magazine article calls your attention to the growing popularity of computers in drugstores (the author owns a computer-service business), and you decide to write the author for an appointment at her place of business to learn firsthand about the applications of computers in small businesses.

Analysis of the Letter

1. *Tell who you are and how you learned about the recipient, complimenting her in an appropriate manner.*

2. *Indicate your interest in the increasing use of computers in pharmacies and your desire to learn more.*

3. *Ask for an appointment, mentioning your forthcoming trip and the time you will be in town.*

4. *If your time is flexible, give the recipient the option of suggesting a particular day and hour.*

5. *Inviting the recipient to call you collect is a courteous gesture; she may prefer that to writing a letter.*

The Letter

Dear Dr. Crain:

One of our clients is a chain of six pharmacies in the Greater Amarillo area. In the last few years, we have become greatly concerned about the increasing cost of maintaining an adequate information system. I was much interested in your excellent article, ''Drugstores Control the Paper Blizzard,'' in The American Pharmacist. You are right on target in saying that in some pharmacies about one-third of the manager's time is spent on paperwork.

I was especially interested to learn that pharmacies are turning to computers to solve the paperwork problem, many on a time-sharing basis. This may be a good solution to our client's problems, and I would like to know more.

I will be in Houston the week of July 18. Would it be convenient for you to talk with me then? I'd especially like to see a computer installation in operation.

If you will set a date and time, I'll be there. My schedule the week of July 18 is quite flexible. If you'd prefer to telephone me rather than write, you may call me collect at (806) 257-1818.

Sincerely,

8-2

REQUESTING ADVICE AND PRODUCT INSPECTION—FOR DEFINITE MUTUAL BENEFIT

Situation

As administrative services manager of an insurance company in downtown Baltimore, you face a serious problem of inadequate office space. You have seen an impressive office setup in which modular units have been installed, and you want to visit the manufacturer of these units in Syracuse to see a display of different types of modules and get some advice from experts. You will be accompanied by two other people.

Analysis of the Letter

1. *Start with background information, which establishes the setting for the request.*

2. *Tell what you already know about the product and where you learned it. The references to Landover Data Systems and Mrs. Robbins will enable you to establish rapport.*

3. *Make the request for an appointment, indicating the number of people in your party and suggest a date and time. Leave open the possibility of a better time for the recipient.*

4. *To help the recipient prepare for the visit, ask for suggestions about what you might bring with you.*

5. *Since your visit represents a sales opportunity for the recipient, there is no need to go overboard in expressing gratitude.*

The Letter

Dear Mr. Margolis:

The rapid growth of our company has made office space a real problem in recent months. Rather than buy or lease additional space, we believe our immediate problem might be alleviated by making more efficient use of the space we now occupy.

On a visit to one of our suppliers (Landover Data Systems), I saw how well that company utilizes every available square foot without sacrificing privacy or efficiency. Mrs. Robbins, the administrative vice president, told me that the modular units installed there were purchased from you. She also said that you have many different types of modular equipment and suggested that I make a trip to Syracuse and talk with you.

Two of my associates and I would like to visit you and discuss our special problem. Would Wednesday, April 18, at 9:30 a.m. be a suitable time for you? If not, please suggest another date during the week of the 16th, and we'll arrange our plans accordingly.

We will bring with us the dimensions and layouts of the three floors of our building involved. If there is any other information you would need, please let me know.

Yours very sincerely,

8-3

REQUESTING INFORMATION AND A SPECIAL FAVOR—FOR REQUESTER'S BENEFIT

Situation

The company you work for is investigating the possibility of sponsoring a Junior Achievement program, and you were asked to write to the organization's headquarters for information. You did so and were referred to a successful Junior Achievement program in another part of your state, with the suggestion that you write the director of the chamber of commerce for details. You decide to ask for an appointment with the director, realizing that the request is solely for your benefit.

Analysis of the Letter

1. *Provide background for the request.*
2. *Next, ask for an appointment, giving your time preferences. This is solely for your benefit, so make it easy for the recipient.*
3. *Also request that arrangements be made to visit certain schools. This could be somewhat troublesome for your host, so be very tactful.*
4. *End with a warm and personal wind-up.*

The Letter

Dear Mr. Talley:

I recently made inquiry to Junior Achievement about the possibility of establishing such a program in Clarkton. In the response I received, there was mention of the very successful Junior Achievement program in Bensonville and a recommendation that I write you for information.

May I come to see you some time in March? The date and time aren't important—whatever is convenient for you. Perhaps you could arrange it so that I could see the Junior Achievement program in action by visiting one or two schools that are participating in it? This would be extremely helpful.

Let me know, please, when we can get together. I would be very grateful for the opportunity to meet and talk with you.

Sincerely yours,

REQUESTING FAVORS

From time to time you will have to write letters to people who may be inconvenienced by the response required of them and have little to gain by cooperating with you. Although most people are generous in this regard, some may require persuasion.

Here are four guidelines for letters requesting special help:

1. *Establish the reason for your request at the outset.*
2. *Emphasize the valuable service the recipient would be rendering by cooperating.*
3. *Make it as easy as you can for the recipient to respond.*
4. *Use more than ordinary tact.*

8-4 REQUESTING SPECIAL ASSISTANCE BY LETTER

Situation

Computer Innovations Inc., a manufacturer of computer equipment, learns that several customers are having difficulty finding competent computer specialists. The supervisor of customer services is asked to write several companies about this matter and share the findings with customers.

Analysis of the Letter

1. *Opening with a question that indicates the subject of the letter is often effective.*

2. *State the purpose of the request, along with a tactful plea for their participation.*

3. *The table provided requires a minimum of writing.*

4. *Enclosure of a stamped, self-addressed envelope is referred to in the last paragraph, along with an expression of thanks. Both are very important.*

The Letter

Gentlemen:

From what sources do you obtain new employees for computer/data processing activities?

This is the subject of a study we are undertaking as a service to companies and government agencies that use our electronic equipment. I hope I can count on you to participate by filling in the brief table below.

Sources of Computer/Data Processing Employees	
Source	Approximate Percentage
State employment services	_____ %
Commercial employment agencies	_____ %
School and college placement offices	_____ %
Employees holding other jobs	_____ %
Employee recommendations	_____ %
Direct application	_____ %
Other _____	_____ %
_____	_____ %

Please use the stamped envelope enclosed to return this letter. Thank you!

Sincerely,

REQUESTING SPECIAL ASSISTANCE BY QUESTIONNAIRE

Situation

You are making a study of employee publications in various companies before starting to publish an employee magazine in your own company. You decide to send a questionnaire to the editors of several employee newspapers.

Analysis of the Letter

1. *Use salesmanship in the first paragraph to gain the recipient's favorable attention. Nothing will please an editor more than seeing his or her magazine praised. (We assume, of course, that it is honest praise.)*

2. *State the purpose of your letter in the second paragraph.*

3. *In the third paragraph, tactfully ask for help. Always include a stamped, self-addressed envelope. This is not only a courteous gesture, but it increases your chances of getting the questionnaire back.*

4. *In the last paragraph, you reemphasize your high opinion of the editor's magazine and promise to send him a copy of yours upon publication.*

The Letter

Dear Mr. Askanazi:

Last month at the DMMA Convention in Atlantic City, I had a chance to examine a special display of employee publications issued by various companies. Among those that impressed me most—in terms of copy, graphics, and general reader appeal—was your magazine, Together.

Our company is planning to publish an employee magazine, and I've been asked to do some research on size and format, personnel required, printing methods, distribution, costs, and so on. I would especially like to have your input to this study.

The brief questionnaire enclosed will, I hope, require no more than a few minutes for you to fill out. Would you please supply the information requested and return the questionnaire to me in the stamped envelope provided. Obviously, if you want to say more than I've asked for, I would be delighted to have your suggestions and recommendations—on the reverse of the questionnaire, if you desire.

I hope eventually to publish an employee magazine that is almost as good as Together. It won't be easy! Anyhow, I'll send you a copy of the first run.

Thank you!

Yours very sincerely,

Analysis of the Questionnaire

1. Give your questionnaire a title.

2. Set up your questionnaire so that it can be filled out quickly. This means:

  a. Designing it so that a minimum of writing is required.

  b. Providing side headings for each major category.

  c. Making sure that every question is clear. (Beware of ambiguities.)

The Questionnaire

INFORMAL STUDY OF EMPLOYEE PUBLICATIONS

Please supply the information asked for below.

SIZE AND FORMAT

1. What is the trim size of your publication? _____

2. Please state briefly the main reason you chose this size.

   _____

3. How many pages does a typical issue contain? _____

4. Is there a restriction on the number of pages allowed for your publication?

   Yes _____ No _____

If yes, what is the number? _____

STAFF

Please indicate the number of people on your editorial/production staff.

Executive editors _____

Copy editors _____

Production specialists _____

Photographers _____

Design and graphics personnel _____

Other: _____ _____

_____ _____

FREQUENCY AND DISTRIBUTION

1. How often is your publication issued?   (Check one.)

   Monthly _____ Biweekly _____ Quarterly _____

   Other _____

2. How many copies are generally printed? _____

3. If it is not important to you, don't ask for the recipient's name and company. The recipient may not be as generous in providing information if identification is required.

3. Is distribution limited to employees?   Yes _____

   No _____ If no, who else receives the publication?

   _____

COST AND PRINTING

1. What is the average cost of producing a typical issue of your publication?$_____

2. Where is the printing done?   (Check one.)

   a. In your own organization _____

   b. At a commercial printing firm _____

READING LEVEL

   Is the reading level of your publication checked against a readability formula?   Yes _____ No _____ If yes, please indicate:

1. The formula you use _____

2. The reading level you aim for _____

REMARKS

   Please include any other information about your publication that you think might be helpful to me in my study. (Use reverse of this sheet if necessary.)

   _____

   _____

   _____

4. Even though the enclosed envelope is addressed, always include your name and address on the questionnaire. The envelope may get lost.

(Please return to A. J. Hamilton, Nu-Age Products Corporation, 3800 Fleur Drive. Des Moines, Iowa 50321.)

REQUESTS FOR SPEAKERS

Occasionally you will need to obtain a speaker for a program. If the person you want is a professional speaker—one who commands a sizable fee for his or her services—writing the invitation is no particular challenge. To the recipient, it is a sales opportunity. If, however, you have little or no money to spend, you may have to use salesmanship in your letter. Even though the person you invite may accommodate you, you are the one who usually benefits most.

Here are guidelines for writing letters to obtain speakers.

1. *Supply complete information about the meeting or conference, including its purpose, its theme (if any), the size of the expected audience, and the time and place.*

2. *If you want the speaker to talk on a particular topic, say so and indicate how long the talk should be. However, if the speech is to be mainly entertainment (such as at a banquet where everyone is in the mood to laugh or be inspired or motivated), you may leave the topic up to the speaker.*

3. *Make it clear what you can do financially—pay expenses only, pay expenses plus an honorarium, or nothing. If the invitation is to a professional speaker, it may be a good idea to learn what the fee is before you make a commitment. You may find too late that the fee asked is well beyond your budget.*

4. *You don't need to give the speaker all the details in the first letter—travel suggestions, hotel accommodations, how expenses are to be submitted, and so on. You provide this and other information after you receive a favorable response.*

5. *The theme of your invitation, especially to "free" speakers, is: "You're the ideal person to address our group, and you would do us a great honor in accepting the assignment."*

8-6 REQUESTING A PROFESSIONAL SPEAKER

Situation

The head of the program committee of the American Association of Travel Agents is to find a speaker for the banquet that closes a three-day meeting. The group has asked for a professional speaker; however, the top fee that can be paid is $1000. Several people have mentioned Raymond Strobel as a good choice.

Analysis of the Letter

1. *Open the letter with a compliment ("You have been highly recommended . . ."); then identify the group and give the place and date.*

2. *Describe the setting in which the speech will be given, the topic, and the time allotted. (In this case, leave the topic to the speaker.)*

3. *Note in the last paragraph that you dodge making a commitment until you know what the fee is. There's still time to back out if the speaker demands more than you can afford.*

The Letter

Dear Mr. Strobel:

You have been highly recommended by several of our members as a speaker for the banquet that closes a three-day meeting of the American Association of Travel Agents. The place is the Sheraton Inn in Myrtle Beach, South Carolina; the date is the evening of October 3.

The banquet is a purely social affair, climaxing three days of hard work, and we prefer an address on the light side, but with an inspirational theme. I would leave it to you to select a topic, which I know will be appropriate for the occasion. A talk of about thirty minutes would be just right.

May I hear from you by June 14? Please indicate in your reply the financial arrangements you require. Just as soon as we have reached an agreement, I will send you more details, including a tentative convention program.

Sincerely yours,

8-7 REQUESTING A SPEAKER— NO FUNDS AVAILABLE

Situation

The executive secretary of a state organization of retired people has been asked to obtain a keynote speaker for the group's annual conference. No funds are available.

Analysis of the Letter

1. *Identify the group and describe the general plans for the conference, including location, theme, and objectives.*

2. *Issue the invitation, reinforcing your special interest in the recipient by complimenting him and giving him a general idea of what he might say. Also indicate the length of the talk and the attendance you expect.*

3. *Be frank about your financial situation, adding that, as a public-spirited individual, the recipient will be more interested in giving a service than receiving payment.*

4. *Offer to send further details just as soon as you have a favorable response. Mentioning the location (hotel) of the meeting is an effective sign-off.*

The Letter

Dear Dr. Burdette:

The Indiana chapter of the American Association of Retired People is holding its annual conference in Terre Haute on June 17–19. The theme of this year's meeting is "The Senior Citizen: A Dynamic Community Resource." As you might guess, most of our discussions will focus on the important role that AARP members can play in community affairs.

Would you be our keynote speaker for this conference? We are well acquainted with your excellent newspaper and magazine articles on the importance to older people of keeping involved. Your remarks as keynoter would set the tone perfectly for our conference. A thirty- to forty-five-minute talk would be fine. We expect an attendance of about 275.

Although our limited treasury does not permit payment of fees or expenses for speakers, we are hoping that your interest in the problems of and opportunities for the aging will be a sufficient incentive for you to be with us.

I look forward to a favorable reply, Dr. Burdette, and just as soon as I receive it, I will send you complete details. Our meeting place is the Best Western Statesman Inn Motel on U.S. 41, just north of Indiana State University.

Very sincerely yours,

8-8

INVITING A PANEL PARTICIPANT— PAYMENT OFFERED

Situation

As the leader of a panel discussion at a convention, you are to invite three people to serve on the panel with you. The organization that sponsors the convention will pay expenses for panel members plus a modest honorarium.

Analysis of the Letter

1. *Give the name of the organization, the date and place of the meeting, and your role.*

2. *Describe the nature and proceedings of the meeting; then issue the invitation in a complimentary manner ("no one better qualified").*

3. *Be specific about financial arrangements; then add other details about the time.*

4. *Express the hope that the recipient's response will be favorable and offer to send other details later.*

5. *The postscript is an effective way to end the letter.*

The Letter

Dear Ms. Steinmetz:

The National Advertising Directors Association holds its annual meeting September 4–6 at the Washington Hilton in Washington, D.C. I have been asked to lead a panel discussion on "Media Trends and Developments."

The panel will concentrate on three media—print, broadcast, and direct mail—and a specialist for each medium will speak for about fifteen minutes. These talks will be followed by a question-and-answer period in which members of the audience participate.

Would you serve as our speaker-specialist on direct mail? I can think of no one better qualified to fill this role. NADA is prepared to pay all your expenses, and we can offer you the modest honorarium of $50 as a panel participant. The media panel is scheduled to begin at 2 p.m. on Tuesday the fifth and end no later than 4 p.m.

I do hope, Ms. Steinmetz, that it will be possible for you to undertake this assignment. Let me know as soon as you can, please. If your response is favorable, I'll get other information to you.

Sincerely yours,

P.S.   You'll be interested in knowing that you were the unanimous choice of the program-planning committee for this spot on the program!

REQUESTS TO REPRODUCE MATERIALS

When you want to make copies of materials from magazines, books, and similar sources, you should get permission in writing from the publisher. Most of these materials are copyrighted, which means you could get into trouble if you use them without permission—particularly for commercial (profit-making) purposes. Some publishers allow no reproductions of certain materials (for example, special charts and diagrams that make the publication unique). Many charge a fee when you want to reproduce more than a half page or so, especially if your reproduction will be sold in some form. (This is mainly to protect the author from loss of royalties.) Others— some magazine publishers, for example—make no charge for noncommercial use of their articles; they like the publicity they receive from such reproductions.

Often, magazine publishers make reprints of certain articles, which they sell at a profit. If reprints are available, you're likely to be required to buy them, rather than given permission to make your own copies.

Following are guidelines in writing requests to reproduce materials:

1. *Give specific information about the material you want to reproduce:*
   a. *If the material comes from a book, give the name of the author, the title of the book, the edition, and the page number(s) on which the material appears.*
   b. *If the material comes from a periodical, give the name of the periodical, the title of the article, the date of issue, and the page number(s) on which the material appears.*
2. *Tell exactly how the material will be used. This is especially important if you plan to sell the publication in which the material is used.*
3. *If you expect to make your own reproductions, say how many copies you will make.*
4. *If appropriate, indicate why this material will be especially useful to you.*
5. *Assure the publisher that you will give proper credit to the source. This is vital if you are using copyrighted material.*

8-9 REQUESTING MAGAZINE REPRINTS OR PERMISSION TO REPRODUCE

Situation

You are helping to plan a regional sales conference. In the process, you run across a magazine article that you would like to distribute to those that will attend. You decide to write the publisher asking whether reprints are available and, if not, for permission to make photocopies.

Analysis of the Letter

1. *Refer to your sales conference as background for your request. (This would not be necessary if you were sure that reprints are available and were merely ordering them.)*

2. *Be specific about the material you want and request reprints (eighty-five) at the usual rate.*

3. *Request permission to make copies of the article if there are no reprints. Tell how they will be distributed and pledge to identify the source.*

4. *Because you're in a hurry for an answer, ask for one by a specific date, closing with a "thank you."*

The Letter

Dear Ms. Schuster:

The theme of our Midwest Regional Sales Conference on May 14–17 is "Winning Sales Through Service." The article, "The Sale Doesn't Stop With the Order," which appeared in the January issue of Motivation, is precisely the message we want to get across at this conference.

Are reprints available? If so, we would like eighty-five copies at your regular reprint rate. If there are no reprints, may we have permission to make eighty-five photocopies of the article? The copies will be distributed only to our personnel and without charge. We would make sure, of course, that the source of the article is prominently displayed.

I would be extremely grateful for a quick response, Ms. Schuster. We hope to complete our conference plans by April 10. Thank you!

Sincerely yours,

8-10

ASKING FOR FREE REPRODUCTION PRIVILEGES OF A BOOK ILLUSTRATION

Situation

You are asked to present a paper at a national convention on the preparation of annual reports—a paper that you plan to distribute to those attending. You want to include in your paper a chart from a handbook, and you write for permission to do so.

Analysis of the Letter

1. *Open the letter with a background statement that leads into your purpose in writing.*

2. *Mention next that you plan to make copies (approximate number) of your paper; otherwise, there would be no need to write for permission to use the chart.*

3. *Identify specifically what you want to reproduce—page number, name of book, edition, and author. The last sentence in the second paragraph is a compliment to the author and publisher.*

4. *Give assurance of your plans for limited distribution without charge. Also mention that you will give proper credit.*

5. *It's usually a good idea to send a copy of the publication in which the copyrighted material appears. This is partial proof, at least, that your intentions are on the up-and-up.*

The Letter

Ladies and Gentlemen:

I have been asked to present a paper on the preparation of annual corporate reports at the annual convention of the Finance Executives Association in Dayton on March 5.

I plan to make copies of my paper and distribute them to those present—about fifty. May I have permission to include the chart on page 425 of *Handbook of Public Relations*, Second Edition, by Frank L. Selden? It's the best structure for an annual report that I have seen.

The paper in which the chart would appear will, of course, be distributed without cost and only to those attending my meeting. Certainly, I would make sure that full credit is given to the author and publisher. If you have a standard credit line that you require, I will be pleased to use it.

I would be grateful for your approval of this request. If you would like a copy of my paper when it is reproduced, I'll be pleased to send it to you.

Yours very cordially,

8-11

REQUESTING REPRODUCTION PRIVILEGES FOR COMMERCIAL USE

Situation

As assistant to the director of merchandising for a large franchiser, you are preparing a sales training manual for employees, which will be sold to the franchise stores. You write to the publisher asking for permission to reproduce the chapter, offering a royalty fee on each copy of the book that is sold.

Analysis of the Letter

1. *Get down to your purpose immediately, giving the recipient a clear description of all your plans.*

2. *Make your request and proposal, indicating the number of copies you plan to distribute and suggesting a royalty arrangement.*

3. *Ask for the recipient's permission in writing, including the requirements for copyright identification.*

4. *Offer assurance that you won't use the material without written permission in any manner other than that which is described.*

The Letter

Dear Mr. Kauffman:

I am preparing a special training manual for retail sales employees in our 1620 franchised stores throughout the country. The manual, which will contain 256 pages, will be sold to the franchisees at $2.50 each, which is about half the actual production and distribution cost.

I would like very much to include in the manual the excellent chapter, "The Last Three Feet," from your book, Practical Selling Techniques, Third Edition, by C. A. Dowling. We expect to distribute about 12,000 copies a year and propose a royalty to you of 2½ cents on each copy sold. This would amount to about $300 a year in royalties.

If this proposal is satisfactory to you, please let me have your concurrence in writing, along with information you require for copyright identification. We would not, of course, use your material in any other manner without your permission.

Cordially yours,

8-12

REQUESTING PERMISSION TO REPRODUCE NONCOPYRIGHTED MATERIALS

Situation

A chemical engineer hears a paper presented on dry storage of nuclear reactor fuel at a recent convention of the American Society of Chemical Engineers. He'd like a copy from which additional copies could be made and distributed to the company's engineers, who are debating the pros and cons of wet and dry storage of nuclear wastes.

Analysis of the Letter

1. *Refer to the paper that was presented and the fact that it was of great interest.*

2. *Ask for the paper and for permission to make copies of it for internal use. Mention the value of the paper to the engineers in the company and the caution that will be observed in distributing it.*

3. *The third paragraph anticipates an event that often takes place— good papers presented at conventions often wind up as magazine articles. This suggestion is a compliment to the recipient as is your willingness to purchase reprints.*

4. *The letter ends with a "thank you" for the presentation and for the consideration of the request.*

The Letter

Dear Professor Mangum:

I was greatly intrigued by your paper at the recent ASCE convention in Reno. Certainly, your experience in the TVA project encourages me to suggest that we at Bolling Chemical take a closer look at dry storage. I'm afraid some of our people are not aware of the advantages you described.

Is it possible to obtain a copy of your report and reproduce, say, a dozen copies for our internal use? We're involved right now in discussions of waste control, and I think your paper would provide valuable guidelines in our deliberations. We would not distribute the material outside the company without permission from you.

Perhaps you have plans to publish your paper in one of our trade magazines. If so, you may be reluctant to release it for our use. If that is the case, would you let me know where and when it is to be published? We'll want to order reprints as soon as possible.

Thank you for your excellent presentation and for your consideration of this request.

Yours sincerely,

PART 3

TRANSMITTAL AND CONFIRMATION LETTERS

When you send something important in the mail, such as a check, contract, purchase order, invoice, statement, or promissory note, it's often a good idea to cover what you're sending with a letter. This gives you a chance to explain what is being sent and why, but equally important, a copy of your letter provides a valuable record. Thus you won't have to wonder later, "Did I send that service contract to Nicholls? If so, when did I send it?"

Equally important is the confirmation of agreements by letter. The reason is, of course, that in telephone conversations or face-to-face meetings, people may come away with conflicting ideas about what was said: who is to do what? at what price? in what quantities? And so on.

TRANSMITTING PAYMENT

It's usually wise to accompany a payment with a letter—to settle an account, pay for an order, compensate a speaker, or whatever. Although most businesses keep an accurate record of payments, often the record doesn't show when the check was actually mailed. A copy of your transmittal letter offers solid proof of this fact.

Use these guides in transmitting payment:

1. *Tell what you're sending (usually a check) and indicate the amount.*
2. *Make sure the recipient knows what the payment is for.*
3. *Clarify any points that may be confusing; for example, the amount may be less or more than expected.*
4. *If the check is for valuable services rendered (an outstanding speaker, for example), show your genuine appreciation.*

TRANSMITTING PAYMENT ON ACCOUNT

Situation

As a new business owner, you have arranged sixty-day credit terms with a supplier on a large order, the payments to be made in equal installments. You have made the first payment on schedule and are now ready to transmit the second.

Analysis of the Letter

1. *Refer to the check you're sending and what it's for. (If you'd prefer to say "Enclosed is" . . . rather than "Here is" . . . , that's all right.)*

2. *You may wish to show, for your own records, the check number in the enclosure notation; thus,*

   Enc. Check 117

3. *If a "thank you" is in order, by all means extend it. You may have been short on cash when the order was placed, and the sixty-day credit terms were a godsend.*

The Letter

Dear Miss Fogel:

Here is my check for $2416.40, which represents final payment on my order of February 9.

Thank you for the courtesy extended me.

Cordially yours,

9-2 TRANSMITTING PAYMENT— DISCREPANCY EXPLAINED

Situation

You receive a statement from a supplier, a personal friend, in the amount of $1059.51. According to your accounts payable records, however, you owe only $979.74. You realize that the supplier failed to give you credit for faulty merchandise that you returned, even though you were issued a credit memorandum for the amount.

Analysis of the Letter

1. *Mention the amount of the check and what it is for.*

2. *Then, explain why the amount doesn't agree with the statement. There is no need to mention "faulty merchandise" or indicate alarm; Bert will get the point.*

3. *To avoid sounding self-righteous, leave the door slightly ajar for rebuttal.*

4. *End the letter on a positive, friendly note.*

The Letter

Dear Bert:

Enclosed is my check for $979.74 in payment of the statement I received from you December 11.

You'll see, Bert, that this amount doesn't jibe with your statement. The reason there is a difference, I'm quite sure, is that the credit memo issued to me on December 2 for $79.77 had not been posted to my account at the time the statement was prepared.

If there is any question, please let me know. Otherwise, I'll assume that our records agree.

The Little Furnace kerosene heater is moving very well (you said it would), and it's likely that we'll have to reorder before the month ends. Good news for both of us!

Best regards,

9-3 TRANSMITTING PAYMENT TO AN OUTSTANDING SPEAKER

Situation

The executive secretary of the American Association of Safety Engineers receives an expense statement from a speaker who appeared on a program sponsored by the association. The speaker was also promised an honorarium of $250. He did an excellent job, and in the short time he was there, a good relationship developed between him and the executive secretary. The writer wants to transmit payment and express genuine appreciation for an outstanding performance.

Analysis of the Letter

1. *Mention the two checks enclosed and what they are for.*

2. *Express appreciation in a highly complimentary manner. (Actually the letter could start with the second paragraph shown and the checks mentioned in the next paragraph.)*

3. *End the letter with a friendly invitation, which will be appreciated even though it may not be possible for the recipient to accept it.*

The Letter

Dear Phil:

Here is a check for $417.88 for your expenses in connection with your presentation at the AASE conference in Phoenix. Also enclosed is a check for $250, which is the honorarium you were promised.

From all reports, the Phoenix conference was one of the most successful we have ever had. Certainly, your keynote talk on Tuesday gave us the ideal kick-off, and it was referred to (and praised) often in the sectional meetings that followed. We're glad you came!

If your travels bring you to Chicago, remember that I'm not far from O'Hare. Give me a call (443-3581). I'm a real authority on the area's best eating places!

Sincerely,

9-4 TRANSMITTING PAYMENT TO A DISAPPOINTING SPEAKER

Situation

Each spring, a large university sponsors an educational conference to which high school and college teachers are invited. One of the three speakers engaged for the conference had to bow out at the last minute, and a substitute had to be found on very short notice. His performance was disappointing, yet he is entitled to the $100 honorarium promised. The writer wants to transmit the check and express gratitude in a tactful yet truthful manner.

Analysis of the Letter

1. *Mention the check first.*

2. *Express your gratitude, stopping just short of a compliment. Make no direct reference to his performance, he may infer a compliment if he so chooses.*

The Letter

Dear Dr. Barkham:

Enclosed is a check for $100, your honorarium for your presentation at the Fifth Annual Conference on Educational Innovation.

We are all very grateful to you for accepting this assignment on such short notice, Dr. Barkham. As a whole, we felt the conference was quite productive, and we thank you for participating in it.

Very sincerely yours,

TRANSMITTING OTHER MATERIALS

No matter what you are sending in the mail, if it is important to have a record of what, when, and to whom the material was sent, then accompany it with a letter. Guidelines for writing such letters are:

1. *Mention specifically what is being sent.*
2. *If there is the least doubt in the recipient's mind as to why the materials are being sent, give the reason and any other required explanation.*
3. *Keep the letter as brief as possible, but be tactful, expressing appreciation when appropriate.*

10-1 TRANSMITTING A CONTRACT

Situation

The company you work for provides automobile leasing to various businesses. You've had several meetings with a potential customer in an effort to put together a satisfactory contract. The contract has finally been drawn up, and you are ready to mail it, with instructions on how to handle it and an expression of appreciation with the new association.

Analysis of the Letter

1. *Be specific about what you're sending.*

2. *Give instructions on how the agreement is to be handled (assuming it is approved).*

3. *Since you're writing to a new customer, end the letter with a goodwill– building message.*

The Letter

Dear Margaret:

The original and one copy of the revised leasing agreement are enclosed.

I think the new agreement encompasses all the changes we talked about last week. If it meets with your approval, please sign both copies and return the original to me (an envelope is enclosed).

We look forward to providing the services described in the contract, Margaret, and to a very cordial relationship between our two organizations.

Yours very sincerely,

10-2   TRANSMITTING A DRAFT FOR APPROVAL

Situation

You are secretary of the long-range planning committee in your company. After each meeting you prepare the minutes, which are distributed to all members. The November meeting was an especially important one; its theme was diversification through acquisition. During the meeting, you made notes, but so many ideas were presented in a give-and-take atmosphere that you're not certain you got everything down accurately. You decide to make a double-spaced rough draft of the minutes and get the chairman's approval before releasing the final copies.

Analysis of the Memorandum

1. *Indicate what you are transmitting.*

2. *Identify your problems, emphasizing those that are of special concern, and ask for a double-check and approval.*

3. *Finally, thank the chairman for his help and mention your plan to distribute the minutes to all members.*

The Memorandum

Dear Floyd:

Here is a rough draft of the minutes of the November long-range planning committee meeting.

Although I was careful to take notes of the discussions, so many topics were covered and ideas generated that I'm not certain I got it all down accurately. Would you please make any needed corrections? (You can write directly on the draft.) I am particularly shaky about capital requirements and projected ROI on warehouse leasing and manufactured homes.

Thanks very much for your help. When I have your okay, I'll distribute the final version to all the members.

Sincerely,

10-3 TRANSMITTING MATERIALS SEPARATELY

Situation

See Letter 8-11 on page 75. The training manual has been published, and two copies are being sent separately to the publisher of the book from which a chapter was taken.

Analysis of the Letter

1. *Identify what you are sending and mention that it will arrive separately. (It's also a good idea to say how it is being sent—in this case, by mail.)*

2. *The recipient will understand the reason the manuals are being sent (they were asked for at the time of the agreement), so no explanation is necessary.*

3. *Wind up with a positive and friendly statement, and a "thank you."*

The Letter

Dear Mr. Kauffman:

Our "Training Manual for Salespeople" has just been published, and I am mailing you two copies in a separate package.

We are quite pleased with the result and hope you will like the way we handled the chapter from <u>Practical Selling Techniques</u>. Thanks again for your cooperation.

Very cordially yours,

10-4 TRANSMITTING RESULTS OF A QUESTIONNAIRE STUDY

Situation

Worldwide Personnel Placement Inc. recently conducted a question-naire survey on the use of tests in employee selection. Now that the results are compiled, each participant is to receive a thank-you letter that includes the findings of the study.

Analysis of the Letter

1. *Immediately mention what the letter is about.*

2. *Present the results of the study in the form of a table for ease of interpretation.*

3. *End the letter with a statement of appreciation and express hope that the results will be interesting to the recipient.*

The Letter

Dear Mrs. Rifkin:

I thought you might like to know the results of our questionnaire survey on the use of tests in employee selection. Here they are.

Test	Number of Companies	Percent of Companies
Clerical/stenographic	660	96.1
Mental (intelligence)	537	78.2
Mechanical aptitude	387	56.3
Personality or interest	376	54.7
Performance	324	47.2
Trade knowledge	290	42.2
Dexterity	275	40.0
Other	108	15.7

I very much appreciate your participating in this study, Mrs. Rif-kin. The results will be very useful to us in our counseling, and I hope you will also find them of interest.

Cordially yours,

10-5 TRANSMITTING PRINTER'S PROOFS

Situation

The printing firm you work for has been given the job of printing several personnel forms for the Herrold Corporation. The type has been set, and the customer's approval of the proof is needed before the forms are actually printed. You transmit the proof with a letter.

Analysis of the Letter

1. *Be specific about what you're sending and list the items for easy identification.*

2. *Tactfully suggest quick action so that you can get on with the job.*

3. *Express appreciation for the opportunity given you.*

4. *If you're anxious to schedule the job immediately, the "P.S." may speed things along.*

The Letter

Dear Mrs. McNamara:

Enclosed is printer's proof of the following forms, together with the copy you supplied us:

Application for Employment

Employee Merit Rating

Position Description Questionnaire

Anniversary Reminder

Just as soon as I have your approval, Mrs. McNamara, we can go to press. I know you're in a hurry for these forms, and the job will receive the highest priority at this end.

Yours very sincerely,

P.S. In the interest of time, you may want to telephone your approval or corrections. If so, call me at (457) 762-4869.

CONFIRMATION LETTERS

Confirming an agreement by letter is critical when the discussion involves a serious commitment, such as offering special prices or services, making appointments or reservations, or changing procedures and policies.

In some instances, even written proposals and agreements are confirmed by letter. An example is a telegram or cable, which could be garbled in transmission.

In the models that follow, some of the letters are from the person receiving the services (such as a customer) and others from the person providing the services.

There are three guidelines for writing confirmation letters:

---

1. *Make it entirely clear what it is that you are confirming.*

2. *Leave room for debate if there is any likelihood that the recipient has an interpretation of the agreement different from yours.*

3. *Since you will probably be acquainted with the person to whom you write a confirmation (you've had some sort of previous contact), personalize the message.*

11-1

CONFIRMING A SUPPLIER'S ORAL INSTRUCTIONS

Situation

Customers of a wholesaler of automobile parts and supplies (retail stores) have returned many cans of enamel in recent weeks because of defective spray nozzles. The owner of STANAP Auto Parts visits the wholesaler to discuss the matter. During the conversation, the wholesaler suggests that the parts store owner simply provide a count of returns and send a report of them rather than return the defective cans. The store owner decides to confirm this discussion by letter.

Analysis of the Letter

1. Review the setting in which the discussion took place and the outcome as you view it.

2. Give the recipient an opportunity to supply his own version of the discussion, if different.

3. End the letter with a friendly expression of gratitude.

The Letter

Dear Ward:

Last week, when you and I were discussing the problems our customers are having with defective spray nozzles for Velvetcoast enamels, you suggested that I simply mail you a report each month on the number of returns by customers rather than send the defective containers to you. You mentioned that you would either issue a credit memo or replace the defective cans, according to the preference I indicate in my report.

I plan to put this new policy into effect at once, Ward, but first I want to make absolutely sure that I understood you correctly. If I don't hear from you within the coming week, I'll assume that what I said in the first paragraph is accurate.

Thanks for giving me so much time in your office last Friday. From my point of view, it was a very productive meeting.

Yours sincerely,

11-2

CONFIRMING PRICES AND QUANTITY DISCOUNTS

Situation

You are sales manager for an office furniture manufacturer. A potential customer visits your office to ask about prices and quantity discounts on acoustical partitions. You confirm your quotations in a letter.

Analysis of the Letter

1. *Describe the setting in which the discussion took place.*
2. *Be specific about identifying the products, including catalog page number, regular and special prices, and the closing date for the latter.*

3. *Mention the date of shipment and terms.*

4. *Close with a sales message, encouraging the customer to place an order soon.*

The Letter

Dear Mrs. Zubeck:

This will confirm our discussion on April 3 about special discounts on Modu-Screen acoustical partitions as described on pages 33–37 of our catalog. These prices will prevail through April 30.

Partition Dimensions	Regular Price Each	Special Price Each (12 or More)
4′ × 4′ Straight	$122.75	$ 98.20
4′ × 5′ Straight	$132.00	$115.50
5′ × 5′ Straight	$152.75	$129.85
5′ × 5′ Curved	$191.00	$152.80

The prices indicated apply to all four colors available in mod-acrylic fabric: wheat, gold, orange, and black. All frames (clear, anodized aluminum) and hardware (end legs and top caps to match frames) are provided at no extra cost.

We can guarantee shipment by April 10 (shipping charges are F.O.B. Camden).

We will be delighted to have your order, Mrs. Zubeck. If you address it to my attention, I'll make certain it gets very special handling.

Yours very cordially,

11-3 CONFIRMING ARRANGEMENTS FOR A SPEAKER

Situation

You are in charge of planning the program for a workshop for administrative assistants in your company. You have invited a university professor to address the group, and the invitation has been accepted. You now confirm the arrangements in writing.

Analysis of the Letter

1. *Open the letter with a compliment and "thank you."*

2. *Be specific about the time, place, type and length of speech, and other matters pertaining to the program.*

3. *Offer to pick up the speaker at the airport or, if she's driving, supply the address of the hotel. In the latter instance, she will need directions to the meeting room, which you supply.*

4. *Give advance notice that she should keep track of all expenses and tell her how to submit the expense report.*

5. *Offer additional help and end on a friendly note.*

The Letter

Dear Professor Dickinson:

Everyone is delighted that you can be with us on March 23. Thank you for accepting our invitation.

Enclosed is a rough draft of the program. You will see that the luncheon at which you are to speak begins at 12:30, and your talk should get under way about 1:30. I will introduce you. (Would you please send me a brief biographical sketch that I may refer to?)

I know that our workshop participants will be very much interested in your varied experiences in the business as well as the academic world. I'm sure you have some amusing stories to tell, and a bit of humor will be perfectly in order. I hope you'll devote some time, however, to giving us your view of the role of the administrative assistant and how she or he can prepare for further advancement into management.

As I mentioned earlier, our meeting will be at the John Marshall Hotel. If you plan to fly, let me know the airline and flight number, and I'll meet you at the airport. Or if you plan to drive, the John Marshall is at Fifth and Franklin in the heart of Richmond. You'll find our meeting room posted on the "Today's Events" board in the lobby.

Please keep a record of all your expenses—airfare (or automobile mileage at 25 cents a mile), food, taxis, and so on—and mail me a statement upon your return to Washington. The $100 honorarium will be given to you while you're here.

In the meantime, please let me know if there is anything I can do to help you. We want to make your visit with us completely enjoyable.

Sincerely,

11-4

CONFIRMING AN APPOINTMENT

Situation

As personnel recruiter for a firm of consulting engineers, you must fill six new jobs in the company as quickly as possible. You telephone an agency in Salt Lake City that specializes in engineering placement and are invited to the agency's offices to discuss your needs in person.

Analysis of the Letter

1. *Confirm the place, date, and time of the appointment and mention what you will bring with you. (The latter gives the recipient an opportunity to suggest other information that may be needed.)*

2. *Give the name of the place where you will be staying and when you expect to arrive. It is always a good idea to do this because there may be a sudden change in the host's plans and you will need to be notified.*

The Letter

Dear Mr. DeSimone:

I look forward to seeing you in Salt Lake City on September 6. I will be at your office at 10:30 a.m. and will bring job descriptions of the six engineering positions that we are anxious to fill.

I expect to arrive at the Hotel Utah about 4 p.m. on September 5. You can reach me there if you need to.

Yours cordially,

11-5 CONFIRMING A TELEPHONE CONVERSATION

Situation

The director of exhibits for a municipal convention center receives a telephone call from a manufacturer of musical instruments in which the manufacturer requests exhibit space at a forthcoming convention. The space asked for is available, and the exhibits director now wants to confirm the information that was transmitted by telephone.

Analysis of the Letter

1. Identify what you are confirming, itemizing the main features of the exhibit space: date, dimensions, location, and price.

2. Include other information that is of prime importance to both you and the exhibitor.

3. Provide space for the exhibitor to sign, which in effect makes the letter a contract. Some organizations require this in order to protect themselves in the event of a back-off.

4. If you wish, you can add a postscript something like this:

P.S. I extend to you a cordial welcome to Hartford and express the wish that the NMEA convention will prove very worthwhile for your organization.

The Letter

Dear Mrs. Thomasulo:

We have reserved exhibit space for you at the annual convention of the National Music Educators Association in Hartford as follows:

Date: June 8–11, 1983

Space: 20 by 10 feet

Location: Exhibit Hall, Hartford Convention Center, sixth area to the right of the entrance

Price: $3000, 50 percent payable in advance

The space reserved for you is equipped with eight heavy-duty electrical outlets. There are no other fixtures, and structural changes (walls, ceilings, etc.) are not permitted. Local union regulations require that setting up and taking down your exhibit be done by union personnel. Please make arrangements with James Carmichael, who is our liaison with the union.

If the terms outlined above meet with your approval, please sign in the space below and return this letter to me, along with your check for $1500. A copy of the agreement is enclosed for your records.

Sincerely yours,

Approved: _____
Name

_____
Company

_____
Date

11-6 CONFIRMING A TELEGRAM

Situation

The Cimarron Development Corporation receives permission to construct a new refinery. The president immediately sends a telegram to an important friend and supplier announcing the good news, which he confirms by letter.

Analysis of the Letter

1. *Repeat the telegram exactly as you wrote it.*

2. *Add any other pertinent information, in this case a reiteration of your need for prices and delivery schedules.*

The Letter

Dear Harry:

Today I sent you the following telegram:

CONSTRUCTION OF REFINERY AT MIDLOTHIAN SPRINGS APPROVED BY REFERENDUM. CONSTRUCTION WILL PROCEED IMMEDIATELY. NEED AT ONCE FIRM PRICES AND DELIVERY SCHEDULES ON ION-EXCHANGE DEMINERALIZERS.

I know you share our excitement about this decision, Harry, and that you will get me the information requested as quickly as possible. We fully expect to be in operation no later than November 1 of next year.

Best personal regards.

Sincerely,

PART 4

SALES COMMUNICATIONS

It's no secret, of course, that in every profit-making organization the sale (to paraphrase Shakespeare) is the *thing.* No subject occupies the thoughts of top executives so consistently. No question is asked more often by management than "How are sales?" Even those not directly involved in selling the company's products or services have learned that the answer to that question is critical. When sales are soft over a prolonged period, gloom prevails and sooner or later there are cutbacks in personnel, in costs, in employee benefits, and in plans for growth. When sales are on the upswing, the organization hums with excitement.

There are many facets to selling. In many organizations, sales representatives who call on prospects and customers are largely responsible for sales, and a lot of money is spent in recruiting, training, and motivating these people. In such companies, there are really no effective substitutes for face-to-face, personal selling.

Sales representatives, however, need support: through effective advertising, exhibits and displays, PR efforts, efficient service from the home office, and various promotional devices.

Letters can play an important role in the sales process—responding to inquiries about the organization's products or services, following up on sales representatives' calls, acknowledging orders, supplying information to customers about a product, and ironing out problems that arise between customer and supplier.

A great many companies make extensive use of the sales letter—one written specifically to obtain an order—even though they employ a large field force for personal selling. Enterprises that do no personal selling, such as magazine publishers and mail-order concerns, depend almost entirely on letters to do their selling.

SECTION 12

RESPONDING TO SALES-OPPORTUNITY REQUEST LETTERS

If you work in sales or public relations, you may spend much of your time responding to requests from people who are either customers or potential customers or supporters. The letters you receive from these groups represent excellent opportunities to sell—if not a product or service, then an image of your company that could be profitable in some way. Whenever you stand a good chance of making a sale, attracting an investor, or winning an influential friend, your response should reflect your enthusiasm for the opportunity.

When you receive thousands of inquiries about something you've advertised or promoted, you can't usually respond to each with a personal letter. In these instances, you may have a card, informal memo, or letter printed to use as your response. When sending advertised materials, some companies don't write anything—they merely send the catalog, report, or whatever, with no message. Although printed responses have a "to-whom-it-may-concern" flavor, we think they're a lot better than nothing.

If you can, it is always best to write a personal letter to each person who makes a sales-opportunity inquiry. This is fairly simple today in offices where there is sophisticated word-processing equipment. But even in smaller offices, form letters and form paragraphs may be used with very little expense.

Following are six guidelines for responding to sales-opportunity requests.

1. *If you can do everything the writer requested, introduce the good news early.*
2. *If you can only partially satisfy the writer's request, first say what you can do; then explain what you can't do and why.*

3. *If you are unable to supply **anything** requested, open your letter with an expression of appreciation, then proceed to the bad news.*

4. *Use every opportunity to win the inquirer's good will, whether your response is favorable or unfavorable. In other words, go out of your way to be helpful (see Section 5).*

5. *Personalize your message in such a way that the recipient feels that you are honestly glad to be of service or disappointed that you can't help.*

6. *When sending printed materials—product descriptions, promotional literature, catalogs, etc.—refer only to the features you think will interest your reader most. Don't repeat in your letter everything that has been said in the printed materials.*

SHORT PRINTED RESPONSE FOR A MASS MAILING

Situation

You have placed an ad in a widely read business magazine, inviting readers to write for a free catalog of business gifts. Based on past experience, you predict that you will receive about 5000 requests. You want a printed response that can be affixed to the catalog cover by a foldover flap.

Analysis of the Message

1. You can simulate a salutation by using a heading such as "THANK YOU."

2. Say immediately what you can do.

3. Personalize the message and include a signature (which is also printed).

The Message

THANK YOU –

for asking for our catalog of business gifts. I am delighted to send it to you!
   Please note that the envelopes for your orders are addressed to me. This is because I want every order you send to have my personal attention. You see, we're as proud of our service as we are of our gifts!

Michael D. Schuster

Sales Vice President
MONARCH ORIGINALS INC.

12-2 PRINTED LETTER WITH A PERSONAL NOTE

Situation

As executive director of Junior Achievement, you place an ad in *Fortune*, inviting readers to send for free materials. Nearly a thousand requests are received, and the materials are to be sent out with a printed letter that includes a personal note.

Analysis of the Letter

1. *Simulate a salutation, since you cannot address each reader by name.*

2. *Say immediately what you're sending and describe its general contents.*

3. *Anticipate the question, "How does one start a JA program?" in the second paragraph.*

4. *Make the final paragraph a persuasive invitation to "join the family" and an offer of special help.*

5. *The postscript is typewritten, which personalizes the letter. This is a great gesture—if you can afford it.*

The Letter

HERE'S YOUR JUNIOR ACHIEVEMENT
SPONSOR'S KIT—

It's a pleasure to send it to you. In it you will find complete information about Junior Achievement—who we are, how we got started, how we operate, and some of the wonderful things that have been accomplished by this unusual organization.

There is a special section in the kit on how your company can establish a Junior Achievement program, including ways of enlisting school and community support.

Naturally, I hope that after you get better acquainted with Junior Achievement and its objectives, you will want to join our family. If there is anything I can do to help, please write or telephone me.

Sincerely yours,

P.S. Our membership directory indicates that there is a Junior Achievement program in operation in Bensonville, which is not far from you. If you want to look into it, you might get in touch with the Bensonville Chamber of Commerce.

12-3

SUPPLYING THE NAME OF A DEALER

Situation

As sales correspondent for an aircraft manufacturer, you receive an inquiry from a reader of your company's magazine ad, asking the name of the dealer nearest Minneapolis. You supply the information, encouraging the recipient to visit the dealer. (Refer to Letter 7-3 on page 51.)

Analysis of the Letter

1. *Express pleasure at the inquirer's interest in the Luxury XII and immediately give complete information about the dealer nearest Minneapolis—name, address, and telephone number.*

2. *It is standard practice to pass along to a dealer inquiries that come from his or her territory so that appropriate follow-up can be made. In the last sentence, offer further encouragement to visit the dealer by mentioning courtesy transportation arrangements.*

The Letter

Dear Mr. Weeks:

I'm delighted to learn of your interest in the Luxury XII helicopter. Our dealer nearest Minneapolis is Avitron Inc., which is located at 1872 North Sheridan Road, Waukegan, Illinois 60085. The telephone number is (618) 283-4414.

I'm sending a copy of your letter and this response to the president, Clinton D. Wesley, and I expect he will get in touch with you very soon to issue a personal invitation to visit him. If you plan to fly, just let Clint know how many are in your party and your flight arrangements, and he will provide transportation from O'Hare to Waukegan and back.

Sincerely yours,

12-4

SUPPLYING MORE DETAILED INFORMATION ABOUT AN ADVERTISED PRODUCT

Situation

As manager of a publisher's Executive Book Club, you run a series of ads in a business magazine to attract new members. You receive a request from a personnel executive, asking how adequately the personnel field is represented in the club's publications. You respond with a persuasive invitation to join the club. (See Letter 7-4 on page 52.)

Analysis of the Letter

1. *Acknowledge the inquiry in a friendly way and say what you are going to do about it.*

2. *In the second paragraph, answer the principal question—the proportion of releases that are in the personnel field—which is good news.*

3. *Next you deliver the bad news, but in a very tactful way.*

4. *Enclose a circular that describes the Executive Book Club and its procedures, emphasizing a feature you think is important: savings.*

5. *In the final paragraph, make it easy for von Hoffritz to take action, adding a clincher in the form of a gift if he joins the club now.*

The Letter

Dear Mr. von Hoffritz:

I am delighted to know that you are interested in our Executive Book Club and am happy to answer your questions about it.

Between thirty and forty new books in the field of management are made available each year to the members of the Executive Book Club. And as you have mentioned, the topics treated vary widely. From eight to ten of these pertain specifically to personnel administration; in addition, a similar number of general management books embrace some aspects of personnel management.

Although we have several specialized book clubs—for example, accounting, computer sciences, and marketing—there isn't as yet one in personnel administration. The decision to set up a specialized book club is, of course, based entirely on demand, and it is possible that we will one day establish one in personnel. Certainly, there is a growing interest in this field.

The circular enclosed contains complete information about the Executive Book Club. Please note that the average price of books distributed by the club, if purchased separately, is about $35. However, as a member you would pay only about three-fourths that amount.

I do hope you will want to become a member of the Executive Book Club, Mr. von Hoffritz. You can do so by filling out the coupon on the back of the circular. If you join now, you'll receive absolutely free one of our popular handbooks featured on page 3. Included in this group is the highly praised Handbook of Modern Personnel Administration.

Yours very sincerely,

12-5

SUPPLYING INFORMATION ABOUT AVAILABILITY OF A PRODUCT

Situation

You represent International Air Cargo, which distributes the export guides described in Letter 7-5, page 53. The guides requested are available, and they are free. You will send the materials requested and pave the way for the reader's selection of your company as an overseas carrier.

Analysis of the Letter

1. *Say immediately what you are doing about the request, indicating that there is no charge for the materials.*

2. *Mention the additional guides that are available. Although the recipient may not be interested, you will have at least shown your desire to be helpful.*

3. *In the last paragraph, invite the recipient to come to you with any problems. This, of course, is a hint that your company would be a wise choice as a carrier.*

The Letter

Dear Mr. Cesario:

Export guides for Colombia, Argentina, Brazil, and Venezuela are being mailed to you today with our compliments. If you need additional copies, just let me know.

You'll see in the circular enclosed that International Air Cargo also has available export guides to several other South American countries as well as to Europe, Africa, and the Far East. If you have use for any of the guides listed, just drop me a note and I'll send them.

Please be assured, Mr. Cesario, that if there is any way that International Air Cargo can assist you with your exporting problems, we'd be delighted to hear from you. Thank you for writing.

Yours very sincerely,

12-6

SUPPLYING INFORMATION ABOUT USES OF AN ADVERTISED PRODUCT

Situation

Your company, which manufactures Lancaster brand paper, receives an inquiry about an advertisement that was placed in a national magazine. You are to respond, supplying the information requested. (Refer to Letter 7-6 on page 54.)

Analysis of the Letter

1. *Deliver the good news quickly, being specific in your answer to Pilarski's question.*

2. *Mention that samples (more than requested) are being mailed separately, assuring Pilarski that the results will please her.*

3. *Anticipate Pilarski's question about prices and supply this information, ending with a friendly invitation to place an order.*

The Letter

Dear Miss Pilarski:

I'm delighted to say that our Lancaster paper can be used with excellent results on the four duplicators you mentioned—photocopier, mimeograph, spirit, and offset. This makes it unnecessary, of course, for you to maintain four separate paper inventories—one paper does it all.

Fifty samples are being mailed separately. I'm eager to have you experiment with Lancaster because I know you'll be excited with the results.

A price sheet for Lancaster paper is enclosed. You'll see that sizable discounts are offered for larger orders, and I hope you'll give us the privilege of serving you.

Cordially,

12-7 RESPONDING TO A PRODUCT INQUIRY—TRAINING MATERIALS

Situation

You are employed by a company that produces training materials (See Letter 7-7, page 55). A person who has heard about your materials on listening asks for more information about this program and whether you have others on writing and speaking. You send samples of the listening program and explain your plans for the two other areas. Your objective, of course, is to generate orders.

Analysis of the Letter

1. Say immediately what you are sending, item by item.

2. Point out some things Gagnon will want to know about the program—all sales features that should be convincing.

3. Next, tell what you can't do: the materials on writing are not yet published but are in the works and will be sent when available. Although you have no materials on speaking (and no plans for them), you suggest a possible source. Both gestures will score points for you.

The Letter

Dear Mr. Gagnon:

I'm sending you immediately a copy of ''A Guide to Effective Listening,'' along with an instructor's manual, a sample tape, and a booklet describing other aids for the instructor.

You'll see that the basic textbook is programmed—that is, it can easily be used for individual instruction with immediate feedback and reinforcement. In addition to the textbook, there is a set of tapes on which conversations, directions, speeches, discussions (meetings), and other oral communication situations are recorded. Although this program can be used without an instructor, many companies prefer group instruction under the leadership of a teacher. The instructor's manual provides day-by-day classroom procedures and methods of evaluating performance.

I think this program may be just right for the listening segment of your communication seminars, Mr. Gagnon. It is being used by hundreds of business firms and government agencies, and the reactions we've received have been most enthusiastic.

We're in the process now of putting together a similar program on writing. Publication is scheduled for March of next year—a bit late for your first seminar, but perhaps in time for the second or third. I've made a note to send you a set of these materials just as soon as they are released. A prepublication flyer is enclosed.

At the moment, we have no publishing plans in the area of speaking, Mr. Gagnon. Have you seen ''Speaking Out,'' which is published by New Dimensions Press? I understand it is a multimedia program and that it is being favorably received by users. The address of New Dimensions is 2000 Sheridan Road, Evanston, Illinois 62201.

Thank you for writing.

Cordially,

12-8 RESPONDING TO A PRODUCT INQUIRY—PERFORMANCE AWARDS

Situation

As a merchandising manager for a company that specializes in business gifts, you receive a letter from a person who has seen your ad for the Viceroy desk set. She asks for more details, You respond positively, hoping to generate an order. (See Letter 7-8 on page 56.)

Analysis of the Letter

1. *Open the letter by saying what you are sending.*

2. *Then assure Miss Marcus of your ability to reproduce the company's logo exactly as shown on the letterhead, at the same time suggesting desk set styles with which the logo will look especially good.*

3. *In the third paragraph, stress sales points that you believe will be important—your reputation, different styles of lettering for the nameplate, and discounts on quantity orders.*

4. *Close the letter on a personal note, which includes the responsibility you feel for giving customers precisely what they have a right to expect.*

The Letter

Dear Miss Marcus:

I'm pleased to send you a colorful booklet, "Gifts of Distinction—by Viceroy," which describes in detail our wide selection of gifts, including the desk set you asked about.

Reproducing your handsome logo exactly as it appears on your letterhead will be no problem at all. The color combination of blue and yellow will look very elegant on just about any style of desk set you choose, particularly black onyx or white marble (see page 6 of the booklet).

Some of the best-known companies in the country have selected Viceroy sets as awards to employees as well as gifts to customers, and our feedback has invariably been enthusiastic. Note the different styles of lettering you may choose from for the brass nameplate. Price information, including discounts for quantity orders, is on the back of the brochure.

You may be sure, Miss Marcus, that your orders will receive prompt attention. It's my job to see that you're happy in every respect with your Viceroy gift purchase, and I take it seriously!

Cordially yours,

12-9

RESPONDING TO AN INQUIRY ABOUT CONFERENCE ACCOMMODATIONS

Situation

As sales manager of Arlington Manor, you receive an inquiry about accommodations for a management conference. (Refer to Letter 7-9 on page 57.) In your response, you attempt to persuade the inquirer to choose Arlington House for the conference.

Analysis of the Letter

1. *Open your letter with a friendly welcome, emphasizing why the date is a good one.*

2. *Refer by name to the three booklets you're enclosing. Since this information should answer most of Spingarn's questions, don't repeat what is in the booklets.*

3. *In the third and fourth paragraphs, emphasize two big selling points: the lower rates in October and your expertise in conference hosting.*

4. *In the last paragraph, encourage Spingarn to act quickly, suggesting that a delay may mean disappointment.*

    Note: *This can be a form letter about which we spoke earlier. It would, of course, be used only for summer-rate situations, and names and dates would have to be changed.*

The Letter

Dear Mr. Spingarn:

We'd like very much to be the headquarters for your annual management conference October 22 to 27. You've chosen the ideal time, not only in terms of our ability to offer you all the accommodations you require, but also in terms of weather. It's a glorious time of year in Stockton Springs!

Complete information about Arlington Manor is given in the booklets I'm enclosing: "So You're Having a Meeting," "Getting to Know Us," and "Recreation Unlimited." When you look these materials over, I think you'll agree that Arlington Manor has it all.

Another advantage of the date you selected is that summer rates are still in effect. This means that all rooms are just a little more than half the winter rates that take effect December 1. (For rates, see the back page of "Getting to Know Us.")

We've had the privilege, Mr. Spingarn, of hosting meetings and conferences for hundreds of organizations such as yours; some of these are listed on page 2 of "So You're Having a Meeting." I'd like to share with you some of the letters I've received praising our excellent accommodations and our know-how in looking after our guests. You'll find us just as eager as you are to make your October conference the best you have ever had.

Please let me know just as soon as you can whether I should reserve accommodations for you. While the October 22 date is open now, the situation could quickly change. In the meantime, if there's anything you would like to know that isn't covered in the booklets, please telephone me collect at (915) 453-9762.

Sincerely yours,

RESPONDING TO AN INQUIRY ABOUT QUANTITY DISCOUNTS

Situation

You represent the publisher of the book, *Dynamic Supervision* (see Letter 7-10 on page 58), about which a prospective buyer has written to ask if there is a discount on quantity purchases. You are to supply the information requested and encourage an order.

Analysis of the Letter

1. *Deliver the good news first by indicating the discounted price.*

2. *In the second paragraph, reinforce the inquirer's enthusiasm for the book and call attention to the free instructor's guide and supplementary cases.*

3. *Finally, encourage quick action—a good technique for closing the sale.*

The Letter

Dear Mrs. Mattel:

Yes, you would be entitled to a 20 percent discount on orders of ten or more copies of <u>Dynamic Supervision.</u> Thus, instead of paying the retail price of $27.95, you would pay only $22.36 per copy plus shipping charges.

I am delighted that you think so highly of this book, Mrs. Mattel. It has been adopted as a textbook by nearly 100 universities, business firms, and government agencies. You will be pleased to know that we have prepared a special instructor's guide, which also contains supplementary cases. The guide is supplied free to the instructor.

I'd be happy to hear from you. I assure you that the books will arrive in plenty of time for your first seminar in October, provided you place your order within the next ten days.

Yours very cordially,

SECTION 13
SALES LETTERS

A lot of people scream constantly about the quantity of "junk mail" they receive, referring, of course, to any unsolicited material in which there is a sales pitch. Listening to these people, one could easily get the idea that nobody really looks at the stuff and that those who try to sell by mail are wasting their money.

Although many of us are guilty of automatically consigning to the wastebasket some letters that are easily identifiable as promotional material, direct mail is one of the most potent advertising mediums that suppliers can use to sell their goods and services. Millions of people *do* read "junk mail"—or at least respond to it whether they read it or not. If this were not so, we would see a sharp drop in the quantity of unsolicited letters that land in our mailboxes. This has not happened; indeed, the output multiplies year by year.

So let's put to rest the notion that products and services can't be sold by means of letters. They definitely can be and are. But getting people to pay attention to these "silent salesmen" is not as easy as it sounds. What you say and how you say it are, of course, very important. Perhaps even more important, however, is the quality of the mailing list. No matter how well you know your product (and you should know it as well as those who designed and made it) and how clever you are with words, you're not going to do much selling if your letter reaches the wrong people. Letters are expensive—postage, stationery, and preparation costs are high—and you must be selective.

Selectivity is one of the big advantages of direct-mail selling. You can pick the audiences you're pretty certain are likely candidates for your product or service. When you purchase television or radio time or newspaper or billboard space, you can't be sure what proportion of your audience represents genuine prospects. Although there is some selectivity in all media, direct mail is superior to most in this regard. You can pinpoint, with a fair degree of reliability, those who are real candidates for your product—whether they are doctors, architects, dog breeders, hardware dealers, or antique car buffs.

Usually, your best mailing list comes from your own records—those who are or were customers or who have made inquiry. In local situations, you can easily supplement your own list by reading newspapers, using the Yellow Pages, and obtaining lists of various civic, professional, and social groups. If your responsibility for selling by mail includes a large geographical area, you're likely to supplement your own "house" list by purchasing mailing lists. Many companies sell them, and you can obtain a directory of them from the U.S. Department of Commerce.

Once you're sure of the reliability of your mailing list, you can begin to think about the kind of letter that is likely to get the biggest response. This is not easy; even a selected audience of, say, pharmacists or real estate agents will have different motivations for buying. Even the most successful sales-letter writers do not always know the magic formula that inevitably pulls a strong response. On massive direct-mail campaigns where many thousands of dollars are to be spent, you may want to write three or more different letters and test them on fairly small groups—say, 1000 each—and for the big mailing choose the letter that brought the most responses on the test. This takes time and is not always a foolproof technique (people *are* unpredictable), but it usually pays off in the long run.

As mentioned, no one knows in advance whether a sales letter that has been carefully prepared will really do the job. You may gasp in admiration at an appealing sales letter, thinking (as the writer did), "That's really a clever piece of writing." But if that's the only response the letter gets—that is, if it doesn't persuade you to place an order, return the enclosed post card, send for a catalog, or whatever—then it wasn't all that good, especially if most of the other recipients reacted just as you did.

ELEMENTS OF AN EFFECTIVE SALES LETTER

According to the basic rules of selling, you first have to get the prospect's attention. Once you do that, you must build his or her interest to the extent that the prospect has a strong desire for the product. Assuming you've succeeded so far, the battle is still not won. You have to close the sale—that is, get the prospect to say, "I'll take it—where do I sign?"

The elements just described—attention, interest, desire, and action—are often referred to as the AIDA formula, which is just as applicable to sales-letter writing as to personal selling. Thus, in planning your letters, you should concentrate on these four questions:

1. What's the best way of getting the reader's attention so that she or he will want to read on?
2. When I have the reader's attention, how can I create genuine interest in my product?

3. Once I have created interest, how can I persuade the reader that he or she really should buy what I have to sell?
4. Finally, how can I get the reader to take action—that is, respond in some way?

Although each of these considerations is essential in a good sales presentation, they are not always separate and distinct elements. Thus, you might open your letter like this:

Just fill out the enclosed card to receive—absolutely free—a box of four of our Super-Write pens.

Here you have not only gained attention in the first paragraph, but have triggered action. And the elements of building interest and creating desire are not necessarily separate entities; they may be intertwined throughout the message.

LENGTH OF SALES LETTERS

Opinions vary on how long a sales letter should be. Common sense would tell us that most people don't have the time or patience to plow through eight or ten pages of "sales puff," and that a shake-hands-and-run approach makes more sense. Yet, day after day mailboxes are stuffed with sales letters that range from four to twelve or more pages in length. Most of them are from publishers of magazines and other periodicals or from mail-order distributors. They've all been writing long sales letters for many years and obviously get good results from them or they wouldn't spend the extra money they cost. It's probably safe to say that few people really read every word of a seller's long letter but, the "medium is the message"— that is, any product that takes that much space to crow about must be worth having. But you have to give the writers credit: letters from periodicals like *Time, Esquire, The Wall Street Journal,* and *National Geographic* are genuinely interesting to read and often models of persuasive writing.

Only experience will tell you what length of letter is best for your product or service. We recommend that, at the start, you try to do the job in a page or two; some of the most successful sales letters ever produced were one-pagers. Many companies hold their sales letters to a page or so, using the letter mainly to draw attention to a colorful brochure that is enclosed. Others use colorful folded circulars that are written as letters rather than as advertisements. These are expensive methods, of course, and only you will know how far you can stretch your advertising budget.

In the examples that follow, we've assumed that the writers attempted to do the entire job by means of letters unaccompanied by supporting materials.

SALUTATIONS IN SALES LETTERS

When possible, it's best to use the reader's name in your salutation. It's costly, even with the help of computers, and many companies think a personal salutation *(Dear Mr. Mowbray)* isn't worth the extra money.

When either money or the type of mailing list you use prohibits a personal salutation, you can use a general label you know to be correct, such as *Dear Subscriber, Dear Reader, Dear Policyholder, Dear Ford Owner, Dear Doctor,* and so on. Probably the most popular impersonal salutation is *Dear Friend,* but some writers (and readers) object to it because they believe you shouldn't call someone "friend" who isn't.

If you can't identify your reader by name or label, you can simulate an inside address and salutation in various ways. Following are examples.

If you could increase the value of your home by 25 percent, wouldn't you be interested?

I know it sounds hard to believe, but . . .

LAST YEAR 50 MAJOR CORPORATIONS CHOSE MARBOROUGH MANOR FOR THEIR CONFERENCES AND CONVENTIONS

We're delighted, of course, that . . .

May I send you . . . WITH MY COMPLIMENTS . . . a handy pocket calendar bound in handsome Duravinyl?

I make no bones about it, I want to . . .

Colorado Springs: A Think Tank as Big as the Rockies!

Now there is more reason than ever to . . .

At Midland Savings and Loan We Do More Than We Have To. (We Have To.)

This has been our byword for twenty years, and . . .

Chances are 10 to 1 . . . friend . . . that you never owned a pair of all-leather shoes

Take leather insoles, for example . . . 95 out of 100 American men have never experienced the luxury . . .

STATIONERY FOR SALES LETTERS

There is a wide variety of colors and sizes of stationery used in sales letters. The most common size is 8½ by 11 inches, although you'll often see odd sizes such as 7 by 11, 7½ by 10½, 8 by 9½, 7 by 10, and so on. The effect of paper size on the reader may be insignificant, but those who choose offbeat smaller sizes believe they are more personal in appearance—a departure from the traditional 8½ by 11 business letter.

Slightly tinted paper—blue, green, gray, cream, salmon, canary, and so on—also adds a personal touch. However, a good-quality white paper is still the most popular.

GIMMICKS IN SALES LETTERS

Hundreds of gimmicks have been used in sales letters to attract attention. Here are a few examples.

1. Typing the letter upside down. The theme here is "I'd stand on my head to get an order from you."

2. Creating illustrations by type placement. For example, a resort hotel "drew" likenesses of North and South America by arranging the words so that they formed a rough outline of the two continents. The theme was: "Our clientele is the whole world."

3. Printing excerpts from headline news stories that tie in with the need for the product being sold.

4. Affixing inexpensive miniature gadgets at the top of the letter:
   a. A pair of plastic scissors ("You can cut your costs in half . . .")
   b. A plastic wrench ("Tighten up your fuel costs . . .")
   c. A bright new penny ("In buying fuel, pennies *do* count . . .")
   d. A sharpened pencil (We sharpen our pencils when we set our prices . . .")
   e. A loving cup ("You, too, can be a winner when . . .")
   f. A pencil stub with no eraser ("Make no mistake about it—we save you money . . .")
   g. A short ruler ("Your increase in profits will be easy to measure when . . .")
   h. A swatch of material ("Feel the ruggedness of Brand X vinyl sheeting . . .")
   i. A strip of sandpaper ("Things are rough all over . . .")
   j. A packet of seeds ("These seeds won't grow unless they're planted in the right place—neither will your investments . . .")
   k. A fake check ("This money can be yours if . . .")

There is no doubt that some of these devices attract attention and often lead to a sale from people who admire your ingenuity. If you have trouble getting people to respond to your sales letters, you might experiment with something similar—some people are reluctant to throw away a device that is the least bit useful.

On the other hand, we think most of them are a bit too corny for the more or less sophisticated reader and that they detract from, rather than add to, the sales message. Admittedly, we are prejudiced. We think you can do a better job with a well-written message that is interesting and quietly persuasive in tone.

GUIDELINES IN WRITING SALES LETTERS

We offer four general guidelines for writing sales letters:

1. *Keep the letter of reasonable length, say, a maximum of 1½ pages.*
2. *Make sure you have skillfully covered the four elements of AIDA, but avoid huckstering.*
3. *Use language that your reader will understand and relate to.*
4. *Make it as easy as possible for the reader to take action.*

13-1 SELLING A PRODUCT

Situation

A manufacturer of portable electronic refrigerators obtains a mailing list of members of an organization of camping enthusiasts, and decides to write a letter to obtain orders or requests for a catalog.

Analysis of the Letter

1. *Painting a word picture in everyday language is often an exciting opening. Camping enthusiasts are likely to relate to this story.*
2. *The story continues in paragraph two, ending with a whimsical twist that starts to whet reader interest.*

The Letter

Dear Fellow Camper:

It's a great day to start your vacation. The sun is ablaze, the van or wagon is humming nicely down the Interstate, and the family is settled comfortably in anticipation of what lies ahead. Even the dog is amiable.

Can you guess what happens next? Suddenly there are echoed demands for a rest stop and something to eat. The rest stop idea you take in stride, but the "something to eat" shakes you a little—visions of hauling out the old billfold and plunking down fifteen bucks or so for snacks at a fast food place.

BUT NOT IF YOU HAVE LEKTRON-KOOL WITH YOU!

3. *The third paragraph is a simple statement that begins the process of creating desire in the next two paragraphs.*

4. *The testimonial in the sixth paragraph is an effective device for stressing product appeal and helping to build desire for it. ("If other campers like this product so much, maybe I should have one.")*

5. *The seventh paragraph reinforces desire by stressing savings and emphasizing the necessity for immediate action.*

6. *The final paragraph is specific as to what the reader is to do: either place an order by phone or mail, or send for a free catalog.*

The Lektron-Cool is the greatest little portable fridge you've ever seen. Pack it with sandwiches, drinks, fried chicken, fruit, whatever, and you'll have at your fingertips really cold food and drink day and night.

The Lektron-Cool is not an ice box. It's a lightweight but roomy electronic refrigerator that you can plug into your car or a 110 volt adaptor that we make available, assuring you of fresh edibles for days and days. The secret is in Lektron-Kool's thermoelectric solid-state module, which replaces all the bulky piping coils, compressors, and motors you find in conventional portable refrigerators.

One enthusiastic owner of Lektron-Kool writes: "Last summer our family took a camping trip to Canada. It was one of those 'perfect' vacations; everything went just as we had planned. But when we got back to Atlanta all of us agreed that, aside from our new Caprice Diesel wagon, the most indispensable item of equipment we carried was our Lektron-Kool. Not only was it a convenience, it saved us a bundle!"

Now you can own the Lektron-Kool for $40 to $50 less than the regular price. That's right. Our three models ordinarily priced at $139, $179, and $199 can now be had for $99, $139, and $149. But you must hurry because this offer will be withdrawn April 1.

Call us toll free at 800-622-0391 to place your order, or mail us your check or credit card number. But if you want more information before you order, the enclosed postage-paid card will bring you a complete catalog of our three Lektron-Kool models.

Yours very sincerely,

13-2 SELLING A SUBSCRIPTION TO A NATIONAL PUBLICATION

Situation

The Wall Street Journal sent the following letter to a large mailing list of people made up largely of those who subscribe to other fairly literate publications. The writer's objective, of course, is to persuade readers to subscribe to *The Wall Street Journal.*

Analysis of the Letter

This is an excellent sales letter in all respects. Note the following:

1. *The opening, with its storylike quality, not only is interesting to read, but carries the reader skillfully to the first center head and the copy that follows it.*

2. *The use of center heads throughout the letter is a good device for breaking up copy in a relatively long letter (three pages), but the heads themselves are attention-getting devices, not only in terms of placement, but in terms of copy.*

3. *As you read the letter, observe the way in which the writer leads the reader from attention to interest to desire to action.*

4. *Especially good, too, are the short paragraphs, the personal tone of the letter, the simplicity of style, and the white space provided to make the letter look easy and interesting to read.*

The Letter

THE WALL STREET JOURNAL

PUBLISHED BY DOW JONES & CO., INC. 22 CORTLANDT ST. N.Y., N.Y. 10007   JOSEPH J. PERRONE, CIRCULATION MARKETING

Dear Reader:

On a beautiful late Spring afternoon, twenty-five years ago, two young men graduated from the same college. They were very much alike, these two young men. Both had been better than average students, both were personable and both--as young college graduates are--were filled with ambitious dreams for the future.

Recently, these men returned to their college for their 25th reunion.

They were still very much alike. Both were happily married. Both had three children. And both, it turned out, had gone to work for the same Midwestern manufacturing company after graduation, and were still there.

But there was a difference.

One of the men was manager of a small department of that company. The other was its president.

What Made The Difference

Have you ever wondered, as I have, what makes this kind of difference in people's business lives? It isn't always a native intelligence or talent or dedication. It isn't that one person wants success and the other doesn't.

The difference lies in what each man knows and how he makes use of that knowledge.

And that is why I am writing to you and to people like you about The Wall Street Journal.

For that is the whole purpose of The Journal: to give its readers knowledge--knowledge that they can use in business.

5. *This particular letter was written on a single sheet of good-quality white paper, 10 by 14 inches, then folded lengthwise to make a 7-by-10 four-pager. Only three sides are used, however; the last page is blank. The only color used is in the letterhead (THE WALL STREET JOURNAL) and the signature—both blue. The message is in black typescript.*

A Publication Unlike Any Other

You see, The Wall Street Journal is a unique publication. It's the country's only national business daily. Each business day, it is put together by the world's largest staff of business news experts.

Each business day, The Journal's pages include a broad range of information of interest and significance to business-minded people, no matter where it comes from. Not just stocks and finance, but anything and everything in the whole, fast-moving world of business.

Knowledge Is Power

Right now, I have in front of me a recent issue of The Journal. On the front page alone, I can see stories originating in the following cities: Stockholm, Washington, Orlando (Florida), Paris, Chicago, Havana, Seattle, New York.

I can see articles on inflation, taxes, jobs. I can see an up-to-the-minute appraisal of current trends in business and finance; I see an article on food prices; I see information about wholesale prices, car prices, the fuel shortage. I see facts and news about certificates of deposit, tax incentives for industry, wheat exporters, wiretaps, Cuba, Israel and retail chain stores.

And there is page after page inside The Journal, filled with fascinating and significant information. If you have never read The Wall Street Journal, you cannot imagine the breadth and scope of its coverage. Nor can you imagine how useful it can be to you.

Much of the information that appears in The Journal appears nowhere else. The information you get, you get when you can use it. The Journal is printed in twelve different plants across the United States and rushed out to subscribers by truck, plane and mail, so that you get it early each business day.

Your Own Personal Subscription

Will you put our statements to the proof--over a trial period for as many weeks as you like? (20 weeks--or 30 weeks.) At just $1.10 a week. You may prefer to take advantage of the Journal's best buy--two years for $99. This subscription offer represents a saving of more that 26% from the published newsstand price of 30¢ a day ($1.50 per week). We also pay the postage to your home or office.

Simply fill in the term you wish on the order form
and mail it today. We'll send you The Wall Street Journal
each business day for the term you indicate. And here's The
Journal's guarantee: Should The Journal not measure up to
your expectations, you may cancel this trial arrangement at
any point and receive a refund for the undelivered portion
of your subscription. And we'll be glad to bill you later.

If you feel as we do that this is a fair and inexpensive proposition, then you will want to find out without
delay if The Wall Street Journal can do for you what it is
doing for more than four million readers. So please mail the
enclosed Acceptance Card now, and we will start serving you
immediately.

                                   *   *   *

Do you remember the two college classmates I told
you about at the beginning of this letter? Two men graduated
from college together, and together started out in the business world. What made their business stories different?

Knowledge. Useful knowledge. And its application.

An Investment In Success

I cannot promise you that success will be instantly
yours if you start reading The Wall Street Journal. But I
can guarantee that you will find The Journal always interesting, always reliable, and always useful.

Sincerely yours,

Joseph J. Perrone
Circulation Marketing Director

JJP:ks
Encs.

P.S. It's important to note that The Journal's subscription
      price may be tax-deductible.

13-3

SELLING AN EDUCATIONAL COURSE

Situation

Cameron Career Institute offers home-study courses in various trade occupations. The sales promotion director has obtained a list of subscribers to a practical mechanics magazine, who are often good candidates for home-study training. He writes a sales letter, the purpose of which is to persuade readers to send for a free catalog, which describes a course in small-engine repair.

Analysis of the Letter

1. *The headline salutation is designed to capture the reader's attention. Many people with mechanical skills who work for somebody else dream of being their own boss.*

2. *The first paragraph by itself would make an effective opening (an "if" beginning stirs the reader's imagination). Here it adds support to the attention-getting headline.*

The Letter

Cameron Career Institute
766 Highland Avenue
Orlando, Florida 32802

WOULDN'T YOU LIKE TO
OWN YOUR OWN BUSINESS?

If you're looking for the chance to be your own boss . . . or earn extra income in your spare time . . . or a way to achieve independence when you retire . . . SMALL-ENGINE REPAIR could be the answer.

CCI can quickly train you—in your spare time at home—to service and repair mowers, tillers, chain saws, outboards, garden tractors, mopeds, motorcycles, snowmobiles, and dozens of other types of small-engine equipment. It's a great way to get your own business, full- or part-time, with a minimum investment. And it's a field with growing opportunities for qualified people.

3. *Paragraph three zeros in on developing interest (by emphasizing the ease of learning, the practical training, and the fact that all tools are supplied), at the same time creating a desire for the product (the course).*

4. *In paragraph four, the writer continues to build desire. The catalog sounds good, it is free, so why not get it?*

5. *The final paragraph is a direct request for action and suggests the ease in taking it.*

6. *The "P.S." is used to allay any fears the reader may have about being pursued by salespeople. This fear discourages many people from putting themselves on a mailing list.*

CCI's Small-Engine Course contains forty-five lessons, each easy to read and understand. Every lesson is short and fully illustrated with step-by-step diagrams and photographs. It's "hands-on" training—you actually build a 3½-horsepower four-cycle engine. You also perform experiments that show you how every part of an engine works. And we supply you with professional tools—a complete set of wrenches, electrical system tools, inductive tachometer, engine overhaul tools, volt-ohm-milliammeter, and others. Everything you need!

Our big catalog tells you all you need to know. It describes the content of each lesson (and there are sample pages of the actual study materials), plus illustrations and descriptions of the equipment you will use. By the way, the instructor you will be assigned to has been a professional small-engine mechanic. He will be your "partner" in your studies.

Just fill in and mail the enclosed post card for your free catalog today. It needs no postage.

Sincerely,

Roger F. Frye

Director of Studies

P.S.   No sales representative will call you!

SECTION 14

SALES, SERVICE, AND PROMOTION COMMUNICATIONS

Letters written expressly to sell a product or service, such as the three illustrated in Section 13, represent only one method of generating business by mail. Any communication that attempts to attract favorable public attention, make new friends, generate additional business, keep present customers buying, or reawaken interest from old customers who have strayed comes under the broad heading of "promotion."

There is virtually no limit to the promotional methods that can be employed, and in this section, we illustrate twelve different promotional letters that have been used successfully.

14-1 PROMOTING A SPECIAL SALE

Situation

A retail store owner has obtained a list of new home buyers in the community and decides to write a letter to attract them to his store.

Analysis of the Letter

1. *The big attention-getter in this letter is, of course, the illustration of a thermometer and the cartoon drawing. Such a visual device has great appeal; the magnified section of the thermometer adds interest and realism.*

2. *Question openings are often used with excellent effect in promotional letters. Like this one, they should be worded to evoke a positive response.*

3. *The second one-line paragraph is a good kick-off for stirring interest, which is fully developed and intertwined with desire in the five paragraphs that follow.*

4. *The central theme of the letter is saving money, but it is reinforced by the use of a brand name that most people are familiar with—no fly-by-night outfit, this!*

5. *Note the short paragraphs, short sentences, lively writing, and friendliness. The folksy tone should have great appeal to prospective customers; the writer comes across as a friendly neighbor.*

6. *The letter is one page in length, and it need not be longer—the catalog that is being sent will do much of the selling job.*

7. *The letter was written on good-quality white paper, 8½ by 11, with black printing. The illustration itself, however, is in five colors—black, dark yellow, red, green, and blue.*

The Letter

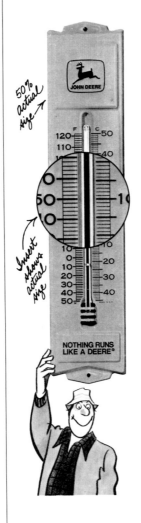

John Deere Lawn and Leisure Center

Dear Mr. Roy:

Looking for help with your lawn and garden chores? Help you can count on year after year? So you can give your lawn and garden that showcase look you admire...and still have time to enjoy them and other leisure-time activities?

Then this is your year for a Deere!

Right now, during our "Down to Earth Values" Sale, you'll find bargains galore waiting for you here at Wilmington Lawn & Leisure.

For openers, there's the attractive, accurate John Deere Outdoor Wall Thermometer. It's yours for just 99¢ if you come in before May 4, 198_.

Want BIG savings? Then take a look at our Great Horsepower Sale coupon. With it in hand, you can save $10 per horsepower--anywhere from $80 to a whopping $200 on a John Deere Lawn & Garden Tractor, depending on the model.

And there's more. A whole sheet of valuable coupons to help you save. There's a John Deere to make it easier, whether you're planning to till...or drill... or even grill. And there's a coupon to make your John Deere product an even better buy right now. Just remember, come in before those coupons expire.

We've enclosed a 198_ Lawn and Leisure catalog to give you ideas. But we'd like you to come in and take a personal look. That's the best way to appreciate John Deere quality.

So please stop by. Bring the family and the coupons along. If you simply want to browse, fine. If you want to talk, terrific! And if you decide to buy, well, you couldn't have picked a better time.

There's a warm welcome waiting for you in Deere country, so drop in soon -- before our sale ends.

Cordially,

Archie Herring

Archie Herring

P. S. Call us any time you have a question about Lawn and Leisure products or service. Our number is 799-6359.

121

14-2 ACKNOWLEDGING A FIRST ORDER

Situation

The sales manager for a paper manufacturing company receives her first order for paper from a large book publisher from whom the company has tried for years to get business. She considers this a genuine breakthrough and decides to acknowledge the order, express pleasure in receiving it, and create a climate for additional business.

Analysis of the Letter

1. *Graciously acknowledge the order and what is being done about it.*

2. *Express pleasure at being chosen a supplier to such a prestigious publishing house, thus complimenting your reader.*

3. *The mention of Dave Cunningham (your Eastern representative) gives assurance that your service extends well beyond merely supplying paper.*

4. *The last paragraph is optional and whether you use it or not depends on how you view your reader. Some people might consider this "hard sell," but we think tactful hints about new products are expected and often welcomed.*

The Letter

Dear Mr. Sargent:

Your order for Fine-Text paper arrived yesterday and is being shipped today to Kingston Press in Providence, as you requested.

Naturally, I am delighted that you chose Fine-Text for your science lab manuals. For a long time, we have all wanted to be a paper supplier to the Bolton-Krantz Book Company, and to us this first order is more than a sale—it's a "happening" that gives us much pleasure and pride.

I wish you great success with this new series, Mr. Sargent. Our Eastern representative, Dave Cunningham, is well acquainted with the folks at Kingston Press, and you can be sure he'll be at the plant when the presses start to roll.

I've enclosed samples of a new paper we recently developed for four-color offset reproduction. We call it "Intensity," and I think you'll know why when you examine the sharp color reproductions.

Very sincerely yours,

14-3 | INTRODUCING A NEW SALES REPRESENTATIVE

Situation

Paul Russon has recently joined Tinley Corporation, manufacturers of electrical fittings and boxes, as a sales representative. The regional manager writes a letter to Tinley customers in the territory that Russon will cover. He believes such a communication will open the door for Russon and make it easier for him to establish rapport with his customers.

Analysis of the Letter

1. *The first paragraph is a quick introduction to Paul Russon—brief but purposeful.*

2. *In the second paragraph, the regional manager supplies information about Russon's education, experience, and general personality—an effective build-up for the new person. Note the reference to the previous representative. This is a good idea, because many of the customers were probably personal friends of his, so a compliment to him (without denigrating Russon) should be well received.*

3. *The final paragraph is a positive way of ending the letter. Note the compliment in the phrase, "that made Fred's visits so rewarding," and the expression of personal gratitude.*

The Letter

Dear Mr. Krafft:

Within the next few weeks you will be visited by Paul M. Russon, our new representative in southern Indiana. Paul replaces Fred Norcross who, as you probably know, recently retired.

Paul is a graduate of the Capper Technical Institute in Shelbyville, where he studied electricity and electronics. For five years he worked with his father in the wholesale electric supply business and, in 1980, joined our company as a technician, later moving up to a position in our quality control department. When the opportunity in sales arose, we thought immediately of Paul. He is highly personable, but even more important, he is thoroughly familiar with our products. You'll find that like Fred, Paul is completely committed to customer service and satisfaction.

I'm sure you will extend the same courtesies to Paul that made Fred's visits with you so rewarding. I really think you'll like him—and I'll be most grateful.

Sincerely yours,

14-4 INVITATION TO AN OPEN HOUSE

Situation

The National Association of Teachers of Homemaking is having its annual convention in Minneapolis on June 4 to 7. Sterling Mills, manufacturer of flour and other food products, has its main headquarters in Minneapolis. The director of educational relations invites each member of the association to an open house during the convention.

Analysis of the Letter

1. *The letter, although processed, is personalized. In the first paragraph, the writer refers to the forthcoming convention, the fact that Minneapolis is the home of Sterling Mills, and the honor of having the NATH convention there.*

2. *She then announces the open house, giving general details (specific information will be printed and distributed at the opening of the convention).*

3. *Transportation plans are described briefly—a matter of great importance.*

4. *In the final paragraph, the writer asks that the enclosed card be returned and expresses the hope that the recipient will be coming to Minneapolis.*

The Letter

Dear Friend:

I hope you are planning to attend the annual convention of the National Association of Teachers of Homemaking in Minneapolis June 4 through 7. Perhaps you know that Sterling Mills calls Minneapolis home, and I consider it a rare opportunity for our city to host such a distinguished group.

While you're here, we'd like you to visit us, so we have arranged a special Open House for all members of NATH on Thursday, June 6, at our main plant from 5:30 until 8:30 p.m. (This is a free evening, according to the officers of your organization.) We'll have refreshments and a buffet, followed by a guided tour of the sections of our plant that we think will interest you most, including our famous recipe testing center.

We're only about twenty minutes from the Radisson, your convention headquarters, and will have courtesy limousines to pick you up there and return you to the hotel at the end of the tour. Full details will be provided at the registration desk.

If you are planning to attend the convention, would you please indicate on the enclosed card whether you are likely to attend the Open House? I certainly hope you will be with us!

Sincerely,

Situation

Excello Illumination Corporation plans to exhibit at a convention of the American Institute of Architects at the Cow Palace in San Francisco. The sales manager reserves space for the exhibit plus a conference room adjoining it. The conference room will be converted into a "little theater," where a promotional movie will be shown continuously. A formalized invitation is sent to all members of AIA.

Analysis of the Invitation

The invitation is printed in black on heavy paper similar to a wedding or graduation announcement. To be effective, the copy should be arranged by a graphics specialist.

The Invitation

EXCELLO ILLUMINATION CORPORATION

cordially invites you to

visit its exhibit at the American Institute of Architects at

THE COW PALACE, SAN FRANCISCO

March 6 to 9, 19—

and to view an exciting new film

"LET THERE BE LIGHT"

at the "Little Theatre" that adjoins the exhibit.

The film briefly traces the history of artificial
illumination and presents startling new developments
and innovations in the science of lighting.
It will be shown every hour from 9 a.m. to 5 p.m.

14-6 ANNOUNCING NEW PRODUCTS AND SERVICES

Situation

Cannon and Burnett, a leading retail office supply store, has added a new department—Business Machines and Services. The following announcement is sent to the store's regular mailing list as well as to others listed in local business directories to attract new customers.

Analysis of the Announcement

The announcement can be printed on heavy white paper (such as the invitation in the previous example) or on regular stock, possibly tinted and printed in a complementary color other than black.

The Announcement

SPECIAL
ANNOUNCEMENT!

CANNON AND BURNETT—for over fifty years, Boise's leading office supply house—is proud to announce the establishment of a new department, Cannon and Burnett Business Machines and Service featuring:

- Electronic calculators
- Desk-top computers
- Electric and electronic typewriters
- Billing and accounting systems
- Other high-quality business equipment plus
- A thoroughly modern service department with factory-trained service technicians

Same location: 1102 Hays, Boise

Same telephone number: (208) 622-4500
and the same dedication to courteous, dependable service

14-7 ANNOUNCING A NEW LOCATION

Situation

Becker Financial Services, a consumer loan company that has occupied the first floor of a downtown office building in Austin, has constructed its own building just outside the city. The company sends a notice to all its customers, former customers, and various others in the community. The same notice appears in local newspapers.

Analysis of the Announcement

The announcement may be on the firm's present letter-head or one designed especially for the purpose. The architect's drawing of the new building is a good eye-catcher.

The Announcement

BECKER FINANCIAL SERVICES

Phillips Building • Austin, Texas 78701
Telephone 444-0679

We are pleased to announce that on March 15 Becker Financial Services will be in our new location at: 7400 Interregional Highway, Austin

We're easy to get to. Off I-35, take St. John's Exit 2, and look for the building you see above (we're just five minutes from downtown Austin). Expanded parking, expanded services, expanded hospitality!

Our telephone number after March 15 will be: 796-4077

We look forward to seeing you in our new home!

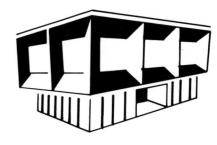

14-8 FOLLOW-UP AFTER SERVICES HAVE BEEN RENDERED

Situation

Shortly after DataComp ends its conference at Arlington Manor (see Letter 12-9, page 106), the manager writes a follow-up letter to the conference leader. Its purpose, of course, is to build goodwill and encourage DataComp to return for another stay at the hotel.

Analysis of the Letter

1. The opening is warm and friendly, yet appropriately brief.

2. Pollock uses the opportunity to persuade Spingarn and DataComp to revisit Arlington House—effective selling that is almost certain to evoke interest.

3. She invites suggestions about improving accommodations and services which, even if Spingarn does not choose to make, will show her eagerness to please.

The Letter

Dear Mr. Spingarn:

I hope you were pleased with your conference at Arlington Manor and that all the participants returned to work with pleasant memories of their stay here. We certainly enjoyed having you and look forward to seeing you again.

Meanwhile, we're enlarging our accommodations—the addition of an Olympic-size indoor pool, a superb nine-hole golf course, three paddle tennis courts, and a sauna. Incidentally, if you plan a winter conference, you'll find this area outstanding for skiing and other winter sports. The famous Cascade Trails is only a half hour away, and we provide free transportation.

If there is anything you can suggest that will help us improve our accommodations or services, Mr. Spingarn, I hope you'll write me.

Yours very sincerely,

14-9

FOLLOW-UP ON A PREVIOUS ORDER

Situation

Hoffstedder Inc., a mail-order distributor of sporting goods, receives numerous orders for "junior" golf clubs (ages 7 to 11) that are often shipped to an address other than the buyer's. Thus it can be assumed that the clubs are a gift for a grandson, niece, and so on. After three years, the sales manager writes each buyer a letter encouraging him or her to invest in standard-size clubs.

Analysis of the Letter

1. *The writer first reminds Corbman of the order placed three years ago.*

2. *He then proceeds to suggest that the time may be at hand for standard-size clubs and that an "almost grown-up" would be excited to receive such a gift.*

3. *Attention is then directed to the catalog enclosed, with specific mention of the special bargain on standard-size clubs.*

4. *In the final paragraph, the writer encourages immediate action and indicates the ease with which an order can be placed.*

The Letter

Dear Mr. Corbman:

About three years ago you purchased a set of Commodore junior golf clubs as a gift to a special boy or girl—perhaps a grandchild, a niece or nephew, or other young friend.

It occurred to me that that young person is getting very close to the age when he or she has outgrown the junior-size clubs and is now ready to graduate to standard size. What a wonderful way to acknowledge the youngster's grown-upness as well as a certain mastery of the game!

Christmas isn't far away, and we've put out a special catalog for the occasion. It is enclosed. Note that a complete set of standard Commodore clubs (four woods, eight irons, and expanded vinyl bag) ordinarily priced at $350 is now on sale for just $299.95. The same applies to Lady Commodore clubs. And there are great savings on other golfing needs—gloves, carts, headcovers, balls, and weekend bags.

Just indicate your needs on the order blank/envelope (note that we now accept major credit cards) and put it in the mail. If you do it now, I absolutely guarantee delivery no later than December 21.

Sincerely,

14-10 FOLLOW-UP LETTER TO AN EXHIBIT VISITOR

Situation

Excello Illumination Corporation has kept a guest log of the visitors to its exhibit in San Francisco. (See the invitation on page 125.) Later the sales manager writes each guest and encloses a promotion brochure prepared especially for the occasion. The letter and enclosure will reestablish contact with the visitor and keep the company's name and products up front.

Analysis of the Letter

1. *The writer thanks the recipient for visiting Excello's exhibit at the convention—a short, effective opening.*

2. *He then calls attention to the enclosed booklet, describing briefly the product feature and the break-through it represents.*

3. *The sign-off is an invitation to request additional materials.*

Note: *This very brief letter strikes us as much more effective than a long, detailed sales pitch.*

The Letter

Dear Mrs. Ramos:

Thank you for visiting our exhibit at the AIA convention in San Francisco. I hope you enjoyed the film, "Let There Be Light," and that you helped yourself to the free materials on display.

Since the convention ended, Excello has published a colorful booklet, "Low-Energy Lighting," a copy of which is enclosed. The 24-volt lighting system described draws only 2½ watts per lamp with a life expectancy of fifty years. We think this is one of the most exciting developments to come along in recent years.

Please let me know if you would like additional copies of this booklet and any of the materials that were handed out at the convention.

Sincerely yours,

14-11 WELCOMING A NEWCOMER TO THE COMMUNITY

Situation

In small towns and suburban areas surrounding large cities, it's fairly easy to keep track of local events by means of the newspaper. New residents are of special interest to local retail stores, and often these people are welcomed to the community by a personal letter. Mr. and Mrs. George Bryson and their three young children have recently moved to Springdale (he will be the new high school principal) and receive a welcome letter from a clothing store.

Analysis of the Letter

1. *The writer first welcomes the Brysons to Springdale and mentions the importance of Mr. Bryson's new position.*

2. *The second paragraph builds up the Walton Family Clothiers as an old and respected store that (according to the brand names given) is synonymous with high quality.*

3. *An invitation is then extended to visit the store and receive a gift (perhaps relatively inexpensive items of clothing or accessories).*

4. *The sign-off, a bit shopworn, perhaps, will still be appreciated by most people who have made few, if any, acquaintances in their new surroundings.*

The Letter

Dear Mr. and Mrs. Bryson:

We may not be the first to welcome you to Springdale, but count us among those who are genuinely glad you chose our community to live and work in. As the new principal of Springdale High School, Mr. Bryson will, we are confident, bring a new standard of excellence to that institution.

For over twenty-five years, Walton Family Clothiers has been Springdale's favorite shopping place for women's, men's, and children's wear, featuring such well-known brands as Botany, Kingsridge, Palm Beach, Cardin, LaCoste, Levi, Florsheim, Buster Brown, Red Cross, Arrow, and Sero. You can charge your purchases with one of our convenient charge accounts; we also accept major credit cards.

But whether you need anything now or not, please come to see us. We'd like to meet you and present each member of the family with a special gift. Just bring this letter with you.

We hope you'll like living in Springdale. We do. What we lack in size we make up for in down-home friendliness!

Sincerely,

14-12

WINNING BACK AN INACTIVE CUSTOMER

Situation

Hoffstedder Inc. (see Letter 14-9 on page 129) has in the past received sizable orders annually from certain customers who, for some reason, have ordered nothing for the last two years. The president sends each of these customers a printed, personalized letter, along with an announcement of a special sale.

Analysis of the Letter

1. *The writer sets the stage in the first paragraph for the questions that follow.*

2. *In the second paragraph, the attempt is made to find out why the customer has stopped buying. Note the frankness of the questions.*

3. *Reference is made in the third paragraph to an enclosure on which the recipient can respond to the questions posed.*

4. *An attempt is then made to sell. The writer suggests that the bargains may be so attractive that the questionnaire can be ignored.*

The Letter

Dear Friend:

We've had the happy experience of receiving one or more orders from you every year for several years. But, as I study our list of faithful customers, I note that you haven't bought anything from us for the past two years.

This set me to wondering: Did we goof on a shipment? Was the merchandise you last ordered not exactly what you wanted? Maybe you've been too busy lately to indulge in your favorite sport? Or is it simply because you haven't needed anything?

Whatever the reason, I'd really like to know it, and I hope you'll tell me on the enclosed form, which you can mail in the postage-free envelope.

In the meantime, I'm sending you a flier describing our special "rock-bottom prices" sale on all Commodore Golf equipment and Grand Prize tennis gear. Maybe when you see the bargains offered, you won't even need to fill out that form I referred to—just the order blank that's on the flier.

Sincerely,

PART 5

LETTERS TO CUSTOMERS

One of the odd things about some business organizations is that they spend so much money to lure new customers and spend so little to keep them after they've been landed. It just doesn't make sense. Taking customers for granted is routine in some larger organizations, where mere bigness generates an attitude of indifference.

Loyal customers are an organization's only protection against bankruptcy, and losing them because of neglect or indifference is downright sinful. Not only do satisfied customers continue to fatten the till, they often encourage others to buy. This is advertising that doesn't cost a penny. And although there are always problems in giving good service to customers, maintaining their patronage isn't all that difficult. It's a matter of attitude, of believing that everyone who buys from you is entitled to the best treatment you can deliver. Plus giving just a little more than you have to.

We said there are always problems in giving good service to customers. The reason, of course, is that no organization is perfect, and there's many a slip 'twixt the cup and the lip: unreasonable delays in filling orders, shipping the wrong merchandise, making errors in invoices and statements, writing cranky letters to customers for no good reason, failing to answer letters promptly, and so on.

Sometimes these errors or failures can't be helped. For example, if you can't get parts because of material shortages or a transportation strike, customers may be denied the goods they've ordered. And not infrequently the customer is to blame—for example, failing to clearly identify the article or service required.

133

Yet no matter who is at fault, customers whom you value highly should generally be given the benefit of any doubt. Note that we said "customers whom you value highly." The old saw that all customers should be treated alike is a myth. Customers who repeatedly place large orders and pay for them will naturally get more attention than those who buy infrequently and have to be badgered to pay what they owe. However, you have to make the assumption that all customers are good unless proved otherwise.

Still, you should not get the impression that you always have to turn the other cheek. Some customers—even highly valued ones—may make demands that are impossible to accommodate or ask for exceptions to standard company policy. So there will be instances when you have to say no. Yet there are ways of doing so without creating animosity.

SECTION 15

LETTERS OF APPRECIATION AND CONGRATULATION

No doubt the most effective way of pleasing customers and keeping them active as buyers is to provide the best possible products or services at the lowest possible price, give prompt and courteous service, maintain close lines of communication, and deal fairly. Customers have a right to expect these things, and suppliers who fall short are sure to have high customer turnover.

But you can enhance customer relations by doing more than is expected. One way is to keep in touch with customers by letter—for orders, payments, courtesies extended to sales representatives, and general support, and to acknowledge special achievements, whether personal or professional.

The guidelines for such letters are simple:

1. *Make them warm and friendly, but don't gush.*
2. *Give them a sales flavor, but avoid hard sell.*

15-1 THANKING A CUSTOMER FOR COURTESIES TO A SALES REPRESENTATIVE

Situation

As the district manager of a textile firm, you supervise several sales representatives who travel the assigned territories to call on buyers and purchasing directors. Each time you receive the report of a representative's visit with a customer or prospect, you follow up with a letter of appreciation.

Analysis of the Letter

1. *Immediately express your thanks for courtesies extended to your representative.*

2. *Say how valuable the meeting was to Beth, adding a personal statement from Beth that will surely win points for her with the buyer.*

3. *End the letter with your assurance that what Beth promised will be sent and with an offer to be of service. (The latter is obviously an invitation to place an order.)*

The Letter

Dear Mrs. Himmelfarb:

Thank you for the courtesies you extended Beth Holloway when she called on you last week.

Beth is one of our newest and most promising representatives, and she was delighted to have the chance to meet and talk with a person of your background and experience. From her report, I gather that you were very generous with your time, and she came away, in her words, "far more knowledgeable about my own products than when I went in."

The swatches of our new Sheer Sheen drapery fabrics that Beth promised are being sent to you today, along with a special brochure that contains complete specifications and descriptive information. I hope you will let me—or Beth—know how we can be of service.

Sincerely,

THANKING A CUSTOMER FOR PAYMENT AND FOR AN ORDER

Situation

A good customer and personal friend has sent a sizable check in payment of an invoice and in the same letter placed a larger order for a new product. It is your policy, as the supplier, to acknowledge payments received as well as all big orders.

Analysis of the Letter

1. *Acknowledge with thanks the check, mentioning the amount; then express your appreciation for the order and plans for shipment.*

2. *When you have good news (here, extra time in which to earn a cash discount), report it early.*

3. *Tell why the customer's choice was wise, thus building his confidence in the new product.*

The Letter

Dear Max:

Your check for $4884.60 is greatly appreciated. Thank you! Thank you, too, for your order for 200 Gem-Con rotomolded LLDPE motorcycle tanks. These will be shipped at once.

We're offering special discount terms on the Gem-Con. In addition to the trade discount of 33⅓ percent, we're giving a cash discount with terms of 10/EOM. This means you have have an extra month to make payment and still receive the cash discount.

A lot of our customers are switching to the rotomolded LLDPE tank as a replacement for metal original equipment. They report hearty endorsements from participants in motocross competition—the tanks are very light in weight, but extremely tough. We predict you'll have a similar experience.

Very cordially yours,

EXPRESSING APPRECIATION FOR PAST SUPPORT

Situation

The president of a small corporation that has been in business only a short time takes the opportunity, on the company's third anniversary, to write its loyal customers to thank them for their support.

Analysis of the Letter

Observe the warmth and friendliness of the letter.

1. *Name the occasion being celebrated and your pride in your success.*

2. *Acknowledge the fact that only because you have had loyal friends have you grown and prospered—not because of your own genius.*

3. *End with a strong "thank you" and an expression of faith in the future.*

The Letter

Dear Mrs. Bueno:

On March 16, Cordon Products will celebrate its third anniversary. It's a wonderful occasion for us, and we're naturally strutting a bit about the progress we've made in such a short time.

Yet we're fully aware that our accomplishments are not simply attributable to "genius" leadership or hard-working employees. We grew and prospered only because we found great friends like you who have given such loyal support along the way.

So this is a thank-you note—for buying and pushing Cordon products, putting up with occasional errors due to "growing pains," and just helping to put Cordon on the map. The future looks bright, and we want to acknowledge your contribution to this rosy outlook. As we say in Georgia, "'preciate it!"

Very sincerely yours,

15-4

CONGRATULATING A CUSTOMER ON A PROFESSIONAL ACHIEVEMENT

Situation

A food wholesaler learns that one of her long-time customers has just been elected president of a state retail food association. Like many business owners and executives, the wholesaler keeps track of such things by reading the trade journals and writes congratulatory messages to customers and friends who have received recognition.

Analysis of the Letter

1. *Express your pleasure at the good news and say specifically why. (Note the compliment to Curtis and your pride in counting him as a friend.)*

2. *Extend good wishes and a sincere offer of assistance.*

3. *Keep the letter brief, but personalize it.*

The Letter

Dear Curtis:

I was delighted to see in the September issue of <u>Food Retailer</u> that you have been named president of the Missouri Association of Independent Grocers. This pleases me for two reasons: first, because I think you will bring dynamic leadership to this important organization, and second, because the honor was bestowed on a long-time friend and customer.

I extend hearty good wishes and, at the same time, an offer of any help our company can give to the MAIG. We're behind you all the way!

Very sincerely yours,

Situation

Johnstown Motors sells a new car to a customer who, just before driving it away, says, "You people certainly rate high with Smith's Car Care Center in Centerville. Mr. Smith and his mechanics all recommended that I come here first." The general manager writes Smith, a parts customer and friend, to thank him for the referral.

Analysis of the Letter

1. *Open with a short paragraph that quickly tells the story, thanking the recipient for the referral.*

2. *Then show pleasure at the confidence expressed by Smith and his mechanics, stressing its special meaning because it came from such a knowledgeable source.*

3. *Thank the reader again and invite him to lunch the next time he is in town.*

The Letter

Dear Jim:

Yesterday I sold a new Triton Nautilus to a young lady named Marsha Wescott, and I have you to thank for the transaction. She told me that you folks at Smith's Car Care Center recommended that she shop us first.

I'm mighty proud that you think well enough of us to refer people to us. I can't think of a higher compliment, especially when it is bestowed by such knowledgeable people as Jim Smith and his skilled mechanics. I am determined to live up to your high expectations, Jim, and I hope you'll let me know if you ever have reason to suspect differently.

Thank you, Jim. If I can find a way to reciprocate, you can be sure I'll take advantage of it. When are you planning a visit to Johnstown? If you'll make it around noon, I'll treat you to the best chili this side of San Antonio—the Tex-Mex Place just opened down the street—and those fellows have the magic formula.

Sincerely,

SECTION 16

APOLOGIZING FOR DELAYS AND ERRORS

As we mentioned earlier, nobody has found a way to bat .1000 in serving customers. No matter how hard the seller's employees try to avoid mistakes, they are bound to occur. But it is no disgrace to make errors; the customers you serve make them, too. The sin is in failing to acknowledge or apologize for them. More often than not, the person who must write the letter of apology had nothing to do with error, but he or she represents the company and therefore accepts the blame on its behalf. It is a distinct "no-no" to single out the guilty party and lament to the customer about the inefficiency of the shipping manager, the accounts receivable supervisor, or whoever. As far as the customer is concerned, it is not an individual but the company that is at fault.

Here are five guidelines for writing letters apologizing to customers for errors for which your company is to blame:

---

1. *Say first what you are doing or have done to correct the error.*
2. *Tell the customer how the error happened (if you know).*
3. *Apologize for the error; however, unless it is extremely serious, don't wring your hands in remorse.*
4. *Don't say that such an error will never happen again (it probably will). Simply reassure the customer that you will do everything possible to reduce the chances for error.*
5. *Close the letter positively—that is, with the assumption that all is forgiven and normal relationships can be resumed.*

16-1 DELAYED SHIPMENT

Situation

The manufacturer of institutional furniture receives an order from a Topeka wholesaler for twelve posture swivel chairs for a special customer. Ten days later the customer writes that the chairs have not arrived. The reason, the manufacturer discovers, was that they were shipped to another wholesaler. In the response, the manufacturer tries to set things right and retain the wholesaler's good will.

Analysis of the Letter

1. *Say immediately what you are doing to solve the problem.*

2. *Explain how you think the error came about, without naming specific individuals.*

3. *Apologize in an indirect manner by mentioning the rush shipment and your willingness to make amends if the error causes the wholesaler problems with the customer.*

4. *Close with a friendly expression—an assumption that the reader will bear no grudge.*

The Letter

Dear Mr. Barrett:

The twelve posture swivel secretarial chairs you ordered July 14 are on the truck (Reynolds Transport) and should be at your place by Friday of this week.

When I investigated the original shipment, I was astounded to learn that your chairs were sent to another customer (in Iowa of all places!). It's hard to account for such an error, and the only excuse I can offer is that we've had several part-time warehouse people this month to fill in for some of the regular crew who are on vacation.

I hope, Mr. Barrett, that this special shipment will compensate in part for the trouble I know we have caused you. Please let me know if this delay represents any real problem with your customer. It would be unthinkable for you to be penalized on account of our poor performance.

Best personal wishes.

Sincerely yours,

16-2

UNEXPECTEDLY OUT OF STOCK

Situation

While visiting a technical bookstore, a publisher's sales representative promises the owner that sixteen copies of a handbook will be sent to her immediately. The representative then discovers that there are no copies in stock due to an unexpected purchase by a foreign distributor. The sales manager writes the customer to apologize for the representative's unfilled promise and retain the order for filling later.

Analysis of the Letter

1. *Quickly review the promise of delivery.*

2. *Explain tactfully why the promise cannot be kept, giving full backing to the representative.*

3. *Say exactly when you expect copies of a new printing, offering to ship the order directly from the bindery.*

4. *Reinforce the importance of the handbook that was ordered by mentioning the success of all the publications in the series, taking the opportunity to promote a new handbook that is now available.*

5. *End the letter on a friendly, positive note.*

The Letter

Dear Mrs. Cassone:

When you placed an order with David Wolff last week for sixteen copies of Handbook of Plastics Engineering, he was so certain we could make immediate shipment that he promised you your copies by September 9.

I would have made that promise, too, Mrs. Cassone, because our inventory of this handbook seemed adequate for at least six months. However, neither of us was prepared for the news that, just three days ago, a European distributor cleaned us out of stock with a huge order, and not a single copy is left.

Of course, we immediately ordered a large reprint and have been promised delivery from the manufacturer by October 22. May we hold your order for later fulfillment? To speed things up as much as possible, I'll have your sixteen copies sent directly to you from the bindery (in Radnor, Pennsylvania). This should mean that you will receive the books by October 22—possibly a day or two earlier.

We're feeling very good about our new Technical Handbook Series. Every one of the twelve we have published has had a far better sale than we predicted. Handbook of Compressed-Air Systems is just off the press, and I've enclosed a new-book information release that may interest you.

Dave Wolff joins me in wishing you a smashing fall season at Cassone's.

Sincerely yours,

16-3

WRONG MERCHANDISE SHIPPED

Situation

The Trophy House produces, among other things, sports trophies and awards. A good customer and personal friend orders sixteen miniature watches with a tennis motif, and receives instead sixteen watches with a golf motif. The watches are to be presented to the winners of a tournament conducted by Lakeside Tennis Club. The manager writes to relieve the customer's anxiety and seek to win his continued friendship and patronage.

Analysis of the Letter

1. *Say immediately what you are doing or have done about the mistake.*

2. *Apologize tactfully for the error and tell what you know about it (nothing).*

3. *Express confidence that the right watches will be on hand for the presentation.*

4. *Tell how the watches that were sent in error are to be handled; then end your letter cheerfully.*

The Letter

Dear Cliff:

Sixteen "Gemset" miniature pocket watches with a tennis motif case were sent today by Blue Label Air Express to replace the watches you received in error. You should have them by now.

You know, one would think it would be impossible to make an error like this one, Cliff. You clearly specified in your letter that these watches were to be awarded to winners of the Annual Lakeside Tennis Club Tournament on August 18. The stock number you supplied was correct. There was no reason for a slip-up at this end, and I can't even guess now it happened.

I am much relieved, however, that you will have the <u>right</u> watches in time for the awards dinner. I really don't know what a tennis player's reaction would be to having a classic golf swing in bas relief on his prize!

When you get around to it, would you please ship the golf watches to me by UPS collect? I apologize for the anxiety we've caused you, and I truly hope that everything turns out just the way it's s'posed to.

Yours very sincerely,

16-4

WRONG SIZE SHIPPED TWICE

Situation

Mid-Continent Distributors is a wholesaler of hardware. A building supply dealer, who purchases much of her merchandise from Mid-Continent, orders six 48-inch ceiling fans with globes. The fans she receives are 36 inches. When the mistake is discovered, another shipment is made—this time 56-inch fans. The dealer writes a letter with an edge to it—she has customers waiting. The wholesaler writes a letter that he hopes will pacify the dealer and retain her as a loyal customer.

Analysis of the Letter

1. *Say at once what is being done about the error. Here, your personal assurance that the right fans were sent is important.*

2. *Admit whimsically that the way in which this order was handled is downright ludicrous.*

3. *Apologize and assure the customer that she's too important to deserve this kind of service.*

4. *End the letter with a warm expression of appreciation.*

The Letter

Dear Mrs. Hotchkiss:

Six 48-inch Victory ceiling fans, with globes, were shipped to you this morning. I know because I saw them loaded on the truck.

By this time you must be convinced that we take special delight in mixing up your orders—two careless errors in a row. I suppose, according to these exhibitions, if we had had a fourth sweep dimension we would have sent that before getting your order right!

It's embarrassing to inconvenience any customer, but unforgivable when that customer is so highly valued as you. Red-faced and contrite, I ask your indulgence and offer you my personal assurance of better service in the future.

Thanks for your patience, and best personal regards.

Sincerely,

16-5

ERROR IN AN INVOICE

Situation

A sales promotion manager sends a special announcement to dealers, telling them that, in addition to the usual 25 percent trade discount on carpeting, they will receive an additional 10 percent on certain lines for a limited time. When buyers who took advantage of this offer received their invoices, they discovered that the additional discount promised was not deducted. The promotion manager writes each customer a letter of explanation and apology.

Analysis of the Letter

1. *It's always a good idea to assure the customer at once that he or she is right and you're wrong.*

2. *Tell what happened, but don't make a big thing of it. Nobody has been hurt yet.*

3. *Say explicitly what is the next step for the customer to take, using exact figures where appropriate.*

4. *Offer an appropriate but mild apology (note the use of the word "oversight" rather than something like "this terrible error") and end the letter with the assumption that all is well.*

The Letter

Dear Mr. Rogovin:

You're entirely right. In our January 16 statement, we neglected to deduct the extra trade discount of 10 percent to which you are entitled.

As sometimes happens, the folks who prepare the invoices don't always get the message. And this time for good reason: I simply didn't get the word to them about the additional discount, so I'm the culprit.

Please deduct $462 from the statement you received. Then the net amount due will be $4158 instead of $4620.

I want you to know that I'm very sorry about this oversight and that I'm grateful to you for pointing it out to us. We appreciate your business!

Cordially yours,

SECTION 17

HANDLING MISUNDERSTANDINGS WITH CUSTOMERS

Customers are *not* always right. They submit garbled orders, take advantage of discounts to which they are not entitled, return merchandise that is not salable, and expect favors that are costly and inconvenient to grant. Every respectable company has policies to deal with such problems, but sometimes these policies have to be adapted to fit particular situations. You might grant a struggling dealer a 90-day extension of credit (though it's against policy to do so) if you believe it could save his business and in the long run result in some healthy orders. And you're not likely to risk losing a $500,000-a-year account because of company policy when only a minor inconvenience or a few dollars are involved.

However, you can't be Santa Claus in every situation. There are times when you must say no to customers—even valued ones—and this is never easy. Your mission is to persuade them to accept your unfavorable response and still retain their friendship and patronage. When you can bring this off consistently, then you've earned the appellation of "master writer"!

Here are guidelines for handling these misunderstandings with customers:

---

1. *If it is possible for you to share some of the blame for the misunderstanding, bend over backwards to admit it.*
2. *State specifically how the misunderstanding came about.*
3. *Say as tactfully as possible what you can and can't do about the misunderstanding. If your decision is "no," use velvet gloves to convey it—not a sledgehammer.*
4. *Make the assumption that, when customers learn of their mistakes, they will appreciate the necessity for the action taken and will continue to do business with you.*

17-1

WRONG MERCHANDISE SENT— CUSTOMER PRIMARILY TO BLAME

Situation

A dealer places an order with a manufacturer for eight outboard motors. A number of errors are made in billing the order, and as a result, the dealer is shipped motors that she doesn't really want. The dealer is primarily to blame, but the manufacturer must also share some of it. The manufacturer writes the dealer a letter of explanation and apology.

Analysis of the Letter

1. *Apologize at once for the mix-up, but don't put all the blame on the customer, even though she deserves most of it.*

2. *Refer to the copy of the order that is enclosed, so that the customer will see how the mix-up could have happened. This is the place to accept your share of the blame ("We should have checked with you . . .").*

3. *Tell what you are doing about the shipment of the 6-hp motors. The suggestion about keeping the 7.5s is, of course, a sales pitch; use it only if you think appropriate for that particular customer.*

4. *Use a friendly sign-off, which in this case, has a sales flavor. Nothing wrong with that!*

The Letter

Dear Miss Claybaugh:

I am very sorry you did not receive the eight 6-hp Sea Serpent outboards you wanted, and I guess both of us share the blame.

Your order (photocopy enclosed) lists the 7.5-hp motor along with its stock number, yet the price indicated is for the 6-hp motor. Since you've regularly ordered the 7.5, we assumed that this one was what you really wanted, and we went ahead and shipped it. We should have checked with you, and I'm sorry we didn't.

We will, of course, ship the eight 6-hp motors immediately. Do you think you might sell the 7.5s? If so, you may wish to keep them awhile, and if they don't move you can return them to us. In any event, we'll pay all shipping charges.

I'm delighted you're having such a good season with the Sea Serpent line. We'll be ready for your next order; I promise no mix-ups!

Very cordially yours,

17-2

CUSTOMER TAKES UNEARNED DISCOUNT

Situation

A housewares manufacturer sends a check to a supplier of plastics in payment of an invoice. However, a cash discount has been deducted from the amount shown on the invoice—a discount to which the customer is not entitled. The supplier writes to accept the check, point out tactfully that money is still due on the invoice and, at the same time, retain the customer's friendship.

Analysis of the Letter

1. *First, thank the customer for the check; then give the bad news—more money is due.*

2. *Review the terms of sale, but be gentle. Don't say, "You failed to meet the terms agreed upon." Simply say, "Unfortunately, these terms were not met."*

3. *In the third paragraph, tell why you can't make exceptions. It is probable that your customer enforces a similar policy, and saying so reinforces the logic of your action.*

4. *Assume that the customer agrees with you and that there are no hard feelings. Sending the reprint is simply a gesture that all is well between the two of you.*

The Letter

Dear Mr. Garvin:

Thank you very much for your check dated September 7 for $927.96. We have credited your account in this amount, leaving a balance of $48.84.

The terms of sale, you will recall, were 5/10 ROG. Since you received the merchandise August 12, you would be entitled to a 5 percent discount only if the invoice was paid within ten days of that date. Unfortunately, these terms were not met.

Although I would like to make an exception in your case, Mr. Garvin, such an action would penalize those who are not accorded the same privilege. I expect you enforce such a policy in your own organization, even though—as in this instance—it isn't a pleasant thing to do.

I think you might be interested in the enclosed reprint of an article written by our New Product Research Group, which appeared in the October Plastics Engineering.

Very sincerely yours,

17-3

UNAUTHORIZED RETURN OF MERCHANDISE

Situation

The customer relations manager of a paint manufacturing firm receives a report from the receiving department that 34 gallons of paint have been returned by Cabrizzi's Building Supply. There has been no advance warning, but it is assumed that the customer wants full credit for the returned paint. This particular brand was discontinued many months ago, and all dealers were notified, and there is no satisfactory way to dispose of it. The customer must be told that full credit for the returned paint cannot be allowed and a compromise suggested that is fair to both parties.

Analysis of the Letter

1. *Although you may suspect a bit of skulduggery here, open the letter in a low key, rather than with an outburst.*

2. *Then say you can't accept the paint for full credit and why. The customer probably knew this before he returned the paint, but make no accusations.*

3. *Suggest what you can do. If this is not acceptable to the customer, then suggest the only other alternative and ask for a quick decision.*

4. *End the letter with a lively sales message— an assumption that he will continue to buy from you.*

The Letter

Dear Mr. Cabrizzi:

Early this week we received 34 one-gallon cans of exterior white Dura-Perm paint from you. I assume that you wish us to issue a credit memorandum for $261.12 (34 gallons @ $7.68).

I am very sorry, Mr. Cabrizzi, that we cannot allow you full credit on this paint, which you purchased over eighteen months ago. As announced to all our customers, we discontinued the Dura-Perm brand last April, at which time we cleared out our entire inventory. We are now handling only Luxor Sheen house paints.

I have a suggestion that may save time and effort for both of us. At the time we discontinued Dura-Perm, we marked it down to our actual cost of $5.76 a gallon. We are willing to give you credit for the difference between $7.68 and $5.76—or a total of $65.28. Or, if you prefer, we can return the paint to you for disposal at the price you choose.

Please let me know your decision right away, Mr. Cabrizzi, and I will take immediate steps to handle the matter accordingly.

We've had wonderful success with the new Luxor Sheen line. Dealers are delighted with consumer acceptance—some reporting up to 40 percent increase in paint sales since they took on Luxor Sheen. We'd be mighty happy to have an order from you!

Best wishes,

17-4　DAMAGED STOCK RETURNED FOR CREDIT

Situation

A dealer in interior furnishings has a policy of accepting returns of merchandise within six months of the date of purchase. Customers receive credit, however, only if the merchandise is in salable condition. A decorating consultant returns sixteen framed art reproductions that are so badly damaged that they cannot be resold. The dealer writes refusing to accept the damaged articles for credit, while salvaging as much goodwill as possible.

Analysis of the Letter

1. *Because you're almost certain the customer knew she was returning unsalable merchandise, you get right down to business without the usual pleasantries.*

2. *Describe the condition of the returned reproductions in such a way that the customer has no doubt that you don't plan to be stuck with unsalable merchandise.*

3. *Ask for instructions for disposing of the merchandise and describe your only alternatives.*

4. *Try to salvage some goodwill by expressing your regret and your confidence that the customer will not be upset by your decision.*

The Letter

Dear Ms. Farnsworth:

When I talked with you on the telephone about returning the sixteen reproductions in our Art Masters Series, I said that our policy is to accept for full credit all merchandise returned <u>in salable condition</u>.

When we received the reproductions, we quickly learned that they were not in salable condition. Apparently, they were stored in a damp place: the pictures are faded and the canvas warped; what's more, the finish on the frames contains blisters—in some cases, loose chips.

Would you like me to return the reproductions to you? Perhaps you can dispose of them at a special reduction in price. Since we cannot sell them to our customers, the only thing we can do is donate them to local schools, hospitals, and so on, who may find a use for them.

I am sorry that I must disappoint you, Ms. Farnsworth, but under the circumstances I am confident that you will fully appreciate my position.

Yours very sincerely,

Situation

Dykstron Computers Inc. has service contracts with many of the firms that use the company's equipment. These contracts stipulate that the company will provide service on Dykstron computers only. It comes to the service manager's attention that at one customer's place of business, Dykstron technicians are being asked to service other brands. The service manager wants to put a stop to it and writes the administrative services manager, a personal friend, to tactfully explain the situation and have the practice stopped.

Analysis of the Letter

1. *Since you and your customer are personal friends, the best way to handle this problem is to identify it immediately and ask for help.*

2. *Review the terms of the contract to lead up to your explanation of what has been going on.*

3. *Be explicit in stating the reasons why you object to the extra services being asked for.*

4. *Dignify your customer by letting her know that you believe she is not aware of the situation and is therefore blameless.*

5. *The ending, "okay?", is effective in this instance. What more is there to say?*

The Letter

Dear Linda:

I have a knotty little problem that I want to unload on you. As you know, our contract with Great Western Insurance stipulates that we will provide services to all Dykstron equipment over a three-year period. I hope you feel that our service so far has been prompt and professional in every respect; certainly, we have been happy with the arrangement.

Until now. Our service personnel report that lately they have been asked by some of your supervisors to service equipment other than our own. In some cases, our men have actually done the work merely to be as helpful as possible. I have asked them to politely decline these requests and for two reasons:

1. They are already hard-put to keep up with the job of fulfilling other service contracts.

2. I think those who produce competing computers are in a better position than our people to provide the professional service you require.

I suspect, Linda, that you have known nothing about this, and I bring the matter to your attention only because I believe you, too, will feel it is not a satisfactory arrangement for either of us.

Okay?

Sincerely,

17-6

DAMAGED SHIPMENT— CARRIER TO BLAME

Situation

Jackson-Holloway Inc. places an order with Wonderbuilt Interiors for six carrels for the company library. The shipment arrives in damaged condition; the enamel on most of the metal panels is scratched and there are numerous dents. The purchasing manager for Jackson-Holloway telephones the supplier about the damaged panels and asks for a replacement. The supplier writes the customer, granting the request and explaining exactly what happened.

Analysis of the Letter

1. Say immediately what is being done about the damaged shipment because this is what the customer is most interested in.

2. Give a brief explanation for the damage and assurance that any problem with the shipment will be resolved by the supplier and the carrier—the buyer will not be involved.

3. Give a quick apology in the last paragraph (no wringing of hands—the incident is not unusual) with assurance that the delay will be minimal.

The Letter

Dear Mr. Rafferty:

Just as soon as we finished our telephone conversation this morning, I ordered a duplicate shipment of carrel panels sent to you. They're being sent by our own truck, and you should have them by the time you receive this letter.

We're quite certain that the damages you reported on the first shipment were the result of careless handling by the trucking company—the fixtures were expertly crated and left our plant in perfect condition. We will, of course, take this matter up with Blue Dart Transport—but that's our problem, not yours. Just store the damaged materials somewhere out of your way, and we'll have them picked up.

I'm very sorry about this incident, Mr. Rafferty, especially because I know how eager you are to complete your library renovation, and I am confident that the delay will be a short one.

Sincerely yours,

17-7

DAMAGED SHIPMENT— CUSTOMER TO BLAME

Situation

Assume that Wonderbuilt Interiors (see previous letter) receives a copy of the trucker's waybill, signed by a responsible employee at Jackson-Holloway, showing that the carrels arrived in good condition. In this case, Wonderbuilt has no claim against Blue Dart Transport and can only conclude that the damage occurred after the shipment was delivered. Wonderbuilt writes to the customer, suggesting that neither the supplier nor carrier can accept the responsiblity for the damaged shipment and offering a possible solution to the problem.

Analysis of the Letter

1. *Make the opening friendly but noncommital.*

2. *Furnish proof that the shipment was certified as acceptable upon arrival at Jackson-Holloway. This clears the carrier of responsibility.*

3. *Then tactfully suggest what might have happened and ask for the customer's explanation.*

4. *Offer to ship replacements, with the provision that the customer pay the cost of repairing the damage to the original carrels. However, indicate that the shipment will not go forward until the customer approves the adjustment.*

5. *Give a quick apology in the final paragraph, but temper it by expressing confidence that the suggested solution to the problem will seem reasonable to the customer. In the final sentence, leave the door slightly ajar for a favorable settlement, provided the customer has the necessary proof.*

The Letter

Dear Mr. Rafferty:

I was glad to have the chance to talk with you this morning concerning the six carrels that were scratched and dented. I can understand your wanting to get complimentary replacements at once.

However, my copy of the waybill from Blue Dart Transport, signed by one of your employees (B. R. Understadt), indicates that the shipment arrived at your place in good condition. This evidence makes it impossible for us to put in a claim against the carrier—the okayed waybill clears him of responsibility.

Is it possible, Mr. Rafferty, that the damage occurred in uncrating the panels or in assembling the carrels in the library? I can think of no other explanation, and I would appreciate your assessment of the situation.

We will be glad to ship another six carrels at once—this time by our own truck. However, it is likely that you will be billed for repairing and finishing the panels that were damaged, the cost of which can only be determined when we inspect them. If this arrangement seems fair to you, please let me know, and I will authorize shipment at once.

I'm sorry, of course, for this delay in completing your library renovation, but under the circumstances I think you will understand why we propose the solution referred to above. On the other hand, if there is conclusive proof that the fault is ours, we will certainly want to make whatever adjustment seems appropriate.

Sincerely yours,

17-8 SUGGESTING A SUBSTITUTE

Situation

Dehnert-Robbins, a manufacturer of filing equipment, systems, and materials, produced a training film on filing techniques several years ago for loan to various institutions as a promotional device. The idea behind the film was that students who viewed it would, upon graduation, think of Dehnert-Robbins as *the* name in records management. The film is now out of date, and the company has produced a new one. Instructors continue to ask for the old film, perhaps because they do not know there is a new one. The manufacturer writes each instructor for permission to substitute the new film—a much more potent promotional device.

Analysis of the Letter

1. *Indicate immediately your willingness to send the old film that was requested.*

2. *Then, mention the newer film and describe briefly what it covers, referring to an enclosed booklet if further information is desired.*

3. *Finally, suggest the substitution, sending a reply card for the recipient, and wind up with a "thank you."*

4. *Do not criticize the old film as out of date and unsuitable for today's student—some teachers may have a special fondness for it. Offer suggestions in a low-key but convincing manner.*

The Letter

Dear Ms. Vereen:

The film you asked for, "Filing and Finding," is certainly available, and I'll be happy to send it to you for use in your course in administrative procedures.

However, you might like to know that we have just released a new 16mm color film, "Modern Records Management," which was produced as a replacement for "Filing and Finding." The new film covers the traditional methods of "paper" filing—alphabetic, subject, numeric, and geographic—along with the procedures and equipment accompanying these methods. But it also presents the many new aspects of records management that have emerged in recent years—in short, "electronic record keeping." As you know, records management has undergone a dramatic revolution, triggered, of course by the advances in computer technology and the advent of film (microfilm, microfiche, etc.). I think you and your students will find "Modern Records Management" exciting and highly informative. A booklet describing the film is enclosed.

May I send you this new film instead of "Filing and Finding"? I expect a copy to be available within the next ten days, and I will reserve it for you if you wish (use the enclosed postcard). There is no charge, of course, but we do ask that you return it within a week—the demand for the film is very great.

Thank you for writing.

Cordially yours,

PART 6

CREDIT AND COLLECTION LETTERS

It is an undeniable fact that buying on credit has become a way of life. Well over 90 percent of all business is transacted on credit. This includes customers who have charge accounts at various retail stores or use their bank credit cards, business firms that use credit to buy supplies and equipment for use in the business or to manufacture other products, and those that purchase merchandise that is to be immediately resold.

Businesses offer credit simply because it increases sales. Buyers expect this privilege, and if it is denied them by one organization, they turn to another that provides it. It stands to reason that with so many people charging their purchases, there will be some who will not honor their obligations. Yet no one has yet found a foolproof method of determining in advance who will and will not pay. Even some of those who score very high on the so-called three C's of credit—character, capital, and capacity—wind up on the list of uncollectible accounts. Workers with the most honorable intentions get laid off unexpectedly, and businesses that looked so promising at birth go bankrupt because of economic conditions not of their own making. And there is that relatively small minority who use credit as a means of obtaining something for nothing.

Offering credit can be hazardous, and the bankruptcy cemetery is well populated with businesses—some small and some not so small—that were put there by their nonpaying credit customers. To reduce chances of loss from bad debts, credit personnel get as much information as possible about applicants before they grant credit privileges.

The first step is to ask the applicant to fill out an application for credit. Applicants for consumer credit are generally required to supply such information as the name of their present employer, the applicant's position, salary received, and how long employed there; the names of previous employers and dates of employment; credit references, including places where they've had charge accounts, banks where they have accounts or from whom they've borrowed; and the approximate amount of their debts. Those seeking commercial credit are usually asked about their type of business ownership, principal owners or stockholders, the insurance carried, the name of their bank, and names of businesses from whom they've bought on credit or borrowed money. If the initial order is fairly large—say, over $1000—the applicant may also be required to submit a current balance sheet and income statement.

Beyond the information supplied by the applicant and the references given, the seller may refer to other sources, such as Dun & Bradstreet (for commercial credit) and a local retail credit association (for consumer credit).

ACCEPTING A CREDIT APPLICANT

When a consumer applicant is approved for credit, he or she may be notified by means of a printed "welcome" message, which may also include such information as the rate of interest charged (required by law) and the monthly payment required for varying amounts of indebtedness. A similar message is sent to those accepted for commercial credit, although instead of disclosing the interest rate (interest is not ordinarily charged on commercial accounts), the supplier describes its credit policy, discounts allowed, and how payment is to be made on the account.

Some sellers write personal letters to their new credit customers. Of course, the tone of such letters is warm and friendly, making the recipient feel that she or he is highly valued.

TURNING DOWN A CREDIT APPLICANT

Some of the people who apply for credit have to be turned down. This is one of the hardest of all letters to write, for in denying credit privileges the writer is saying, in effect, "We don't have sufficient trust in you to allow you to buy on credit." And no matter how tactfully this message is put, it is always a bitter pill to swallow. Here are three guidelines for turn-down letters:

---

1. *Express appreciation for the opportunity to consider the applicant's request.*
2. *Say as tactfully as possible why the request must be denied. (Retail stores often try to convince the applicants that they're being done a favor since additional debts would simply add to their burdens.)*
3. *Leave the door open for future credit privileges, and, in the meantime, encourage the applicant to pay cash.*

18-1

REQUESTING COMMERCIAL CREDIT

Situation

The Computer Place in Wichita provides not only computer services to local businesses, but sells computer equipment as well. At a recent business show in Omaha, the owner of The Computer Place, Gretchen Rivers, sees a thermal printer terminal that sells for $525. She thinks it will be a popular item for the small businesses she serves, and she writes to the manufacturer requesting credit terms.

Analysis of the Letter

1. *Providing information to the manufacturer about how you learned about his product, including a favorable impression of it, is an effective opening.*

2. *Place the order, requesting the terms desired and ask for a continuing credit arrangement up to a certain amount.*

3. *Indicate the amount of the initial order and how it was computed. Be explicit, to avoid misunderstanding.*

4. *Next, review briefly the history of the business you own, expressing confidence in its future.*

5. *Supply credit references—firms that will vouch for your reliability and promptness.*

6. *Finally, offer to supply additional financial information and give the name of your bank. Even if this information is not used by the supplier, your willingness to provide it reveals your confidence in your local reputation and your accountability.*

The Letter

Gentlemen:

When I visited the Omaha Business Show last week, I saw your new thermal printer terminal (RC 720) and was very much impressed by its features and relatively low cost. I think this terminal would meet the needs of a number of my small-business customers.

I would like to order three RC 720s on sixty-day credit terms and, at the same time, establish similar terms for future purchases up to $2500 monthly. As I understand it, the RC 720 is priced at $525, plus $50 for transportation, terminal checkout, and one 15-inch, 400-foot roll of paper. This means that my first order would amount to $1725.

The Computer Place was established two years ago, and since that time we have grown very rapidly. My associates and I are convinced that the services and equipment we offer will be in increasing demand as businesses discover that only by applying sophisticated technology to their operations can they remain competitive.

For information concerning our financial responsibility and promptness in paying our obligations, I refer you to the following:

Rontech Inc., 6200 Newman Avenue, Huntington Beach, CA 92647

Allied Data Associates, 4406 Cromo Drive, El Paso, TX 79912

Winthrop Systems, 16536 Stone Avenue North, Seattle, WA 98133

If you would like additional financial information, I will be glad to supply it. Our bank is The First National Bank, 106 West Douglas Street, Wichita 57202.

Very truly yours,

REQUESTING INFORMATION FROM A COMMERCIAL CREDIT APPLICANT

Situation

Upon receipt of the order and credit application from The Computer Place (see previous letter), the manufacturer responds promptly and with appreciation. However, many computer stores have been opened lately, some of which went out of business very quickly. The manufacturer decides to tactfully ask the credit applicant for additional financial information.

Analysis of the Letter

1. *Thank the credit applicant for her interest in the product and compliment her on making such an intelligent assessment of its principal marketing target.*

2. *Express appreciation for the initial order and the request for credit terms, indicating the importance of the references supplied. If the figure given by the applicant on the first order is correct, no reference need to be made to it.*

3. *Ask for additional information, mentioning the forms enclosed for the purpose.*

4. *Finally, assure the applicant of quick action on her request and of your eagerness to have her as a customer.*

The Letter

Dear Ms. Rivers:

Thank you very much for your interest in our RC 720 thermal printer terminal. This instrument was designed with the small business in mind, and I think your assessment of it is right on target; this is where most of our orders are coming from.

I also appreciate your request to purchase three RC 720s on sixty-day credit terms and to establish similar terms for future purchases. The references you supplied will be very helpful—thank you.

Would you please send me a copy of your most recent statements of ownership and results of operations? Or, if you prefer, you can use the forms enclosed to supply the required data.

You may be sure, Ms. Rivers, that just as soon as we have the information we need we'll attend to your request. We're eager to have the RC 720 in the hands of your customers, and we'll do our best to expedite shipment.

Very cordially yours,

18-3 REQUESTING INFORMATION FROM REFERENCES SUPPLIED

Situation

Refer to Letter 18-1 on page 160 and Letter 18-2 on page 161. The manufacturer of the RC 720 thermal printer terminal writes to the references supplied by The Computer Place.

Analysis of the Letter

1. *Make a brief reference to the applicant and the fact that she listed the recipient as a reference. There is no reason to mention what is being purchased or the amount involved.*

2. *Make it easy for the recipient to respond by supplying space for the information requested.*

3. *Assure the recipient that information supplied will remain confidential. Note that an extra copy of the letter is being sent, along with an envelope—an important courtesy gesture.*

The Letter

Gentlemen:

I have received a request for credit privileges from The Computer Store, Wichita (Ms. Gretchen Rivers, owner). Your company was listed as a credit reference.

I would be very grateful if you would supply the following information about this customer:

1. Credit terms extended to the customer, including limits _____

_____

2. A brief statement concerning the customer's promptness in

meeting obligations _____

_____

3. Your reservations, if any, about the customer's financial condi-

tion and general reliability _____

_____

I assure you that the information supplied will be treated as confidential. Thank you. (A copy of this letter and an envelope are enclosed for your reply.)

Cordially yours,

18-4

Accepting an Applicant for Commercial Credit

Situation

Johnson and Hall, a wholesale auto parts distributor, receives an order and request for short-term credit from Live Oak Auto Parts, a new retail store owned by J. C. Laughlin. The information supplied by Laughlin himself and from various credit references is very favorable. The wholesaler welcomes Laughlin as a credit customer and encourages him to use the privilege frequently.

Analysis of the Letter

1. Open the letter with a warm welcome and assurance that the order is being filled immediately. Rather than describe credit terms in the letter, enclose them on a separate sheet.

2. In the final paragraph tactfully suggest that the customer think first of Johnson and Hall when buying parts.

3. The "P.S." is simply additional evidence that Live Oak Auto Parts is now part of the family.

The Letter

Dear Mr. Laughlin:

It's a genuine pleasure to welcome you as a credit customer of Johnson and Hall. Your order for four 4-way convertible tops with sun roof (totaling $799.80) is being shipped immediately by truck on credit terms described on the enclosed sheet.

We look forward to serving you and hope you will call upon us often for your parts needs. In the meantime, we wish you outstanding success in your new store.

Sincerely yours,

P.S.   I'm placing your name on our list to receive our monthly newsletter, *Auto Spotlight*, which will give you up-to-date information on everything new in automotive parts.

TURNING DOWN A CONSUMER CREDIT APPLICANT

Situation

Kermit Forstner, 29, is single and lives in an apartment on which his monthly payment is $375. Forstner's take-home pay is just over $1250 a month, and his monthly payments, exclusive of rent (on a car, a loan, furniture, and credit-card purchases) amount to over $600 a month. He applies to Richert's, a department store, for a revolving credit account. The credit manager at Richert's decides that Forstner is a poor risk (he has frequently been behind on his bank credit-card payments).

Analysis of the Letter

1. *Express appreciation for the applicant's interest in opening a charge account.*

2. *Give a tactful denial of the application along with a thorough explanation of the facts that led to the turn-down decision. Note that the language is soft, but the message is straightforward. There is no mention of the credit-card payment defaults; the evidence is sufficient without it.*

3. *Leave the door open for future consideration of credit privileges, and extend an invitation to shop at Richert's on a cash basis in the meantime.*

The Letter

Dear Mr. Forstner:

I appreciate your interest in establishing a charge account at Richert's.

I have tried very hard to find a way to give your application favorable consideration, Mr. Forstner. However, the fact that your present monthly payments are so perilously close to your net monthly earnings leads me to believe that it would not be wise for you to undertake further obligations at this time. If these debts were to be paid off soon, the picture would be more favorable. Yet some of your payments, such as on the car, the loan, and furniture, have from one to three years to go before they are paid off. I think that once you have thought the matter through carefully, you may feel as I do that you have possibly overextended yourself already.

When the situation changes, we will be pleased to have you reapply. In the meantime, it will be a pleasure for us to serve you on a cash basis.

Yours very sincerely,

18-6 TURNING DOWN A COMMERCIAL CREDIT APPLICANT

Situation

Rhodes Furniture and Equipment receives an order from Premier Career Institute, a vocational school, for classroom furniture in the amount of $2800, asking for 120-day credit terms. The financial statement supplied by the school, as well as information furnished by credit references, indicates that the school's financial situation is very shaky. The most damaging information shows a current ratio of 1 to 4.7 and less than 1 percent net profit on operations during the past year. The credit manager of Rhodes writes a turn-down letter.

Analysis of the Letter

1. *Express appreciation for the order.*

2. *In the second paragraph, tell the applicant why credit privileges must be denied "at this time." The statement is tactful and completely honest.*

3. *Express hope that the situation will change and encourage the customer to pay cash for the furniture she needs.*

The Letter

Dear Mrs. Ashforth:

I appreciate your order for furniture in the amount of $2800 in which you request credit terms of 120 days.

Unfortunately, Mrs. Ashforth, the information supplied me was not at all favorable concerning the financial condition of Premier Career Institute. Not only are current liabilities far in excess of current assets, but it would appear that the school is experiencing serious difficulties in producing a reasonable profit. Under the circumstances, we feel it necessary to defer credit privileges at this time.

Of course, the situation may change. Indeed I hope so because we would be pleased to be in a position to provide the privileges you request. In the meantime, we will be happy to ship your order immediately on receipt of your certified check for $2716 ($2800 less cash discount of 3 percent).

Cordially yours,

COLLECTION LETTERS

Most credit people assume at the start of the collection process that those who owe money fully intend to pay. And they usually have every reason to feel this way. After all, the applicants were carefully investigated as to character, capital, and capacity, and the seller was satisfied that they were good risks. It makes no sense, then, to bombard them with ugly, threatening letters the minute they fall behind in their payments.

Yet the patience of the seller varies. Some credit managers will threaten legal proceedings after sending only two or three messages (especially to people they've had previous difficulty with); others will make six or more attempts to collect the money before writing an "or-else" letter.

Most large companies and retail firms have developed a collection system that, once tested adequately and found effective, is used consistently. This is often called a collection letter series, although some (often most) of the communications sent are not actually letters. A national retail chain may have four or five series of letters, each designed for a particular type of customer.

Following is the collection system used by one large company. Although the situation pertains to commercial credit, it also applies to many consumer credit situations as well.

---

1. *A monthly statement is sent to those who have account balances.*

2. *Those who do not make payment within ten to twenty days (depending on the collection policy) are sent a second statement, this time with a tactful personal message or a brightly colored sticker (available at stationery stores) on which is printed a message such as: PLEASE! or HAVE YOU FORGOTTEN? (with a drawing of a finger with a string tied around it) or SECOND REMINDER or PAYMENT OVERDUE!*

3. *If there is no response to the second statement, two or three additional statements may be sent, each with an increasingly persuasive, yet low-key appeal.*

4. *If there is still no response (perhaps three months have now passed), the customer is placed on a special follow-up list and given personal attention: telephone calls, Mailgrams, and personal letters.*

5. *The final step is usually a threat to take legal action of some sort or a notification that it has already been done. (In consumer credit situations, if the amount is small, say, $25 or so, the store may decide to write it off—the cost of collection may exceed the amount owed. In this case, the "or-else" letter is never sent. Retailers must be very wary of harrassing customers lest they violate the provisions of the Fair Debt Collection Practices Law.)*

19-1   FIRST REMINDER AFTER MONTHLY STATEMENT

Situation

On February 3, Greenacres Nursing Home purchases supplies and equipment from Walton Hospital Supply Company on thirty-day credit terms. Although the nursing home has been in operation only a short time, the information concerning the enterprise was favorable and credit was granted. A regular statement is mailed on March 10. When no response is received by March 20, a second statement is sent.

Analysis of the Reminder

The reminder is simply a duplicate of the statement mailed earlier, except that it includes a sticker to draw attention.

First Reminder

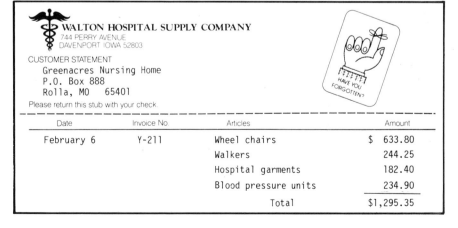

WALTON HOSPITAL SUPPLY COMPANY
744 PERRY AVENUE
DAVENPORT IOWA 52803

CUSTOMER STATEMENT
Greenacres Nursing Home
P.O. Box 888
Rolla, MO   65401
Please return this stub with your check.

HAVE YOU FORGOTTEN?

Date	Invoice No.	Articles	Amount
February 6	Y-211	Wheel chairs	$ 633.80
		Walkers	244.25
		Hospital garments	182.40
		Blood pressure units	234.90
		Total	$1,295.35

19-2 SECOND REMINDER

Situation

Greenacres Nursing Home makes no response to the first reminder. Ten days later a second reminder is sent.

Analysis of the Message

The writer reviews the situation, suggesting that payment has merely been overlooked. She also invites the customer to let her know if there are other problems and, if none, asks for a check.

The Reminder

This is a copy of the regular statement on which the following message appears at the bottom:

Mr. Montgomery: To date, no payments have been received from you, and we're curious to know why. Perhaps it is merely an oversight. If there are other reasons we should be aware of, please let us know. Otherwise, may we have your check for $1295.35?

19-3 THIRD REMINDER

Situation

Greenacres Nursing Home still has not responded to the previous reminders. A third reminder is sent ten days after the second one went out.

Analysis of the Message

The message is simply a plea for some type of response, with the suggestion that the seller is entitled to some kind of communication.

The Reminder

This is a copy of the regular statement on which the following message appears at the bottom:

Mr. Montgomery: Is there some reason we have not heard from you? The amount you owe us is now long past due and is beginning to concern us. Don't you think we are entitled to an explanation? Please let me hear from you at once.

19-4 FOURTH REMINDER— TELEPHONE CALL

Situation

The credit manager at Walton Hospital Supply Company has heard nothing from Greenacres Nursing Home and, on April 3, decides to telephone the owner, Mr. Montgomery.

The Telephone Call

When the credit manager reaches Mr. Montgomery, she may start off something like this: "Hello, Mr. Montgomery. I'm Beth Kroll at Walton Hospital Supply Company, and I'm calling to ask about your plans for paying your account which, as you know is now over thirty days past due." Montgomery is given an opportunity to tell his side of the story (he has just been so busy putting the nursing home in operation that he has had to let some of his paperwork slide). At the end of the conversation, Montgomery promises to send his check right away.

19-5 FIFTH REMINDER— TELEGRAM

Situation

A week has passed since the credit manager spoke on the telephone with Montgomery, and no payment has been received. She decides that the next step is to send a telegram (a day letter or Mailgram).

Analysis of the Telegram

The telegram, which is written in stiff language, has an urgent tone yet there is no threat of any kind.

The Telegram

DURING OUR TELEPHONE CONVERSATION ON APRIL 3, YOU PROMISED IMMEDIATE PAYMENT OF YOUR ACCOUNT. YOUR CHECK HAS NOT ARRIVED, AND IF IT IS NOT ALREADY IN THE MAIL, I URGE YOU TO SEND IT TODAY.

19-6 SIXTH REMINDER— PERSONAL LETTER

Situation

The telegram has elicited no response from Montgomery, and the credit manager decides to write a personal letter.

Analysis of the Letter

1. *In the first paragraph, the credit manager reviews the situation to date. The tone is businesslike—no personal warmth here!*

2. *In the second paragraph, the writer emphasizes the fair-play theme—we did our part; why don't you do yours?*

3. *In the third paragraph, the writer hints at other action (which means turning the account to an agency for collection), but stops just short of naming it. Suggesting damage to one's credit reputation is often a powerful collection weapon.*

4. *A final plea is made in the last paragraph. Montgomery should know what comes next if he doesn't pay what he owes.*

The Letter

Dear Mr. Montgomery:

On February 3, we sent you hospital equipment and supplies in the amount of $1295.35. You agreed to make payment within thirty days—or by March 4. Now, sixty days later, and after four reminders, a telephone call, and a telegram, you still have made no effort to settle your account or even give us a valid reason why you have not done so.

I had every faith—especially after our telephone conversation—that you would abide by the credit terms offered you. We did, after all, supply you with materials and equipment you needed and which, so far as I know, were entirely satisfactory. Don't you think you have an obligation to reciprocate?

The idea of using other means of collecting the money owed to us has not even occurred to me until now because I know what this can mean to one's credit reputation. I know you value yours just as we do ours.

Please help me avoid other action by sending your check the minute you receive this letter.

Very truly yours,

Situation

When, after a reasonable period of time, say, ten to fifteen days, Montgomery has not sent a check, he is sent a final letter.

Analysis of the Letter

The customer is given one final chance to avoid legal action, and nothing more needs to be said. The time for gentle persuasion has passed.

The Letter

Dear Mr. Montgomery:

This is to notify you that unless your check for $1295.35 is received by May 1, your account will be placed in the hands of our attorneys for collection.

Very truly yours,

PART 7

LETTERS
TO SUPPLIERS

All too often, business executives and others take their suppliers for granted. "We're valuable customers," they say, "and the people we buy from should be made constantly aware of our importance." Then they proceed to make unreasonable demands, fuss about inconsequential errors and delays, and exert their "authority" in numerous other ways.

Yet some suppliers are every bit as important as loyal customers. When you find an organization that provides you with competitive merchandise or services at competitive prices, gives you unfailingly good service, and bends over backwards to help you in times of crisis, then you should reciprocate by treating that supplier with courtesy and respect.

At the same time, there are occasions when customers have reason to be dissatisfied with a supplier's service, merchandise, policies, or treatment. And, of course, they should not hesitate to call attention to these problems and insist on a fair solution to them.

In this part, we deal with three different types of letters to suppliers: letters placing orders for merchandise, letters pertaining to problems that arise between supplier and customer, and letters of appreciation for special services and favors.

PLACING ORDERS
BY LETTER

In ordering merchandise, you will generally use your company's purchase order form or an order blank provided by the supplier. In the absence of a form or, in special cases in which a form isn't adequate to communicate your needs, you can place your order by letter, observing these guidelines:

1. *Give specific details about what you want—stock number (if any), description (name of product, size, color, etc.), catalog page reference (if appropriate), price per unit, extension, and total.*

2. *Leave no doubt about where the merchandise is to be shipped. If it's important to you, specify the method of shipment—parcel post, UPS, air freight, truck, and so on.*

3. *Mention payment if you have not established credit with the supplier—an enclosed check, COD, credit card, and so on.*

4. *Deduct any trade and/or cash discounts to which you are entitled, and show how the computation of the total amount due was made.*

5. *Mention your desire for fast shipment if speed is imperative.*

20-1

PLACING A CASH ORDER

Situation

A partner in a small, new consulting business decides to order stationery from a mail-order supplier. There is a 5 percent discount for cash, and the supplier pays shipping charges for orders over $250. No order form is available, and a letter must be written.

Analysis of the Letter

1. *On first orders, where the buyer has not established credit with the supplier, advance payment is often required. Refer to the check and its amount in the first paragraph. (You might rather place the order first and refer to the check at the end of the letter.)*

2. *Be specific. Note references to catalog page number, style or stock number, and copy for letterhead and envelope.*

3. *Specify the quantity of each item, the price, and the total; then, compute the discount and the net amount due.*

4. *If you prefer, you can remind the supplier that he pays shipping charges. We think it isn't necessary here.*

The Letter

Dear Ms. Lobdell:

Enclosed is my check for $992.46 in payment of the following items (see page 16 of your catalog):

5000 letterheads to match style 1412, including logo, type face, and color	$384.50
5000 envelopes to match style 6840	455.00
3000 second sheets, catalog number 1637	205.20
Total	$1044.70
Less 5%	52.24
Net amount due	$ 992.46

Here is how the letterhead should appear:

VICTOR ENGINEERING GROUP
4005 Center Street
Omaha, Nebraska 68105
(402) 763-3877

The envelope should contain the same information as the letterhead, except that the telephone number should not appear.

Yours very truly,

20-2 PLACING A C O D ORDER

Situation

The owner of a small retail store wants to order goods from a supplier with whom credit has not been established. Therefore, the order must be placed on a C O D basis. The supplier, in this case requires a minimum cash payment of 25 percent before shipment is made.

Analysis of the Letter

1. *In this letter, the order is placed first (note that the preferred method of shipment is indicated) and the bank order enclosed is referred to later. However, it could be the other way around.*

2. *Supply the catalog number, name of the article, quantity, unit price, extension, and total.*

3. *If your need is urgent, say so. You may not receive the merchandise when you want it, but it doesn't hurt to ask.*

The Letter

Ladies and Gentlemen:

Please send me the following by United Parcel Service C O D :

No.	Item	Quan.	Price	Extension
PM 41	Price marker	2	$64.90	$129.80
L24	Red labels (store name: RITTER)	20M	51.25	51.25
			Total	$181.05

A bank money order for $45.29 is enclosed, which represents the minimum payment of 25 percent.

Would you please give this order high priority? I would like these articles by March 12 if you can manage it. Thank you.

Yours very truly,

20-3

PLACING A CREDIT CARD ORDER

Situation

Marilyn Fortunato sees an ad in a magazine for "Classic Automobile Miniatures" that she wants to order as a Christmas gift for her nephew. She places the order by letter, having it sent directly to her nephew, and asks that the amount be charged to her credit card.

Analysis of the Letter

1. *Identify what is being ordered and refer to the ad. (The note about the coupon is optional.)*

2. *Make it clear that the article is a gift, and supply the name and address of the person to receive it. (Indenting this information and the writer's name and credit card number makes them stand out.)*

3. *Refer to the price and give specific details about the credit card.*

4. *When you have a preference as to date of arrival, state it.*

The Letter

Dear Mr. Boyers:

This is my order for the "Classic Automobile Miniatures" advertised in the November <u>National Geographic</u>. (The magazine did not belong to me, so I could not use the coupon supplied.) The set of miniatures is to be a Christmas gift and should be sent to:

Mr. Keith Leavitt
Box 54B
Coyle, Oklahoma 73207

Please charge the amount ($45) to my VISA account as follows:

Ms. Marilyn G. Fortunato
Number: 5242 0431 4301 3842
Expiration date: 09-88

Is it possible to schedule shipment so that the gift arrives no earlier than December 15? I would greatly appreciate it if you could. Thank you!

Sincerely,

PROBLEM LETTERS
TO SUPPLIERS

Problem letters to suppliers are of an almost infinite variety. In this section, we deal with poor service on a special order, poor performance on a service contract, receipt of unsatisfactory merchandise, suspected error on an invoice, and complaint about a supplier's sales representative.

Guidelines for writing such letters as those mentioned above follow.

---

1. *Describe clearly, tactfully, but firmly the situation that triggered your letter.*
2. *Explain what you expect the supplier to do—improve service, change his policy, send a new shipment, offer an adjustment, or whatever.*
3. *Avoid showing anger (unless, of course, the problem you're writing about has occurred repeatedly and previous letters have produced no results).*
4. *If you expect some kind of adjustment, your letter falls in the sales category, and you're more likely to get what you want if your message is persuasive rather than threatening.*

21-1

POOR SERVICE ON A SPECIAL ORDER

Situation

Lomack's, a retail gift shop, places a special order with a long-time supplier for monogrammed crystal stemware. The stemware is to be a wedding gift, and delivery is promised by May 15. Not only does the order arrive after the wedding; the monogram is wrong and two pieces are cracked. The owner of Lomack's, Mrs. Lydia Lomack, writes the supplier about the problem.

Analysis of the Letter

1. *Start off by referring to a copy of the order so that there will be no question about what was ordered and when delivery was expected.*

2. *Then describe exactly what happened.*

3. *In the third paragraph, express your annoyance firmly but not angrily, and indicate the likely results of this fiasco.*

4. *The supplier knows what must be done, and there is no reason to go into detail about it. However, make a special plea for quick action, reinforced by mentioning the loss of a customer and the possibility of patronizing another supplier.*

5. *End on a positive note, which says, in effect, "I still want to do business with you." This may get more positive action than an angry closing would.*

The Letter

Dear John:

I'm enclosing a copy of my order, dated February 17, for Prestige crystal stemware: eight 11-ounce goblets, eight 5½-ounce wine glasses, and eight 7-ounce champagne glasses. As you will see, these pieces were to be monogrammed ''G'' in Old English lettering, and delivery was requested not later than May 15.

Well, John, here is what happened:

1. The stemware was finally received May 28. Because I became anxious about delivery before the wedding (for which the stemware was to be a gift), I telephoned your customer service department twice—May 4 and May 11—and in each case was assured that delivery would positively be made by May 15.

2. The monogram on the stemware was ''C'' in block lettering.

3. Two of the wine glasses were cracked.

I think you will understand, John, why I am upset at the manner in which this order was handled. My excuses and apologies to the customer (an aunt of the groom) are of no comfort; to her, the incident was ''terribly embarrassing—unforgivable,'' and I confess that I agree with her. I did persuade her not to cancel the order simply because there were no other gifts of this nature, but I had to promise very fast delivery.

Obviously, you know what must be done: get the *right* stemware to me as fast as you can. I'd like to save this good customer, and if you don't turn handsprings to expedite delivery, I don't have a prayer. But let me know so that, if necessary, I can make other arrangements.

Incidentally, John, the Colonial ironstone is going very well. If you're bringing out new patterns, be sure to let me know.

Cordially yours,

Situation

Severn and Kearns, an architectural firm that occupies its own one-story building, has a two-year contract with Universal Maintenance Service to provide complete janitorial services. During the eight months the contract has been in effect, the firm has been frequently dissatisfied with the service given, and the administrative services manager, Kathleen Malette, has discussed the problem numerous times with the manager of Universal. The situation has not improved to Malette's satisfaction, and she puts her case in writing, describing explicitly the reasons for dissatisfaction with the service given and putting Universal on notice that the contract is in jeopardy.

Analysis of the Letter

1. Open the letter with a quick review of the situation that triggered it.

2. Then, enumerate and describe the failures of the supplier in meeting the terms of the contract.

The Letter

Dear Mr. Weidner:

You will recall that you and I have discussed at least four times during the past eight months the low quality of service provided by your company. After each conversation, service improved for a short time only to revert back to the old standard that brought about my original complaint.

I will summarize in this letter my previous discussions about your performance. You may wish to refer to our contract as you read my comments.

1. *Windows.* According to the contract, all windows are to be cleaned once a month. This is not being done. Often from six to eight weeks elapse between cleanings. Even when the windows are cleaned, the job is less than satisfactory. But you are aware of this—you've seen the results on several occasions and always promised a better job "next time." It has not happened.

2. *Floors.* The floors throughout the building are to be cleaned after each workday—the carpeting is to be vacuumed and tile and wood floors cleaned with special solvents. Although your service people do show up each day, their efforts can only be described as careless.

3. *Furniture and Equipment.* Furniture and equipment are to be dusted or vacuumed daily, and once a month desks, chairs, tables, and other furniture are to be cleaned and polished. Neither of these two contract stipulations is being met to my satisfaction.

4. *Walls and Drapes.* Walls and drapes are to be vacuumed every week. I'm convinced that this is not being done in several offices.

3. *Indicate the possibility of canceling the contract if service does not improve. This threat is perfectly justifiable, since there have been at least four confrontations between the two parties without satisfactory results.*

4. *Finally, offer to give the supplier one more hearing (and probably a tour of the building) before taking further steps. However, leave no doubt that the matter is urgent.*

Note: *Some will think this letter is too tough. We think, however, that it is more than fair. After all, the supplier has had at least four warnings, so he should not be surprised at the writer's straightforwardness.*

5. *Miscellaneous.* I could mention a dozen other cleaning responsibilities that are not being met satisfactorily—pictures, glass-front cabinets, lavatories, and ash trays, for example.

I call your attention to paragraph 7c in the contract, Mr. Weidner, in which the provisions for revocation of the contract are described. I do not like to consider such a possibility, but I must unless I have your written assurance that all provisions of the contract will be met.

I will be pleased to meet with you once more to discuss this situation and again point out to you why we are not satisfied with the present arrangement. I assure you that this is a matter of some urgency to me.

Yours very truly,

RECEIPT OF AN UNACCEPTABLE SUBSTITUTE

Situation

Harbor Light Press, a book publisher, has had great success with *The Handy Desk Companion*, a style manual for secretaries. Long published as a traditional hard-bound book, the publisher, because of customer demand, has also recently made it available in a spiral binding. Laughlin's Book Nook has placed two orders for *The Handy Desk Companion* in spiral binding over the past three months, and each time received the hard-bound book with the note on the shipping ticket, "Please accept this substitute; we're temporarily out of stock on the spiral binding." The owner of the Book Nook, Mary Beth Laughlin, writes the publisher to call attention to the recurrent out-of-stock situation and receive assurance that in the future no substitutions will be sent.

Analysis of the Letter

1. *Review in the first paragraph the two incidents that prompted the letter.*

2. *Then present the seriousness of the problem and indicate that a quick solution is imperative. (Note the hint that if the writer can't get what she wants, she will be forced to change her one-book policy.)*

3. *In the third paragraph, place a new order, with the stipulation that it be canceled if it cannot be filled as given.*

4. *End on a positive note.*

Note: *In responding to this letter, the supplier ought to thank the customer for her letter and tell her that she is perfectly right in feeling as she does. The supplier should offer a full explanation, then give assurance that the problem is being solved and that no further substitutions will be made without the customer's advance permission.*

The Letter

Ladies and Gentlemen:

During the past three months I have placed two sizable orders for The Handy Desk Companion, by Mauck, specifying the new spiral binding that you are advertising in Publisher's Weekly. Both times you sent me the hard-cover binding because you were out of stock on the spiral.

Fortunately, I am still selling quite a few of the hard covers, but more and more customers ask for the new spiral-bound book (at least two of your competitors have similar reference books in this easy-to-use binding).

I'm frankly concerned that unless you solve this out-of-stock problem, we're both going to be hurt. Up to now I have stocked only the Mauck book—my customers tell me it is the best of its kind on the market—but I may have to change my policy in self-defense. It may sound a little foolish that people will choose a book because it's easier to use rather than on the merits of the content, but it really seems to be happening.

Enclosed is my order for 75 copies of The Handy Desk Companion in spiral binding. Please do not, under any circumstances, send me anything else. I have plenty of the hard-cover copies in stock.

The new Recipe Date Book is a winner. I sold 162 of them in April and will soon have to place another order. Please don't be out of stock!

Sincerely yours,

21-4

RECEIPT OF UNSATISFACTORY MERCHANDISE

Situation

Among the hundreds of products sold by Meritt-Clayton Office Supplies are various stick-on mailing labels, typewriter correction tape, and so on. The brand featured by the store for many years is Marvello, which has sold in large quantities with satisfactory results. The most recent shipment of self-adhesive correction tape, however, indicates that a low quality of paper is now being used. Many customers have returned the tape saying that the paper is so thin that it does not cover the error being corrected. The store manager, Claudia Halperin, writes the supplier's sales manager whom she knows personally. She explains the problem fully and asks to receive credit for the full shipment of tapes and for assurance of the original quality on future orders.

Analysis of the Letter

1. *Immediately express dissatisfaction with the new quality of the product, using customer returns as the main basis for your complaint.*

2. *Then, ask the supplier to make his own comparison between the new and the old. Warn him that you will stock another brand if the latest shipment reflects a new standard of "quality."*

3. *Next, request full credit on the return of remaining stock and give the reason.*

4. *Finally, ask for an immediate response.*

The Letter

Dear Marvin:

For the first time in my memory, I have a complaint to make about the quality of one of your products—Marvello self-adhesive correction tape. My customers are returning the tape I sold them from my last order (August 11), saying that it is very nearly transparent and does not satisfactorily cover the error being corrected. The people in my office tell the same story: there is a definite lowering of quality in the paper used.

Are you aware of this situation, Marvin? If not, would you please take the time to compare the new with the old? I think you'll find, as I did, that my customers are fully justified in returning the tape and selecting other brands carried by my competitors. If this latest batch was simply a fluke and subsequent shipments will match the quality of the tape we've sold so successfully for many years, then I will be content to stick with the Marvello brand. However, if the August 11 shipment is to be the new standard, then I will have to stock another brand (Bannion's is far superior).

I'm returning what I have left from the last shipment (116 rolls), and I ask that you give me full credit on the entire order of 124 rolls. The reason is that I have no way of knowing how many more returns I'll get. In the meantime, I will simply have to refer my customers to another stationer, offering the excuse that I'm temporarily out of stock. I'd rather do that than risk driving away customers.

I know you will understand that I must hear from you within the next few days—and I hope the news is favorable.

Sincerely yours,

21-5

SUSPECTED ERROR IN AN INVOICE

Situation

Neilsen Inc. is a wholesaler of restaurant equipment and supplies. The purchasing director, Lloyd Edgerton, is visited by the sales representative of an automatic ice machine manufacturer and promised that, during January, the price of the Wizard icemaker to dealers will be $147 each, rather than the regular price of $183.80. On that basis, Edgerton orders six icemakers on January 17, but the invoice that accompanies the shipment is figured at the regular price rather than the sale price. Edgerton writes the manufacturer about the oversight, saying that he expects to pay the lower price that was promised by the sales representative.

Analysis of the Letter

1. *Explain the source of your information about the special price and the error in the invoice.*

2. *In the second paragraph, express the assumption that the overcharge was unintentional and that the enclosed check is for the correct amount. Then, tactfully suggest that if the assumption is wrong, you want permission to return the shipment at the manufacturer's expense.*

Note: There are several ways in which this matter could have been handled. For example, the customer could have opened the letter with reference to the check, then proceeded to explain why its amount is at variance with the invoice. Or the customer might have withheld payment, pending assurance from the manufacturer that $882 is the correct amount. In any case, the message is tactful and reasonable— not accusatory.

The Letter

Gentlemen:

When your sales representative, Molly Kinlaw, called on me in late December, she told me that you were offering a special price of $147 on the Wizard icemaker during the month of January. I ordered six on January 17, figuring the total amount of the order at $882. However, the invoice that accompanied the shipment showed the amount due as $1102.80, so it is apparent that I was charged the regular price of $183.80 instead of the lower price I was promised.

I'm enclosing a check for $882 in payment of the order. Unless I hear from you to the contrary, I will assume that this is the correct amount and that my account is clear. If this is not the case, I would like your permission to return the six Wizard icemakers to you at your expense.

Cordially yours,

21-6

COMPLAINT ABOUT A SUPPLIER'S SALES REPRESENTATIVE

Situation

Bennington High School, like other schools all over the country, is frequently visited by sales representatives of publishers and other firms. At Bennington, each teacher selects the textbooks for his or her classes, thus, this is the individual a book representative likes to talk with. The principal, Frances Morelli, welcomes sales representatives, but she insists that they check in at her office before visiting teachers. One company representative consistently violates this rule, and Morelli decides to write the regional manager about the problem and tactfully request a change in the sales representative's conduct.

Analysis of the Letter

1. *Start off with the admission that you do not enjoy doing what you feel you must do.*

2. *Then, describe fully the policy concerning visits from representatives and explain why it is a reasonable one.*

3. *Be straightforward yet tactful in citing the representative's indiscretions. Strengthen your case by referring to complaints from the teachers themselves.*

4. *Finally, soften the message by paying the representative a compliment. Then, ask the supplier to straighten out the matter.*

Note: Such letters are hard to write, for most people don't like to flog another. This is a very reasonable approach.

The Letter

Dear Mr. Engels:

Although I find it an unpleasant task, I feel that I must bring to your attention a problem I am having with your representative, Graham Wolff.

I am, of course, delighted to have sales representatives call on our teachers. I firmly believe that teachers should keep up to date on everything new in textbooks and other educational products and that no one is in a better position to inform them than the people who sell them.

Yet I have a rule that I feel that I must enforce. Every representative is to check in at my office for clearance before proceeding to the classrooms. The reason is understandable to you, I am sure. I want to be certain that each visitor is one that teachers will want to see and, equally important, I think it is unwise for me to allow teachers to be interrupted while their classes are in session.

Mr. Wolff was informed of this rule when he first began to call on us in September. However, he has repeatedly ignored it. I know only because the teachers themselves have complained to me about his frequent interruptions, often at extremely awkward times.

Naturally, I do not want to cause trouble for this young man. He seems very personable, and I know the teachers he sees have great respect for his knowledge and the company he represents. Yet I am sure you understand my position and will pass the word on to him.

Very truly yours,

SECTION 22

APPRECIATION LETTERS TO SUPPLIERS

As was mentioned earlier, the companies from which you buy often deserve letters of appreciation and congratulation, especially when they go out of their way to give you special favors or service. Obviously, you won't increase sales by writing such letters (which is why so few customers bother about it). Yet there are other reasons for giving credit where it is due. When you compliment people for doing a good job, you build loyalty to your organization. This loyalty could pay big dividends—for example, when you need personal service that you have no right to ask for or when there are material shortages and suppliers must choose which companies are to receive priority. And so on. Finally, there is the simple matter of good human relations. It costs almost nothing to express appreciation to someone, but it can mean a great deal to the individual who is the beneficiary.

22-1

PRAISING A SUPPLIER'S SALES REPRESENTATIVE

Situation

Gulf Cove Marina, a new facility that provides services, equipment, and supplies to boat owners, has recently held its Grand Opening. The sales representative for a manufacturer of inboard and outboard motors has been so helpful prior to and on that occasion that the new owner decides to write the manufacturer's sales manager a letter of appreciation.

Analysis of the Letter

1. *Open the letter with a quick report on the success of the Grand Opening which, no doubt, will be of considerable interest to the recipient.*

2. *Then pay special tribute to the sales representative, mentioning specific ways in which he was helpful.*

3. *Finally, thank the sales manager for "lending" the representative, and end on a positive note concerning the manufacturer's standing with you.*

Note: The sales manager will probably immediately acknowledge the letter, congratulating the owner on his success and mentioning that, although this particular representative is indeed a remarkable young man, the service he rendered is typical of the whole organization's attitude. The sales manager will probably send the representative a copy of both letters.

The Letter

Dear Mr. Swayne:

Last Saturday, Gulf Cove Marina had its Grand Opening. I'm happy to report that it was a great success—the attendance was about three times our expectations. So I think we're off to a fine start.

As I look back on the event and the magnificent confusion that one expects on such an occasion, I think of the wonderful help your representative, Victor Jacobs, was to me and my associates. Not only did Vic show up a couple of days before the opening to help us with displays and other special preparations, he remained on the "big day" to perform numerous chores wherever he was needed—from waiting on customers and demonstrating equipment to serving cold drinks and hot dogs. He was a godsend.

I'm enormously grateful to you, Mr. Swayne, for "lending" Vic to us on this important occasion. As far as I am concerned, he'll be accorded a warm welcome here every time his travels take him in our direction.

Yours very cordially,

22-2

THANKING A SUPPLIER FOR SERVICE AND SUPPORT

Situation

Ranier Wholesale Hardware is celebrating its fiftieth anniversary in business. On the occasion, the president writes many of the company's loyal customers to thank them for their support. About a month later it occurs to the president that several of his suppliers also deserve recognition, and he decides to write them to express appreciation for high-quality merchandise and services.

Analysis of the Letter

1. *A provocative opening sentence is a good way to attract attention.*

2. *Describe the recent celebration of the company's golden anniversary and the tributes paid the customers who made it possible.*

3. *In the third paragraph, emphasis shifts to the manufacturers who supply the products, with a warm compliment to them for their role in the company's growth.*

4. *Make the ending brief, friendly, and direct.*

5. *Consider adding a humorous "P.S." to give the entire message a little sparkle.*

The Letter

Dear George:

Generally, it's the customer who gets all the attention.

When we held our Golden Jubilee Anniversary last month, we had a wonderful celebration. One of the things we thought of first was to write to a couple of hundred of our retail hardware customers to thank them for their loyal support over the years. Without them, we said, we couldn't possibly have become what we are; in fact, we wouldn't even be around to celebrate those fifty years. Of course, we meant it; you know the importance of loyal friends as well as we do.

But later I got to thinking: What about those people who kept us supplied most of those years with quality hardware products that dealers wanted to buy and did buy time and time again? Don't they deserve some credit, too? Of course, they do. We've been buying hammers, saws, blades, wrenches, and a couple of dozen other Mikkelson-brand products from you for how long—thirty-five years? And you've always given us genuine quality at a fair price, plus outstanding service. What more can a wholesaler ask from a manufacturer? Sure, we've had our minor squabbles from time to time, and your attitude was that the customer is always right (in our case, he often wasn't!). Whatever the problems were—I forget—they haven't detracted one bit from our high opinion of your company, your products, and your people.

So, on at least one occasion, I want to direct my full attention not to my important customers, but to my important suppliers. Mikkelson stands very high on our list of those to whom we owe a great big thank you. Thank you!

Sincerely,

P.S.   When a small crisis arises between us—and it will!—you won't hold over my head the nice things I've said, will you?

PART 8

PUBLIC RELATIONS AND PERSONNEL LETTERS

Many of the letters you write will probably fall under the general category of public relations. Of course, the public is *everybody*—including your customers, suppliers, and employees—but in this part, we concentrate on those letters that have to do mainly with a company's image.

Nearly every business wants people to have a good feeling toward it. Many large organizations spend millions of dollars a year toward that end, employing a large staff of PR specialists or engaging consultants to build and maintain a supportive attitude on the part of the public. Among the groups with whom PR departments are most anxious to establish good relations are news media, government (local, state, and federal), organized consumer groups, local civic organizations, professional associations, and others who represent centers of influence. Obviously, paying close attention to the reactions of the public makes good sense; the road to success in any endeavor is a lot smoother when you have influential friends.

But whether you're a member of the PR group or not, you're likely to write some letters to people who ask for favors or solicit donations or merely express their views—pro and con—on what your company is doing.

Although one would hope that all PR letters are friendly, image-enhancing messages, this is not the case. Just consider the kind of mail received by a telephone company, an electric power company, automobile manufacturers, and others when rates and prices hike upwards and performance is not satisfactory. Such letters often find their way into newspapers and other media, along with the responses of the accused. And these aren't the only companies who receive unfavorable (sometimes downright libelous) mail. A large number have their own flock of critics who consider themselves watchdogs on matters concerning the environment, public policy, product safety, political affiliations, prices, and so on. Some people dearly love to write scathing letters to which tactful responses seem only to generate even more critical diatribes.

Writers have to handle these letters in the most tactful way possible, using sound logic and gentle persuasion to present the company's point of view. However, when you've done everything reasonable to mollify your critics without success, you're perfectly justified in simply turning your back on them.

Every day, large organizations receive letters applying for positions for which there are no vacancies or for openings for which the applicants are not qualified. Responses to such letters also fall into the public-relations category.

SECTION 23

GENERAL PUBLIC RELATIONS LETTERS

As we mentioned earlier, some public-relations letters are pleasant messages, whose primary purpose is to build goodwill and enhance the company's image. In tone and style they are very much like the letters you would write to sales prospects and customers. The guidelines for writing them are simple: be warm, friendly, and persuasive.

Other letters deal with matters that are not altogether pleasant, such as saying "no" to requests that you can't grant or responding to outraged critics. In these instances, you are, of course, as tactful and cordial as possible, but you must still deliver a response that is unlikely to win applause from your readers.

In this section, we concentrate on the latter type simply because they are the hardest to write. Here are guidelines for writing such letters:

---

1. *If there's good news to report, do it first; then deliver the bad news.*
2. *When the letter you received contains a compliment, acknowledge it gratefully.*
3. *When you have to say "no," do it as gently as possible, giving reasons why.*
4. *If you're responding to an irate critic:*
   a. *Express appreciation for his or her point of view.*
   b. *Fully explain your point of view.*
   c. *End the letter with a statement that assumes the air has been cleared and no further correspondence is necessary.*

23-1 HANDLING A SPECIAL REQUEST

Situation

A graduate student in communications writes the president of Widmark Corporation. She is making a study of the history of corporate annual reports and requests a copy of each of Widmark's reports for the past fifteen years. Only three can be sent, but the president has a suggestion for getting access to the others.

Analysis of the Letter

1. *Compliment the reader on her choice of a topic and express pleasure that she wants to include Widmark Corporation.*

2. *Say immediately what you can do and explain why you can't send all fifteen reports. Then, invite her to view the microfilms if she wishes and describe the arrangements that can be made.*

3. *End the letter on a friendly, positive note.*

The Letter

Dear Miss Demeter:

Your study of the history of annual reports sounds very challenging, and I'm pleased that you want Widmark represented.

I'm enclosing copies of our annual report for the current year and the two preceding years. Although earlier reports are not available in hard-copy form, they are on microfilm. If you are in Minneapolis, you are welcome to visit us and spend as much time as you wish examining these films. Just let me know ahead of time, and I will make arrangements with the company librarian (J. C. Schultz) to set up a carrel for you with viewing equipment.

I suspect your study will prove to be quite an ambitious one, but certainly useful to a large number of people. Good luck!

Cordially yours,

23-2 REFUSING A REQUEST TO BUY ADVERTISING

Situation

You are promotion manager for a national firm that sells sports equipment to schools and colleges. Every year you receive letters inviting you to buy space in the high school yearbook. Obviously, it's a poor medium—people who see these ads are not prospective buyers of your equipment. The invitation must be declined.

Analysis of the Letter

1. *Use a conversational tone, but don't be condescending.*

2. *In the first paragraph, thank the reader for the invitation and recall your experience in a similar role (if you can do so honestly).*

3. *Move smoothly into the reasons why you can't purchase advertising space, with emphasis on the theme, "If we contribute to one yearbook, we must contribute to all—and we can't afford it."*

4. *Suggest reasons why the reader should concentrate his efforts in his own community.*

5. *Close the letter with a warm and positive message.*

The Letter

Dear William:

I appreciate your invitation to purchase an ad in The Cardinal. I recall my own experience as advertising manager of my high school yearbook and the troubles I had selling space to national organizations.

The answer I got then is the same that I give now. There are so many thousands of yearbooks published each year that it is impossible to support them all. I admit that there is probably equipment in your school that was purchased from Sparling's, but the same is true of thousands of others. And advertisers spend most of their money where the message gets into the hands of purchasing directors and others who buy in large quantities.

I expect, William, that you will have to rely primarily on local community business owners to purchase space in The Cardinal. The readers of the ads are likely to be prospective customers of these advertisers. Moreover, most businesses feel a strong obligation to support worthy community activities; just having their names associated with a local school project is a strong incentive. Indeed, Sparling's feels the same way about Fort Wayne, which is our home base.

Thank you for thinking of us, William, and my best wishes for the most successful Cardinal that has ever been published!

Sincerely,

23-3 ACKNOWLEDGING A REQUEST FOR A DONATION

Situation

Most companies get many requests for donations to various causes; more often than not, they are addressed to the president, for obvious reasons. Although there is usually an amount set aside for contributions, it is almost never enough. To remove the responsibility for decisions from one person, it is standard practice to set up a committee to cull the most worthy causes for support. The first response, however, usually comes from the person addressed. The president of Halpern Associates responds to such a request, explaining the company's position in handling such matters.

Analysis of the Letter

1. *Express appreciation for the letter.*

2. *Explain fully the difficulty in supporting all causes and tell how your company handles such requests. (In this case, you admit that the Duplin Youth Symphony is deserving, but you leave the door open for a "no" response by the contributions committee.)*

3. *State what you are doing and express your wishes for success.*

The Letter

Dear Mrs. Mueller:

Thank you for writing about your need for financial support for the Duplin Youth Symphony.

Each year, our company sets aside a sizable sum of money for distribution to various charitable agencies and other groups. The requests for financial aid have multiplied many times in the past few years, and to make sure our budget is distributed in the fairest manner possible, we have established a special contributions committee, whose members have the responsibility of selecting those organizations they consider most deserving in terms of what we can give. It's a difficult job because most of the requests we receive are, like yours, for worthy causes.

I am handing your letter to the head of the contributions committee, and you may expect to hear from her within the next few weeks. In the meantime, I wish you all success in your endeavor.

Very cordially yours,

23-4

TURNING DOWN A REQUEST FOR A DONATION

Situation

This is a continuation of the situation described in Letter 23-3 on page 194. The contributions committee of Halpern Associates decides against a donation to the Duplin Youth Symphony, and the head of the committee writes Mrs. Mueller, who made the request.

Analysis of the Letter

1. *Open the letter with an update on the committee's deliberations, saving the "no" until later.*

2. *Acknowledge the importance of the cause, and then indicate that the request has been turned down. It's a good idea to tell where the money was placed, but you don't need to be more specific.*

3. *In the third paragraph, admit that the committee is not infallible, but note that the members did what they felt was fair.*

4. *End on a note of optimism and encouragement.*

The Letter

Dear Mrs. Mueller:

Our contributions committee has, after careful study of all the requests for contributions, selected those which we think are in greatest need of our support.

Although the members unanimously agreed that the Duplin Youth Symphony contributes much to the community—as well as to the performers themselves—we can't, unfortunately, provide financial support at this time. There are so many projects that need help desperately, and we have chosen to allot our budget to child-care centers for working mothers, drug rehabilitation programs, parental counseling on child abuse, "half-way" facilities for unwed teenage mothers, and various projects for the aged.

Of course, Mrs. Mueller, we realize that any decisions our committee makes are arbitrary, but I assure you that they were arrived at thoughtfully and, we believe, fairly. I do hope that in the future we will be in a position to provide some funds for the Duplin Youth Symphony. In the meantime, we wish you success with your efforts on behalf of this excellent organization.

Sincerely,

23-5 RESPONDING TO A FRIENDLY CRITIC

Situation

You're in the public relations department of Transamerica Technologies, a large conglomerate that sponsors a public-service television series, "American Issues." It is your job to answer letters from viewers who comment—pro and con—on the program. One viewer writes that he likes the series a lot, but takes issue with the segment that dealt with the environment. You write to the viewer to express appreciation for his interest and point of view, present the other side, and retain his goodwill and support of the series.

Analysis of the Letter

1. *Express gratitude for the letter, mentioning the unexpectedly heavy volume of mail (mostly favorable, including Converse's general assessment).*

2. *Compliment the reader on the study and thought he has given to environmental matters, and say that others also wrote critical letters about that segment in the series.*

3. *Explain the company's eagerness to present both sides of every controversial issue. Then, subtly indicate that you've succeeded, since there were letters in direct contradiction to the reader's views.*

4. *Reinforce the value of the program as a thought stimulant to people who are concerned about difficult issues that are facing Americans.*

5. *End the letter on a pleasant note, inviting the reader to continue to share his opinions of the programs with you.*

The Letter

Dear Professor Converse:

It was very thoughtful of you to write about the television series, "American Issues," sponsored by Transamerica Technologies. Our mail from viewers has been much heavier than we expected but, as we had <u>hoped</u>, overwhelmingly favorable. Certainly, your general assessment of the series is very satisfying to us.

Your comments on "Environment versus Progress" indicate that you have given much study and thought to this subject, and I appreciate your frank appraisal of it. Several other people wrote that they, too, felt it was biased in favor of industry.

The producers were well aware in the beginning that this is a highly controversial subject and were determined not to take sides. Our general mail would seem to indicate that they succeeded, for we received comments from many viewers that the program was biased in favor of the environmentalists!

Indeed, conflicting viewpoints are expected on this series, and as long as they are fairly well balanced (as they have been), we feel that the series is encouraging people to think more intelligently and deeply about the unresolved issues that face our nation.

Thank you for writing. I hope you will continue to watch "American Issues" and that you will let us have your opinions—favorable or unfavorable.

Very cordially yours,

23-6 RESPONDING TO AN OUTRAGED CRITIC

Situation

The president of a large corporation receives a severely critical letter from the owner of a construction business. The writer objects to the corporation's advertising in a magazine called *Bulwark*, which he feels is "militant" and "un-American." He is so incensed at the corporation's "support" of this magazine that he threatens to boycott its products. As assistant to the president, you are asked to respond, expressing appreciation for the letter and explaining tactfully the company's position.

Analysis of the Letter

1. *Express appreciation for the letter, even though it is caustic.*

2. *State quite explicitly how a medium is chosen for advertising, emphasizing that placing an ad is not an endorsement of the medium itself.*

3. *Point out that the reader's view is not necessarily shared by others; yet do not directly accuse him of bias.*

4. *Go into further detail about your standards in choosing a medium and restate your general policy. Then, reinforce your stand by pointing out that most other advertisers follow a similar policy.*

5. *Thank the writer for expressing his views and for allowing you to express yours.*

Note: *We do not claim that this letter will satisfy the recipient, even though it is very tactful. If you hear from him again along the same lines, we recommend that the second letter be ignored.*

The Letter

Dear Mr. Coughlin:

I appreciate your writing about our advertising in Bulwark magazine.

Bulwark was chosen as an advertising medium simply because its circulation (about 300,000) is made up mostly of young men and women in the upper-income brackets whom we consider appropriate targets for our video cassette recorders. Placing advertising in a publication does not necessarily mean that we endorse its editorial views. You criticize Bulwark as "militant" and "un-American"—even "dangerous." I expect, Mr. Coughlin, that some people will agree with you. Yet we also receive letters equally vehement about our advertising in magazines that are broadly labeled as "conservative."

We do have a policy of not advertising in periodicals that are prurient in nature or that are essentially scandal sheets. It is our opinion that Bulwark does not fall into either of these categories. It is quite likely that the people in our advertising department who chose Bulwark do not all agree with its editorial position, but it is their responsibility to place ads where they think our products will get the widest exposure, given the constraints mentioned above. I think most national advertisers use a similar criterion in choosing media. Not one that I know of believes that spending advertising dollars means "support."

Thank you for expressing your views so frankly and for giving us the opportunity to express ours.

Very truly yours,

23-7

TURNING DOWN A REQUEST FOR CONFIDENTIAL INFORMATION

Situation

The president of a group known as The Committee for Clean Children's Literature writes The Smalley Corporation asking for a contribution "to fight smut in children's books." No money is given. The Smalley Corporation then receives a request from the group's president for a list of the organizations to which Smalley did contribute and the amount given to each one. This information is confidential. You respond for Smalley, denying the request.

Analysis of the Letter

1. *In the opening paragraph, indicate the total amount contributed, but decline to disclose the organizations that received the money or the amounts.*

2. *Describe how contribution decisions are made. (In this case, indicate that it is a democratic process in which you do not participate.)*

3. *End the letter with a "thank you."*

The Letter

Dear Mrs. Leyden:

During the past year, The Smalley Corporation contributed a little over $300,000 to various local charitable organizations and other community groups. I am not at liberty, however, to disclose the names of the organizations which received the money or the precise amount given in each instance.

The decision on how to distribute the amount budgeted is placed in the hands of our committee for donations and contributions, which is made up of ten individuals who represent a cross section of the company. The decisions of this committee are final and confidential.

Thank you for writing.

Very cordially yours,

SECTION 24

PERSONNEL LETTERS

Every day, large organizations receive letters from people who apply for a job. More often than not, these applications must be turned down, either because there are no vacancies in the positions applied for or because the applicants are not qualified for openings that do exist.

Saying no to job applicants, for whatever reason, requires the utmost tact, since those who receive such letters are quite likely to think of the turn-down as a *personal* rejection.

In this section, we give examples of "no" letters to job applicants as well as other communications pertaining to employment.

24-1 RESPONDING TO A QUALIFIED APPLICANT— NO POSITION AVAILABLE

Situation

You are in the Personnel Department of Grantham Distributors Inc. and receive an application from a woman for the position of computer programmer. There are no openings; however, you are impressed with the applicant's qualifications and want to leave the door slightly ajar for later consideration. You write to express appreciation, explain the job situation, and compliment the applicant on her qualifications.

Analysis of the Letter

1. *Always thank a job applicant, even though she or he may lack the necessary qualifications. (This one is qualified.)*

2. *Give the bad news, tempered somewhat by the statement that the present situation could change.*

3. *Compliment the applicant on her qualifications.*

4. *To be fair, you may want to suggest that she apply elsewhere. Certainly it would be wrong to give her false hope.*

5. *Promise to let the applicant know if an opening occurs. Even though she may have a job by then, yours could be a better one.*

The Letter

Dear Miss Langston:

Thank you for your application for the position of computer programmer.

At the moment, Miss Langston, there are no vacancies in our data processing division. Of course, the situation may change at any moment, and I would like to keep your résumé handy in case there is a staff expansion or a resignation. Certainly, it would appear that you have excellent qualifications for the position you seek.

Even though I am reluctant to "turn you loose" on the job market, in all fairness to you I recommend that you submit applications elsewhere. I would not want you to pass up an opportunity merely on the hope that our situation will change soon. You may be sure, however, that if an opening does occur here which I think would interest you, I will get in touch with you at once.

Sincerely yours,

24-2

RESPONDING TO AN UNQUALIFIED APPLICANT— POSITION AVAILABLE

Situation

You receive an application for the job of advertising copywriter which was advertised in a local paper. The applicant is poorly qualified in comparison with several others who made application. You write to express appreciation for the application and explain the situation without giving the applicant a definite "no."

Analysis of the Letter

1. *Express appreciation for the application.*

2. *Because you are almost certain that the applicant won't get the job, mention the large number of qualified people who have applied. If the job has already been filled, say so. Since it hasn't, be honest in saying you haven't made up your mind yet.*

3. *The statement in the third paragraph will make it unnecessary to write an actual turndown letter.*

4. *Thank the applicant for his interest in your company.*

Note: Some people may feel that you owe it to the applicant to level with him at the outset and simply say "you're not qualified" and why. This is all right if, say, the ad called for two years' experience and the applicant has none. But if you base your assessment on a very poorly written letter—which would certainly sink a copywriter—you may want to refrain from harsh criticism.

The Letter

Dear Mr. Spillers:

I appreciate your application for the position of copywriter that was advertised in the <u>Denver Post</u>.

The response to our ad has been very gratifying, and we have had applications from several people who are extremely well qualified for the job. However, we shall want to wait until all applications are in and then study each one carefully before making a decision.

Our plan is to fill this position no later than June 10. If you have not heard from us by that time, you may assume that the job has been filled.

Thank you for your interest in Grantham Distributors Inc.

Cordially yours,

24-3 WRITING AN APPLICANT WHO FAILED TO QUALIFY

Situation

Each year the supervisor of editorial training for a magazine publisher hires ten new trainees who are selected on the basis of the scores achieved on an editing test designed for the purpose. After the test is given and graded, the supervisor writes a turn-down letter to the candidates who failed to place in the top ten.

Analysis of the Letter

1. *Thank the recipient for submitting the editing test.*

2. *Announce the bad news gently and be tactfully specific in describing flaws that prevented a higher score.*

3. *In the third paragraph, suggest a source for refresher training—a good PR gesture.*

4. *Close with a note of friendly encouragement.*

The Letter

Dear Ellen:

Thank you for submitting the editing test for the position of editorial trainee.

All the tests from the thirty-three applicants have been graded, and, unfortunately, your score was not among the top ten. According to the grader, your main problem was in spotting several sentence faults in the test—run-ons, fragments, unbalanced construction, and faulty modifiers. Also, there were several notes about incorrect grammar and punctuation.

If you're still interested in doing editorial work, I suggest that you undergo a thorough review of the elements of style. A book that I think you will find helpful is <u>Programmed Handbook of English</u>, by A. C. Skinner, published by Unity Press. It's a self-study manual and very thorough.

Good luck!

Sincerely,

24-4

RESPONDING TO A PARTIALLY QUALIFIED APPLICANT

Situation

Recently, Cent-West Corporation advertised in *Power* magazine for a cost and scheduling manager. An applicant met one of the two experience requirements described in the ad, but did not mention the other. You write to point out to the applicant the experience requirements of the job, leaving the matter open to further consideration in case the ad was misread.

Analysis of the Letter

1. *Thank the reader for applying, mentioning the source that triggered the application.*

2. *Accentuate the applicant's excellent background in general power-plant management. Then, indicate tactfully that the coal power-plant experience was not mentioned.*

3. *Leave the door open for the applicant to supply evidence of coal power-plant experience just in case he misread the ad.*

4. *Ask for a quick reply.*

The Letter

Dear Mr. Jacobi:

Thank you for applying for the position of cost and scheduling manager at Cent-West Corporation, which was advertised in the November issue of Power.

Certainly, Mr. Jacobi, your educational qualifications are superb, and your twelve years' experience in general power-plant projects is most impressive. I do not, however, find any mention in your résumé of coal power-plant experience, which is mandatory for this position (four years minimum).

If I am incorrect in my assessment of your credentials, I would be pleased to hear from you—immediately, please, since we must make a final decision within the next two weeks.

Very sincerely yours,

Situation

Angela Wheaton was employed for five years in the personnel department of a pharmaceutical manufacturer. At the time she left the company (her husband was transferred), she held the position of director of clerical training. She has applied for a similar position in a large insurance company, listing her former boss as a reference. As a personnel supervisor for the insurance company, you write Wheaton's former boss for information about her employment record.

Analysis of the Letter

1. *Immediately mention the applicant's name, the position applied for, and the recipient's listing as a reference.*

2. *Set up the questions as fill-ins, making it easy for the recipient to supply the information. (Questions about applicants vary from one company to another, but the ones shown are typical.)*

The Letter

Dear Mrs. Eller:

Mrs. Angela Wheaton has applied to us for the position of director of office training, and your name was given as a reference.

I would appreciate your answering the following questions about Mrs. Wheaton.

1. How long was she under your supervision?_____

2. What was her position at the time she left your company?

_____

3. What reason was given for leaving?_____

_____

4. How would you rate her overall competence? (Check one.)
Outstanding_____ Good_____ Average_____ Fair_____ Poor_____

5. Please state briefly what you believe to be her greatest strengths
and weaknesses (if any):

a. Strengths_____

_____

b. Weaknesses_____

_____

6. If you had an opening for which she is qualified, would you rehire
her? Yes_____ No_____. If no, please state why.

_____

3. Give assurance that the information supplied will be treated as confidential (a must) and offer to reciprocate should the occasion arise.

Note: *It is customary to enclose a stamped, self-addressed envelope in which to mail the response.*

I assure you, Mrs. Eller, that any information you supply about this applicant will be held in strict confidence. If there is ever an opportunity for me to reciprocate, I will be pleased to do so. Thank you.

Very sincerely yours,

OFFERING AN EXECUTIVE POSITION TO A QUALIFIED PERSON

Situation

Mills-Froman Corporation, in San Francisco, is establishing a new department in the company, to be called organization planning and manager development, and is searching for a director. The executive vice president, C. J. Bouchard, has interviewed several people in various parts of the country and has decided to make an offer to Lawrence A. Margulies in Cleveland, who is extraordinarily well qualified. Bouchard gave no definite promises when he met with Margulies in Cleveland, but is now ready to make a written offer.

Analysis of the Letter

1. *Make favorable reference to the meeting and to the dinner that included Mrs. Margulies.*

2. *Offer the position by exact title, and emphasize its importance. Mentioning the backing of the president and other top executives should be reassuring to the recipient.*

3. *Although the salary and various benefits were discussed at the meeting, it is important that these matters be stated in writing.*

The Letter

Dear Larry:

The day I spent with you in Cleveland was very enjoyable and stimulating, and I appreciate your taking the time to meet with me. Getting acquainted with Sara was a special treat; I am indebted to her for joining us at dinner on such short notice.

I am pleased to offer you the position of director of organization planning and manager development of Mills-Froman Corporation. As I mentioned, this is a new position that we are most anxious to fill. The growth of our company makes it essential that we centralize this function, rather than leave the responsibility with individual executives, committees, and outside consultants. President Froman and all other top executives support this idea enthusiastically. As mentioned, the person who holds this position will report directly to me.

We are prepared to offer you an annual salary of $65,000 at the outset, along with what I think is a very attractive array of fringe benefits. Our personnel policy manual is being sent to you separately, along with Executive Memorandums 14 and 26, which describe various financial incentives for which you would be eligible.

4. Provide a brief description of the position and responsibilities of the person selected for it. All this was probably said at the meeting—and more—but those considering an important job change usually want these things spelled out.

Although we discussed the responsibilities of this new position briefly, I want to outline in broad terms the function as we see it. Obviously, our principal objective is to develop managers for executive responsibilities. At the same time, we are well aware that the first step is to create the appropriate climate in which candidates for leadership can grow and flourish. At the outset, this means intelligent organization planning, which includes the following:

1. Establishing company objectives.
2. Establishing the critical success factors that affect the attainment of those objectives.
3. Developing an ideal organization structure that will favor the activities related to the critical success factors.
4. Modifying the ideal structure to achieve a satisfactory compromise between the existing structure and the ideal structure.

Only when these steps are taken will we be in a position to construct and implement a sound manager development program. As you know, the scope of such a program can be very broad, including on-the-job-training, special task-force assignments, seminars and conferences, business gaming, university-sponsored courses, and so on. The director of this new department will be given wide range in selecting the most effective methods of achieving the ultimate goals.

5. Express the hope that Margulies will accept the position, and ask for a decision by a certain date. Suggest a starting date, but try to keep it flexible. The writer's insistence that Margulies wind up affairs with his present employer amicably is simply good business etiquette.

I hope, Larry, that this opportunity sounds exciting and challenging to you. After our conversation in Cleveland, I'm convinced that you have the depth and experience in this area to perform the duties of this position highly effectively.

Please let me know your decision within the next two weeks. The starting date we have in mind is January 15, but of course that date is flexible, depending on your circumstances. Certainly, we would want you to wind up things at Corcoran amicably.

Sincerely yours,

6. The "P.S." simply reassures Margulies that Mills-Froman will be more than fair in assisting him in dealing with personal financial matters.

P.S.   Although we touched briefly in Cleveland on such matters as moving expenses, per-diem allowances for you and your family while you are being settled in the Bay Area, and certain real estate adjustments, I will provide specific details when I have your acceptance. I assure you that our company policy in these matters is very generous.

24-7 ANNOUNCING AN IMPORTANT APPOINTMENT—NEWS RELEASE

Situation

DeWitt J. Fuller has just been appointed senior consultant in small business management at Harlan Thomas Associates. As assistant to the personnel and public relations manager, you are to prepare a news release, which will be sent to local newspapers and broadcast stations. (The same information, in slightly different form, is also sent to all employees by means of an executive memorandum.)

Analysis of the Release

1. *News releases are usually written on 8½ by 11-inch paper with a pre-printed heading, such as the one shown.*

2. *A headline is usually provided, although it is common practice for news editors to write their own.*

3. *The copy is relatively brief, as it should be. Space is scarce in most publications—and even the copy shown here is likely to be cut by perhaps one-third.*

4. *Avoid sales puff. Only copy that has real news value will be used.*

The News Release

HARLAN THOMAS ASSOCIATES
Management Consultants
1379 Madison Avenue
New York, N.Y. 10028

For immediate release

DEWITT J. FULLER JOINS HARLAN THOMAS ASSOCIATES

DeWitt J. Fuller, former manager of the New Orleans Small Business Administration Field Office, has joined Harlan Thomas Associates as senior consultant in small business management and will assume his duties April 16, 19—.

According to President R. B. Myers, Fuller will establish a new small business management department at Harlan Thomas Associates for the purpose of providing special counsel to those who are considering starting a business, as well as those who are already operating a business and need assistance in financial planning, marketing strategies, and general management techniques. "Small business owners have largely been neglected by management consulting organizations," Myers said, "and we are convinced that an enormous contribution can be made by our company, not only to the owners themselves, but to the business community as a whole. We feel very fortunate in having a person with Fuller's experience to head up this important new service."

Prior to joining the SBA in 1974, Fuller was owner-operator of a small electronics manufacturing firm near Phoenix and for many years taught courses in small business management at Arizona State University. He is the author of Successful Small Business Management (Ploughman Press) and numerous articles in various trade journals.

PART 9

EMPLOYEE RELATIONS LETTERS

In our anxiety to please customers and other people of influence, we often overlook the fact that the employees in the company are the most important "public" of all. Although executives are quick to praise, congratulate, and express appreciation to outsiders, the idea of doing the same for employees rarely occurs to some.

One of the most important rewards an employee can receive costs nothing: recognition of achievement. This can be done face to face (preferably when others are present). But on certain occasions, nothing is so meaningful to an employee as a letter from the boss or fellow employees that says he or she deserves applause. Conversations and public announcements are appreciated, to be sure, but they are fleeting. Words on paper are tangible and permanent; they can be shared with family and friends and read and reread by the recipients when they need a lift.

LETTERS OF CONGRATULATION AND APPRECIATION

Obviously, you don't write letters of congratulation and appreciation to employees for simply doing what they are paid and expected to do. Such letters should be reserved for very special achievements and outstanding performance. The problem arises in determining what is special or outstanding. There are a few people who constantly dazzle their superiors with their ideas, innovations, and productivity, and if you wrote them every time they did something creditable, your letters would soon lose meaning. Although you would certainly tell them in person when they've pleased you, write them only when their achievement falls in the "spectacular" category.

It is the more typical employee—the one who does her or his job well and is only faintly visible to those on the upper rungs of management—to whom a congratulatory letter is truly meaningful when it is really deserved. And you have to define the word "deserved" in terms of the employee. What might be a run-of-the-mill accomplishment for a truly gifted and productive employee could be a grand-slam homer for the average worker. A congratulatory message to a good, solid, unspectacular employee can have a double benefit: it should lift your spirits to have written it, and you may get increased productivity from the worker because of an uplift in morale.

There are occasions, however, when nearly every employee deserves a written congratulation from the boss: upon an anniversary with the company, for recognition achieved outside the company, and on an important promotion.

The guidelines for such letters are quite simple:

1. *They should be warm and friendly.*
2. *They should be very specific about the achievement or occasion being acknowledged.*
3. *They should be believable—that is, not grossly exaggerated.*

25-1

CONGRATULATING AN EMPLOYEE FOR A JOB WELL DONE

Situation

The personnel vice president writes a letter of appreciation to an employee in the marketing department who has served effectively as head of a committee during the past year.

Analysis of the Letter

1. *Introduce the subject of the letter with a "thank-you."*

2. *In the second paragraph, recount the employee's achievements overall and her importance to the company.*

3. *Next, single out the things that were especially deserving of praise, thus giving the recipient assurance that these are not empty words that could apply to anybody.*

4. *Sign off quickly, but with gratitude.*

5. *Send a copy of the letter to the employee's boss. This is extremely important!*

The Letter

Dear Chris:

Thank you for serving as head of the new-employee orientation committee during the past year.

Under your leadership, our employee orientation program has become the most effective instrument we have for educating new people about the company—its past, present, and future; its people, policies, and procedures; its high standing in the industry. I'm confident that new people now adapt more quickly to their new environment and bring to their jobs a good feeling about Boughton's—so important to morale and productivity.

I have been especially pleased at the variety of your programs, the professional yet interesting manner in which the speakers brought off their presentations, the effective use of visual devices, and your allowance for participation by the new employees themselves.

You ran a good show, Chris, and I am deeply grateful.

My best to you,

cc: J. R. Dykman
Director of Marketing

25-2 CONGRATULATING AN EMPLOYEE ON A NEW IDEA

Situation

In visiting the suburban warehousing and distribution center located about thirty miles from the home office, the company president is impressed by the way in which the operations vice president (also housed in the home office) has established communication between headquarters and suburban-based employees. The president writes to compliment the operations vice president on the idea and tell him how well it is working.

Analysis of the Letter

1. *Introduce the subject of the letter with a compliment.*

2. *In the next three paragraphs, review the entire experience and tell the reader why it was so educational and satisfying. (Note the mention of specific ways in which the vice president's idea came off so well.)*

3. *In the final paragraph, offer congratulations and ask to be invited again.*

The Letter

Dear Morrie:

I enjoyed sitting in on your new Joint Management Group get-together at Industrial Park on Tuesday.

I learned a lot from the experience. I realized perhaps for the first time how important it is for home-office brass to make themselves available to employees who labor in warehousing and shipping—miles from the home office—and have up to now been sort of invisible.

Surely this new committee, with its monthly get-together, smooths the lines of communication and gives those in the hinterlands a feeling of importance and belonging. It was easy to see that a lot of problems can be quickly solved when there is complete candor in an informal setting. Everyone seemed to feel free to unload his or her pet peeves without fear of recrimination. Now <u>that's</u> communication!

The plant tour was a treat, too. After it was over, I came away feeling that the employees at Industrial Park know we know what they are doing and how well it is being done.

Congratulations, Morrie, on this idea. I hope you'll invite me another time. Can we have pizza and beer again for lunch?

Yours sincerely,

25-3

CONGRATULATING AN EMPLOYEE FOR AN OUTSTANDING REPORT

Situation

The executive vice president of Engineering Resources Inc. receives a very impressive report from a fairly new employee (an engineer) in which she proposes a new potential market for the company. He writes to offer congratulations for the excellent report and emphasize its importance to the company.

Analysis of the Letter

1. *Begin with an expression of congratulations on the report.*

2. *Be specific in identifying the parts of the report that are of special significance.*

3. *Indicate the importance of the author's conclusions and recommendations by announcing a special meeting, to which the author will be invited, for full discussion. This is praise of the highest order, and nothing more needs to be said.*

The Letter

Dear Clarissa:

Congratulations on the report, ''Energy Management—a New Market for Engineering Resources Inc.''

Although I have been seeing a good deal in the trade press recently about the growth of building energy consulting, I was not really aware that the demand was so explosive. Yet your report makes perfectly clear that this is a logical development in a period of economic slowdown and escalating fuel costs. I especially enjoyed the reprints you supplied of articles from leading business papers and professional journals.

The conclusions and recommendations in your report deserve very careful study, and I am sending copies to all the members of the development and planning group for their reactions. Later this month I will schedule an all-day meeting with these people at the Olympic Club. I want you to be there, and I will let you know the date and time. For the moment, I suggest that you jot down October 26 on your calendar as a tentative date.

Sincerely,

25-4

CONGRATULATING AN EMPLOYEE ON AN ANNIVERSARY

Situation

Martha Olson joined Atlantic Mills fifteen years ago as secretary to the director of purchasing. After five years she was promoted to assistant director, and when her boss retired four years later, she was named director. On the occasion of her fifteenth anniversary, a special luncheon is being held in her honor and hosted by the president. Immediately following the luncheon, the president wants to congratulate Olson again, this time by means of a personal letter (not a memorandum).

Analysis of the Letter

1. *The reference to the luncheon is only one way to open the letter, but it is a good one because it gives the writer a chance to put on record the accolades that were merely spoken about the day before—that is, that all those nice things that were said are really true.*

2. *Lest the employee get the impression in the first paragraph that she is only a "professional machine," the president emphasizes her personal qualities in the second paragraph.*

3. *The letter closes with a quick look at the future, the implication being that the recipient of the letter is an essential part of it.*

4. *The letter is brief, but it does the job—too much praise can destroy believability and prove embarrassing.*

The Letter

Dear Marty:

I meant what I said at the luncheon yesterday: I really can't remember when Marty Olson was <u>not</u> our director of purchasing. Six years isn't that long, but you have filled your role so competently and all of us have relied on you with such confidence that it is hard to separate the name from the function.

But you have won our esteem for personal as well as professional attributes. You have that wonderful gift of gaining friends and loyal supporters while maintaining the highest standards of purchasing management, and few are blessed with it.

As we continue to grow, the purchasing function will have an increasingly important role at Atlantic Mills. I hope you anticipate the challenge; certainly, there's no doubt that you will rise to it.

Warm personal regards,

CONGRATULATING A NEW MEMBER OF THE TWENTY-FIVE-YEAR CLUB

Situation

Robbins Steel Corporation honors employees who have worked for the company for twenty-five years by inducting them into its Twenty-Five-Year Club. It's a gala occasion, held in a hotel ballroom, at which inductees are presented with an engraved silver bowl. Just as soon as an employee's eligibility is announced—prior to the dinner and induction ceremonies—the president writes a letter of congratulation to honor the employee and express appreciation for loyal service.

Analysis of the Letter

1. *Congratulate the employee and invite him to become a member of the Twenty-Five-Year Club (note the words "distinct privilege").*

2. *Emphasize the importance of this group and express personal appreciation for the employee's loyalty and confidence.*

3. *Finally, mention the invitation that will follow and indicate anticipation in congratulating the employee in person at the affair.*

The Letter

Dear Sidney:

I consider it a distinct privilege to congratulate you on the completion of twenty-five years at Robbins Steel Corporation and to invite you to become a member of the Twenty-Five-Year Club.

As far as I am concerned, there is no group as important, for it is they who have contributed the most to our growth and our good name. I hope you look back on those years with great satisfaction and pride. It's a grand achievement, and I want you to know how much I personally appreciate your loyalty and confidence.

Shortly you will receive an invitation to the annual Twenty-Five-Year Club Dinner at which you will be formally inducted. I look forward to seeing you there and congratulating you in person on becoming a member of this very exclusive group.

Sincerely,

25-6

CONGRATULATING AN EMPLOYEE FOR COMMUNITY RECOGNITION

Situation

The owner of a small manufacturing company in a resort area learns that an employee has been elected to the board of directors of the local Chamber of Commerce. The owner writes the employee to extend congratulations and offer support.

Analysis of the Letter

1. *Offer congratulations immediately, designating the specific honor.*

2. *Recount the past achievements of the Chamber of Commerce and express the conviction that even more will be accomplished with the employee on the board.*

3. *Offer the company's intensified support of the Chamber because of the employee's new role.*

The Letter

Dear Julie:

I've just heard the good news that you have been elected to the board of directors of the Ocean Isles Chamber of Commerce. Congratulations!

During the few years the Chamber has been in existence, it has done a remarkable job of attracting new industry, professional people, tourists, and retirees to this community. And now that you're a board member, I expect the Chamber to achieve even bigger things during the next three years.

The Chamber has always had our support, but our resolve is now stronger than ever to contribute to its growth and success. Best wishes and good luck.

Sincerely,

25-7

CONGRATULATING YOUR BOSS ON A PROMOTION

Situation

Your boss, the director of sales training, has just been named staff vice president for marketing. You've enjoyed working with him and have a high opinion of his ability. You write to offer congratulations and express your pleasure at this recognition of his worth.

Analysis of the Letter

1. *Immediately express your personal delight in your boss's promotion and your excitement about it.*

2. *Praise him as a leader who made your work enjoyable and taught you much. Note that the message is sincere but not sticky.*

3. *Make the closing paragraph a warm goodbye and expression of good wishes.*

The Letter

Dear Chuck:

I am genuinely delighted that you now bear the lofty title, staff vice president for marketing. I can't recall ever being so excited about seeing someone promoted.

If you think that means "I'm glad he's gone," you are dead wrong! Because of you, I've really enjoyed my work in sales training. Certainly, I couldn't have had a better teacher—or friend.

We'll miss you a lot, but all of us feel great about this recognition of your ability. You deserve it, and I wish you well.

Yours,

LETTERS ON RETIREMENT

To most people, retirement after many years of employment is a joyous occasion. Not that they haven't enjoyed their work, but they look forward to a different lifestyle and the freedom to do pretty much as they please without pressures, fixed routines, or deadlines.

A few would rather stay on the job for as long as they live. They like what they do, think they are as productive as they were forty years ago, and can't imagine occupying themselves without working. Some are forced into early retirement for health reasons.

In any event, all retirees like to receive letters from fellow employees acknowledging their accomplishments and telling them how much they will be missed.

Here are guidelines for writing letters to retirees:

___

1. *Assume that it is a happy occasion unless you know otherwise, and treat the matter accordingly.*
2. *Recount the retiree's contributions to the company.*
3. *Extend best wishes for many happy and healthy years ahead.*

___

26-1

CONGRATULATING AN EMPLOYEE ON RETIREMENT—A HAPPY OCCASION

Situation

The financial vice president of Watson-Ferguson Corporation, an employee for forty-five years, retires. He is honored at a special retirement party. The president of the company wants to follow up with a personal letter to offer congratulations and express warm appreciation.

Analysis of the Letter

1. *A letter congratulating an old friend who is happily retiring is appropriately personal and light in tone. Mentioning the retirement gift leads the writer nicely into the main message in the second paragraph.*

2. *The retiree's work is praised, using his new hobby as the hook. Again, the message is friendly without being maudlin.*

3. *In the third paragraph, the writer says that the retiree will be missed, but this is done without pathos—still bright and cheerful.*

4. *The writer expresses good wishes and invites the retiree to drop in for a visit when he is in Cleveland.*

The Letter

Dear Herb:

I was a mite surprised at the gift presented to you on the occasion of your retirement party—a really beautiful set of golf clubs. I happen to know that you are not a golfer, and when I asked someone about the gift, the answer was: "That's what Sheila said Herb wanted most of all. He doesn't play now, but he's determined to learn."

Of course, I shouldn't be surprised. You've been constantly pursuing new challenges throughout your forty-five years at Watson-Ferguson, and I can't think of one that you didn't master. It's that fierce determination—tempered with a delightful Hoosier wit and practical-mindedness—that has made you such an outstanding financial executive. Why not golf, indeed!

We will miss you, naturally, but our gloom is brightened somewhat by our vision of your chasing the little white ball all over Hilton Head Island. That, by the way, sounds like a lot more fun than juggling debentures and arguing with security analysts.

Muriel joins me in wishing for you and Sheila many happy years in the Sun Belt. Be sure to drop in on the folks here at W-F when you get to Cleveland.

Best personal regards,

26-2

EXTENDING GOOD WISHES TO A RELUCTANT RETIREE

Situation

Edwin Millspaugh, 70, is being retired by his company. It is not a happy event for him; he is one of those who believe that no one should be forced to retire as long as he or she is productive. However, company policy requires this action. His immediate boss, the controller, writes a letter to express appreciation for past service and extend warm wishes for the future.

Analysis of the Letter

1. *Although Edwin is upset about being retired, the writer makes only a brief reference to it. To sympathize with Edwin, the writer would be saying, in effect, that the company is wrong in enforcing such a policy.*

2. *Edwin's forty-seven years of competent performance are recalled warmly and positively. Note that there is no mention that it will be impossible to replace him.*

3. *In the final paragraph, the writer compliments Edwin by implying that, at 70, he can still be productive. The last sentence wraps up the event in a positive and friendly manner.*

The Letter

Dear Edwin:

I know that you're not especially thrilled to be retiring at the tender age of 70, so I won't congratulate you. But I do want to express my appreciation to you.

You can always look back with pride and satisfaction on your forty-seven years at Gemstrand. No one knows more about manufacturing cost control than you, Edwin, and I can recall hundreds of occasions when your sharp pencil and keen mind guided us in making intelligent decisions. You have been a valuable ally and friend.

I hope you will find new and exciting ways to use your know-how, Edwin. We will certainly miss you, and I extend to you every good wish for health, happiness, and satisfaction in the years ahead.

Cordially,

26-3

WRITING AN EMPLOYEE RETIRING FOR HEALTH REASONS

Situation

Patricia Brogden has been in charge of the library at McKinsey and Knoblett ever since it was set up twenty-two years ago. Recently she has been in poor health, and she has been advised by her doctor to seek a dry climate. She has resigned and plans to live in Arizona. Her immediate superior, the director of personnel services, writes her a letter shortly before her departure to express regret on the condition of her health, review her accomplishments, and extend best wishes for the future.

Analysis of the Letter

1. As mentioned earlier, letters on retirement— for whatever reason— should be as cheerful as possible. Although Patricia's situation is not a happy one, the writer is positive rather than negative.

2. Patricia is heartily commended on her excellent work and the esteem in which she is held by the writer. This particular message brightens an otherwise somber occasion.

3. The writer closes by expressing hope for the future and offering assistance in finding a job if Patricia wants one.

The Letter

Dear Patricia:

I have already told you how distressed I am that, because of health, your doctor has persuaded you to move to a mild, dry climate. The only satisfaction I can get from this development is that where you're going, you'll be a lot more comfortable and stand a good chance at full recovery. That's the important thing; the great void your leaving creates here must not even be considered.

Some people say that those who leave a company are quickly forgotten, and I guess that's true in some instances—but not in your case, Patricia. You've made such an imprint here by establishing and operating one of the most respected professional libraries in the country that your presence will be felt for many years to come. My association with you has been one of the genuine rewards of working at Hargrave Industries.

I hope and expect that you will find living in Arizona truly delightful. I have a suspicion that when your health permits, you may look for an opportunity to use your expertise in librarianship in that area. If you do, I would be honored to have you use my name as reference.

Warmest personal wishes,

SECTION 27

LETTERS OF SYMPATHY

Among the most difficult messages to convey are those that try to console people who have experienced tragedy. Almost anything one can say seems trite because, no matter how sincere the writer is, grief is such a personal thing that only time can erase it. Yet to completely ignore the suffering of close friends seems heartless and uncaring.

Today, most people express their sympathy by means of a personal visit to the bereaved—either in the office or the home—where a physical gesture can be much more consoling than words. Some people send the bereaved a modest gift—a potted plant, a book, and so on—accompanied by a note such as "We loved her too," or "Jack was very special to me, and I will miss him." Printed cards that also contain a personal message are sometimes used.

There are occasions, however, when nothing but a personal letter seems suitable. Only you will know what these occasions are.

Here are four guidelines for writing letters of condolence:

1. *Express your sorrow briefly; a torrent of sympathetic words can make things worse.*
2. *Recall happy personal experiences about the deceased, but don't be maudlin.*
3. *Reveal by some modest gesture your willingness to be of help or comfort.*
4. *Always use personal stationery—never a company letterhead—and write the message by hand.*

27-1

DEATH OF AN IMMEDIATE SUPERVISOR AND CLOSE FRIEND

Situation

Assume that your immediate supervisor passes away. His death was not unexpected—he had been seriously ill for months. You felt very close to him for many reasons, and you feel compelled to write a letter of condolence to his widow, also a personal friend.

Analysis of the Letter

1. *Mention your grief at Larry's passing and how difficult it is for you to accept it.*

2. *In the next two paragraphs, emphasize the influence Larry had on your career, giving him much of the credit for your success, and indicating that, even though Larry is gone, his presence is still felt.*

3. *In the fourth paragraph, express the hope that your friendship with Sarah will continue, which she will appreciate.*

4. *The last sentence is an effective way to show your desire to do something tangible for Sarah. This may not be the offer indicated here, but if possible, try for something more meaningful than an offer to be "of assistance."*

The Letter

Dear Sarah:

Larry's death has saddened me beyond words. Although not totally unexpected, it is still hard for me to accept.

I'm sure you know, Sarah, the enormous influence Larry had on me personally and on my career. He was the first person ever to say to me: "Carl, you have a special gift. I'm going to do all I can to see that it is developed to its fullest." He then proceeded to do just that, and during our eight years together, he never lost faith in me and was, of course, largely responsible for the success I have achieved.

I suppose most successful people somewhere along the line were singled out by a wise and generous mentor who guided and shaped their careers. Mine was Larry. I shall miss his counsel. Indeed, I do already. Every time I have a hard problem to solve, I ask myself, "What would Larry have done?"

I hope, Sarah, that Emily and I can continue our friendship with you. If ever you feel the need to get away for a quiet rest, our little cottage on Sequoia Lake (which I'm sure you remember) is always open to you. I've had a key made for you, and it is enclosed.

Affectionate regards,

27-2 DEATH OF THE SPOUSE OF A FORMER COLLEAGUE

Situation

You have just learned of the death of the wife of a former business colleague (your old boss). You left the company a couple of years ago, but have kept in touch and still considered both good friends. You write to express sympathy and recall the special esteem you held for the deceased.

Analysis of the Letter

1. *Express sympathy in the first paragraph.*

2. *Then, recall the pleasant memories in the home of the deceased and the affection you held for her.*

3. *Next, move on to the present, bringing Alan up to date on your activities. This is done to get away quickly from a depressing subject.*

4. *Your invitation to Alan to drop in to see you and have dinner in your home represents that "something tangible" we mentioned earlier.*

The Letter

Dear Alan:

I was very distressed to learn of Ellen's death, and I express my deepest sympathy to you.

Always in my memory will be the many evenings I and the other members of the planning group spent in the Costello home and the gracious hospitality extended to us by Ellen. As I look back on those evenings, I wonder how she put up with such good grace the noisy discussions, spilled ashtrays and drinks, and the general confusion. But she always kept her cool and really seemed to enjoy our philosophical ramblings as much as we did. Although I hadn't seen Ellen in some time, I haven't forgotten her—a lovely lady indeed.

My work here at Caldwell Universal continues to be interesting, although I confess that I miss many of my friends at CWI. Right now we're involved in several downtown revitalization projects, and I'm learning that there's more politics than planning in these jobs!

If your travels bring you to Philadelphia, I hope I will get to see you. Maybe I could persuade you to come out to Paoli for dinner with Ruth and me. And, of course, meet the newest member of the Hubbard household—Annette, two months old yesterday.

Best personal regards,

27-3

SYMPATHY ON THE EVENT OF A SERIOUS ILLNESS

Situation

Rob Harrell, age 45, is assistant to the president of a medium-size company. Rob is a demon for work—one of those who burn the candle at both ends. Recently he has had a heart attack and is in the hospital. Early reports seem encouraging, but Rob's condition remains serious. The president writes Mrs. Harrell both to express concern and try to ease some of the worries she may be experiencing.

Analysis of the Letter

1. The writer expresses concern about Rob's illness and his anxiety about Rob's recovery.

2. Because the writer knows Rob will stew about being away from his job, he advises Kitty to restrain him, to convince him that his job will still be here when he recovers, and that the company expects him to think of himself first. Such statements are likely to be of genuine comfort to Kitty.

3. The writer mentions his plan to visit Rob when it is appropriate, but the most important thing in the last paragraph is the offer to be of help to Kitty. If she has questions about salary, insurance, and so on, she can call on the writer.

The Letter

Dear Kitty:

I was shocked and distressed to learn of Rob's heart attack, and I won't rest easy until I learn of his full recovery.

Knowing Rob, I suspect that when he surmounts this crisis, he will be champing at the bit to get back to his job here. But you mustn't let him. Although his presence will be sorely missed, we'll find a way to cover his desk while he is away—perhaps not nearly as well as he would like, but as best we can. Please insist that he follow the doctor's prescribed routine for convalescence, with no thought for any other responsibility he may feel. We want him back, of course, but not until the doctor says he <u>should</u> return. In the meantime, Rob will remain on full salary and benefits.

Kitty, please let me know when it is permissible for Rob to have visitors. I want to see him. Now, is there anything I can do for <u>you</u>?

Affectionately,

SECTION 28
LETTERS OF RECOMMENDATION

Often, you will be asked to supply information about former employees who have applied for positions after leaving your company. Some response letters will be a genuine pleasure to write because the former worker can be highly recommended in all respects. Even letters about former employees who were very satisfactory on most counts are no problem; you simply emphasize their strengths and mention only casually (if at all) any minor weaknesses.

In this section, we present two letters in response to requests for information about former employees, the first an unqualified recommendation and the second a recommendation with a slight qualification.

28-1

UNQUALIFIED LETTER OF RECOMMENDATION FOR A FORMER EMPLOYEE

Situation

For five years Edwin Thresher was a copywriter in the advertising department of Riegelwood Distributors. A little over a year ago he resigned to join an advertising agency. As manager of the advertising department at Riegelwood, you receive an inquiry from Newell, Inc. about Thresher, who has applied for the job of assistant advertising manager. Thresher has a fine record, and you want to give him a hearty recommendation.

Analysis of the Letter

1. *Confirm Thresher's employment at Riegelwood Distributors in the first paragraph.*

2. *In the second paragraph, describe both his professional and personal attributes.*

3. *Finally, offer your recommendation, reinforcing it by stating that you would hire him again.*

The Letter

Dear Mrs. Needleman:

Edwin Thresher was a copywriter at Riegelwood Distributors for five years under my direct supervision.

I consider Thresher an excellent employee. He handled all his assignments with imagination and style and, so far as I can remember, never missed a deadline. An extremely likable young man, he had many friends here. He left Riegelwood of his own free will, believing that agency work would be more exciting and offer greater opportunities. I was genuinely sorry to see him go.

I heartily recommend Edwin Thresher to you. I would readily rehire him if a suitable vacancy arose.

Cordially yours,

Situation

L. Richard Maxwell, sales manager for a national sporting goods manufacturer, has received an inquiry from the marketing director of a chain of clothing stores concerning a former employee, Craig Halliburton. The position Halliburton applied for is director of sales training. Although he had an excellent record as a member of Maxwell's department, his experience in training was somewhat limited.

Analysis of the Letter

1. *The writer gives considerably more detail about the employee's record than is typical; yet we think that a recounting of Halliburton's favorable job history will be very helpful.*

2. *The reason given for Halliburton's leaving is made very clear. Although the recipient may jump to the conclusion that Halliburton is restlessly ambitious, this presumably was not the writer's intent. We think it would have been worse to have left out the reason for Halliburton's departure.*

3. *The writer did not have to qualify his recommendation. He could have simply given the minimum amount of information and stopped there. Some will say that Maxwell should have omitted the last paragraph; others will think he was justified in covering himself. In any event, he has not been derogatory—simply honest.*

The Letter

Dear Mr. Maxwell:

I am pleased to write in behalf of Craig Halliburton, who has applied to your company for the position of national sales training director.

Craig joined our organization in 1977 as our sales representative for the state of Arkansas. He quickly proved highly effective in selling, and, during the three years he was in this territory, sales increased nearly 20 percent. He had a special gift for building customer loyalty, and I received many letters of appreciation from these people for his services.

In 1980 Craig was promoted to the position of field manager, with the responsibility for recruiting, training, and supervising eleven sales representatives in Arkansas, Oklahoma, and southern Missouri. He was equally effective in this job, and we saw a very bright future for him. When the southwest regional manager's position became vacant because of a retirement, Craig applied for it. However, he was not chosen for it because we felt that another of our field managers, who had a good deal more experience in management and an outstanding track record in selling, was the more logical candidate. Not long afterward, Craig resigned to accept a sales position with a competing company, where he felt he would have greater opportunities for growth. We were very sorry to lose him; he is an outstanding young man—intelligent, personable, hard-working, and persuasive.

I am not familiar with the requirements of your position, so I cannot speak with any authority about Craig's ability to administer a company-wide sales training program. He did some training, of course, in his field manager's job with us, and he was extremely good at it. I suspect the chances are very good that, even though Craig may lack an in-depth knowledge of training methods at present, he would in time be able to assume the responsibilities of national sales training director very effectively.

Cordially yours,

SECTION 29

UNFAVORABLE REFERENCE LETTERS AND WARNINGS TO EMPLOYEES

One of the most difficult letters to write is one in response to a company's request for your opinion of a former employee whom you rate very low. This can present a real dilemma. If you say exactly what you think, you will almost certainly destroy the applicant's chances for a job that he or she may desperately need. Equally serious is that existing federal laws make it mandatory that employees be given the right to see everything in their personnel files, and a defamatory letter could result in a suit against the former employer.

Before there was a federal law about such matters, many employers felt it their duty to be completely truthful about unsatisfactory employees and expected the same candor from other employers. Today, however, many personnel administrators strongly recommend that only basic data be supplied in writing to those who request information about unsatisfactory employees—dates of employment, job title(s), and salary at the time of departure. If further information is required, they contend, it can be obtained by telephone.

In this section, we give an illustration of a letter that the former employer felt had to be written in spite of the cautions outlined above. It is not a recommendation, yet it is not a particularly harsh condemnation. You can be the judge as to whether the writer did the right thing.

Occasionally, you will have an employee whose job performance is not satisfactory, and you have almost reached the conclusion that the worker must be dismissed. In some companies there is a policy that no one can be fired without first warning him or her that such action is contemplated. An example of such a letter is also included in this section.

29-1

RESPONDING TO A REQUEST FOR INFORMATION ABOUT AN UNSATISFACTORY FORMER EMPLOYEE

Situation

Charles Edwards worked in the mailroom of a large firm for nearly two years. He was a genuine problem to the supervisor—he often arrived late and left early, was absent a good deal, and showed no interest in his work. The supervisor's talks with him were not productive, and she was eventually forced to let him go. A few weeks after Charles leaves, the supervisor receives an inquiry about Charles from a company to which he has applied for a job.

Analysis of the Letter

1. *The writer confirms the dates of employment under her supervision.*

2. *She mentions the favorable attributes first, then honestly (but not viciously) spells out her problems with him.*

3. *In the final paragraph, the writer implies that there may be hope for Charles, provided he can locate a job that really challenges him.*

Note: You yourself will have to decide whether to write this type of letter. Many prefer to say almost nothing for the reasons mentioned earlier. Indeed, some companies have a policy against writing such letters.

The Letter

Dear Mrs. Kimberly:

Charles Edwards worked under my supervision in the mail department of Atkinson-Trickett Company for nearly two years (1979 to 1981).

Although a cheerful and popular young man, Charles showed very little interest in his work, and I was forced to talk with him many times about his tardiness and absences, and his poor work habits and general attitude. I finally concluded that there was no way for me to motivate him and suggested that he find another job.

Perhaps, given another type of work in which he is genuinely interested, Charles would succeed. He is very bright, and perhaps that was the problem here—the work did not challenge him.

Yours very truly,

29-2

WARNING LETTER TO AN EMPLOYEE

Situation

Philip Moore is administrative assistant to an executive in a large corporation. Although highly competent, he has one bad fault: he can't keep secrets. He has been warned repeatedly about his indiscretions, but leaks continue to occur. The most recent incident proved to be very serious, and he was called into his boss's office and read the riot act. The boss writes a letter that tactfully warns the employee that he is in danger of losing his job.

Analysis of the Letter

1. *The writer reviews the favorable traits of the employee and his value to the company.*

2. *He then proceeds to discuss frankly Moore's major weakness and reviews fully the latest incident that proved to be so serious. Although names are not disclosed, there will be no doubt in Moore's mind who the parties are.*

3. *In the third paragraph, the writer recalls yesterday's discussion; this is written confirmation that the employee was given plenty of warning.*

4. *Finally, Moore is given notice, which will support any unfavorable action that may have to be taken later.*

Note: *Generally, it is not necessary to give advance warning in writing to employees of Moore's stature. Many executives simply fire them on the spot, and they have the right to do so. Because the relationship between Moore and his boss has been close, the executive chose to handle the matter as shown.*

The Letter

Dear Phil:

During the three years we have worked together, I have been much impressed with your job competence. You have shown a remarkable talent in managing this office, freeing me of paperwork and people interruptions so that I could spend most of my time on long-range planning for the company. I have looked upon you as an invaluable assistant and confidant.

It would now appear, however, that my use of the word "confidant" is gratuitous. During the past several months, you and I have discussed numerous leaks of confidential information, and you were always courageous enough to tell the truth. Up to this point, these indiscretions were merely embarrassing to me—the damage was slight and no one was really hurt. However, the latest episode, involving an acquisition, is much too serious to pass off. Advance knowledge of our plans by certain individuals has severely hampered negotiations and has put us in a bidding situation for which we are likely to pay a heavy price. Indeed, it is not unlikely that we will remove ourselves from contention.

You and I discussed this thoroughly in my office yesterday. I accept your statement that the leaked information seemed safe since it involved only one person—a department manager—and that you had no way of knowing that that individual was on the verge of leaving the company to join a competitor. But even so, Phil, a confidence is a confidence, and a person in your position should know by now that he can have <u>no</u> intimate friends when it comes to dispensing highly private information.

It is with great reluctance that I inform you that if such a happening recurs—no matter how harmless it may appear to be—you will be asked immediately to submit your resignation.

Sincerely,

29-3

TERMINATING AN EMPLOYEE BY LETTER

Situation

John Coover is a sales engineer for a manufacturer of microprocessor-based communication systems, calling on dealers in three southwestern states to help them with any installation or service problems they may have. Although a knowledgeable engineer, Coover has proved to be undependable in covering the territory assigned him. He often fails to show up for important appointments or to send in the itinerary that he is required to submit each week to his superior, Jeffrey Forstner. Forstner has talked with Coover many times and received the assurances asked for, but the situation has not improved. Two months ago, Forstner wrote Coover a warning letter. Recently a situation arose in which it was made clear that Coover is not going to shape up, and Forstner decides to terminate his employment. However, he has been unable to reach Coover by telephone and writes to him at his home address.

Analysis of the Letter

1. *Mention first the unsuccessful attempts to reach the employee by telephone and the necessity for writing a letter.*

2. *Announce the termination of the employee and the effective date, giving the historical background for the action.*

3. *Describe in detail the most recent events that provoked the final decision.*

4. *Indicate reluctance to take this action, but let the employee know that there is no alternative.*

5. *Finally, mention the severance check and where it will be sent.*

Note: *If a terminated representative has property that belongs to the company, also indicate how the employee is to handle the return of the property.*

The Letter

Dear John:

I have tried several times to reach you by telephone, but have been unsuccessful. Thus I am writing to you at home.

This is notification of your termination from the company effective March 10. You and I have talked several times about your problem in covering your territory properly, John. Each time you gave me assurances that you would shape up and do the job you were hired to do. Yet last week I had clear indications that you have again violated your promise to me.

Your itinerary shows that you were to be in the Albuquerque area last week, calling on dealers and staying at the Best Western Capri. Three dealers in that area who had been expecting you telephoned me to say that you did not show up. All have had serious complaints from customers about the malfunctioning of the Telemaster III communication system and desperately need professional help. When I telephoned the Best Western Capri (every day last week), I was told that you had not registered and there was no record of a reservation. Today, I asked Maurice Taylor in Phoenix to fly to Albuquerque to visit the three dealers and try to solve their problem.

I am sorry, John, that this action is necessary, but I am certain that under the circumstances you will agree that I have no alternative. You will, of course, receive the standard two weeks' severance pay. Indeed, I have already requisitioned a check for you, which will be sent to your home when it is ready.

Sincerely,

PART 10

JOB-GETTING LETTERS AND OTHER EMPLOYMENT COMMUNICATIONS

Some fortunate people don't have to extend themselves much to land their first job. If they specialized in college or graduate school in a field in which the demand for people far exceeds the supply, they may have only the problem of choosing between job offers. Others are channeled into good positions by influential friends and relatives. Some simply join the family business. Most people, however, have to scramble a bit for that first job, against others who are after the same thing.

But for both groups—the shoo-ins and the scramblers—knowing how to sell oneself on paper can be enormously important. True, some people settle happily into their first job and stay with the company forever. On the other hand, people change jobs rather frequently, and the reasons vary. They don't like the company they work for, or they don't get the promotions they think they deserve, or their bosses don't allow them freedom to innovate, or they get laid off for economic reasons. Others change jobs simply because they find a better opportunity elsewhere.

Chances are good, then, that no matter how happy you are in your present setup or how rosy the future looks, you'll one day need to know how to present your employment credentials in the best possible light. That's the main purpose of this part.

JOB-GETTING COMMUNICATIONS

Aside from an employer's own application form, two basic documents are often required to obtain a job of some stature: the résumé and the letter of application.

THE RÉSUMÉ   Vital to your job-searching campaign is a good résumé—that is, a summary of your qualifications. (Some people call it a data sheet.) Although somewhat formal in setup—mainly for quick reading and reference purposes—the résumé is essentially a sales instrument. By this we mean that you emphasize in it those events and accomplishments that make you look good to a prospective employer. While the résumé is not a razzle-dazzle document (except for certain people in the creative arts who choose to make it so), neither is it merely a condensed biographical sketch of your life and work. It is an interesting profile of your best side.

We mentioned earlier that there is no magic formula you can use to produce an effective letter for every occasion. Most of the letters you write must be tailored to fit the particular situation you are faced with. The same is true of a résumé. Although a model will be helpful (we show four excellent résumés in this section), it's not likely that any one is just right for you. You should feel free to make whatever adjustments are needed to best tell *your* story.

Every good résumé contains four basic parts:

1. A heading
2. Experience (a description of the jobs you've held)
3. Education (degrees, major courses taken, special training, etc.)
4. References (a short list of people whom an employer can contact for information about you)

Some job applicants use additional headings, and we'll talk about those later.

To illustrate these four basic parts, let's imagine that you are very much interested in the following job that was advertised in a large-city newspaper:

DIRECTOR OF PUBLICITY for a large corporation. Minimum of three years' experience in publicity, public relations, or a related field required. Must have college degree, preferably in journalism. Position requires heavy writing and ability to deal effectiively with all media. Excellent salary and benefits. Send résumé to Box 457, *Times*. An equal opportunity employer.

Although relatively brief, the above ad says a great deal. You will study the job requirements very carefully; then you can start to put together a résumé that matches what you have to offer with the job requirements.

The Heading   Give your résumé a heading. It will usually contain your name, address, telephone number, and the position you are applying for. Some applicants also include the name of the company to which they are applying.

It's up to you whether you give the résumé itself a title. It isn't really necessary, since the information presented is self-identifying. Here are three examples.

EDWIN R. COULTER
225 Normandy Village
Shreveport, Louisiana 71104
(318) 865-7544

Position applied for: Director of Publicity

Qualifications of

JANET LEE FELDER
Old Lyme Road
Northbrook, VT 05663
(802) 264-5911

for the position of <u>Systems Analyst</u>
Brighton Industries Inc.

JOB RÉSUMÉ

of

P. L. Quackenbush
2160 Shelter Island Drive
San Diego, California 92106
(714) 622-9178

<u>Position desired:</u> Controller

If you're applying "blind"—that is, you don't know whether there is an opening that matches your job preference—you won't know what precise position title to use. Some people believe that naming a specific job on a blind résumé lessens their chances of being hired if that particular position doesn't exist or isn't available. They feel that if they merely indicate a general field of interest, they may find just what they want, even though it doesn't carry the title they had in mind. There is nothing wrong with this, but we think you should come as close as you can to identifying your special interest. For example:

Not: Position desired: Advertising Department
But: Position desired: Advertising assistant (copywriting, layout, etc.)

Not: Position desired: Personnel work
But: Position desired: Personnel recruitment, placement, training

Not: Position desired: Public relations
But: Position desired: Public relations (with a special interest in publications)

Of course, if you're answering an ad that names a specific job or you're applying at the suggestion of someone who knows about a vacancy, use the title specified.

Experience

Generally, your first side head is "experience." (There are two exceptions: when you have little or no experience related to the job you are applying for and when your educational background is far more impressive than your experience. In these instances, your first heading will be "education.")

Experience is mentioned as the first (and probably chief) requirement in the want-ad on page 235, and assuming you feel you meet the requirement, start there. List the jobs you've held (with dates), starting with your present position and working backward. Describe the duties of each job—that is, what you actually did. Here is where your tailoring really begins. When you outline your duties, use every opportunity to capitalize on publicity—the job you're after. Even if most of your experience has been in, say, sales promotion, you can emphasize the publicity aspects of your work (many jobs in sales promotion involve some general publicity). We don't mean that you should fake experience you don't have. We simply encourage you to focus on any relevant experience you *do* have.

Note that the ad mentions heavy writing responsibility. Among your duties in your previous job(s), be sure to mention the volume and type of writing you were required to do.

What about the phrase, "and ability to deal effectively with all media"? If any of your job duties included contact with media representatives, you will certainly say so. For example: "Was responsible for writing all releases on new products and distributing them to the media (often by means of press conferences)."

If you can't glean any media experience from your work experience (or even if you can), you may want to list memberships you hold in organizations that have some relationship to media—an advertising club, public relations group, and so on. Be sure to include any offices you may have held in such organizations.

Education

After you've made the most of your job experience, turn to the second major area—education. First, indicate your degree, the institution that awarded it, and the year. Then, indicate your major.

> B.B.A. Degree, University of Mississippi, 1974
> Major: Accounting

If you're light on experience in the position you're applying for but strong in educational background, you may wish to list the courses you completed that have a direct bearing on the job and any related courses that may add clout to your qualifications.

With reference to the want-ad on page 235, let's assume that you majored in journalism. Since this is what the employer prefers, you may need to say nothing further about your education.

Suppose, however, you majored in English instead of journalism. This doesn't mean that you're automatically ruled out as a candidate for the job—the ad says "*preferably* in journalism." This leaves the door open for other majors—English, personnel administration, public relations, and so. In these instances, however, you will probably want to augment your educational history by listing any courses you took that relate to journalism or publicity—perhaps creative writing, business communications, or copywriting, and so on.

Another thing you can do under the "education" heading is describe outside college activities that relate to journalism or publicity. Perhaps you were an editor or the advertising manager of your college yearbook, or a reporter for the college newspaper, or the publicity director for the college's Spring Festival. If you did none of these things but were an active member of professional and social organizations, you might list them. While none is likely to qualify as education or experience, your participation (especially if you held office) says something about your liking for and effectiveness in mixing with people. Simply identifying yourself as a doer could help persuade the employer that you have the "ability to deal effectively with all media."

References

Finally, list three or four references, giving their courtesy title, name, position, affiliation, address, and, if possible, telephone number. Your most important references will be those for whom you have worked—supervisors, managers, and executives. However, if you're light on experience or have other reasons for not listing former employers, you can use the names of major professors and people of some distinction in your community (a judge, a government official, and possibly a minister, priest, or rabbi). *Note:* Before you list people as references on your résumé, you ought to get their permission. You can do this in person, on the telephone, or by letter. If by letter, enclose a self-addressed, stamped envelope.

If you are presently employed, you probably will not want your company to know that you are looking for another job. In that case, simply use the heading "references" and state "supplied on request." Most employers will know what you mean and will not violate your trust by contacting your present management until they have your okay. (References are usually asked for on the application blank that you fill out.)

Other Headings

In some résumés you will see such headings as "special interests and achievements," "brief personal history," "statement of philosophy," and the like. If you have something really important to say under these headings, by all means go ahead.

At one time it was standard practice to include a heading called "personal data," under which was included such information as date of birth, physical characteristics (height, weight, etc.), state of health, marital status, and so on. You may do this if you wish, but the tendency is to omit this data entirely. The information you supplied earlier in the résumé will reveal all the employer needs or should want to know.

Some applicants attach a photograph to the résumé. There is nothing wrong with this—indeed it might be a good idea. But the decision is yours; an employer cannot require it.

Length of the Résumé

As to the length of the résumé, there is no set rule. A typical résumé is from 1½ to 2 pages in length, but we have seen some excellent ones that are much longer. Everything depends on how much you have to say about yourself that will interest a prospective employer. If you're a highly experienced executive applying for a top management job in a large corporation, your résumé might be five or six pages long. Hiring top people is a huge investment for employers, and most make up their minds slowly, so they're not averse to reading lengthy résumés. Yet they are quick to spot padding, and a long dissertation that consists mainly of babble will simply wind up in the "circular file."

Reproducing the Résumé

You could enhance your chances for a job by having the résumé personally typewritten. This gives the document a "just for you" flavor. Use a good-quality white bond paper of standard size and a well-inked typewriter ribbon.

However, if you're sending your résumé to several companies (untailored, so to speak), you may have to settle for photocopies. This is all right as long as the copies are sharp and clean. The letter that accompanies the résumé (which we'll talk about later) *must* be an original document, so it will atone in part for the duplicated résumé.

Binding the Résumé

If your résumé consists of more than one sheet, we recommend that you mail it flat (unfolded) in a large envelope. Longer résumés will be much more impressive if they are placed in a binder with a transparent plastic cover. Several styles of binders are available at good stationery stores, and if you plan to use one, select it before typing the résumé so that you can allow for the proper margins.

If you decide to staple a multi-page résumé, use three staples in the left margin, vertically placed.

Situation

At the annual convention of the American Association of School Administrators, Russell Buchanan, a field sales supervisor for a book publisher, learns that Kauffman institutional Equipment Inc. has an opening for a regional sales manager. He decides to apply.

Analysis of the Résumé

1. *Buchanan gives the résumé a title ("Qualifications Summary"). This, as was previously mentioned, is optional. He did not name the company even though he knows it, perhaps because he plans to use the same résumé later if he is not successful in this effort.*

2. *Note that Buchanan describes his experience first. The reasons are that he has had very valuable experience that relates to the job applied for, and he is certain that the position of regional sales manager will require field management and sales experience.*

The Résumé

RUSSELL R. BUCHANAN
1416 Saybrook Road
Wellesley Hills, Massachusetts 02181
(617) 944-8778,

QUALIFICATIONS SUMMARY

Position: Regional Sales Manager

EXPERIENCE

1982–present:	Field sales supervisor, Horton-Miller Book Company. Duties: Selecting, training, and supervising a field sales staff of 16. Territory includes Massachusetts, New Hampshire, Vermont, and Maine. During this period, sales in the territory have increased 22 percent.
1977–1982	Sales representative, Horton-Miller Book Company, calling on teachers and administrators in western Massachusetts.
1975–1977	Head of department of business education, DeKalb (Illinois) High School. Duties: Supervised eleven instructors and managed the department with an enrollment of over 800 students.
1971–1975	Instructor in accounting and data processing, DeKalb High School. Also taught evening classes in accounting at Northern Illinois University.

3. *Under "education," Buchanan lists two degrees, the universities that awarded them, and the dates. Also under "education," he describes his college activities. This is not necessarily standard practice, but there is nothing wrong with doing so. He is obviously proud of his participation in various groups; certainly, the employer will be impressed with the applicant's well-roundedness, a genuine asset in a sales management position.*

4. *The brief personal history is a good idea. An employer may wonder how an individual who trained to be a teacher wound up in sales supervision, and the explanation will be welcomed. Note the sales flavor of the third paragraph. Buchanan hints strongly that, although his sales experience has been limited to books, the know-how gained in book selling is easily applied to other educational products.*

5. *Obviously, Buchanan has talked over his aspirations with the marketing director of Horton-Miller (A. J. Sholes). By saying so in the résumé, he gives the potential employer the green light to contact Sholes for information.*

EDUCATION

Degrees | B.S. in Business Education, University of Wisconsin, 1968; M.S. in Business Education, 1971.

Activities | Member of Pi Omega Pi (undergraduate business education fraternity—served as president in junior year), Badger diving team (placed second in 1967 Big Ten meet), and Tau Kappa Epsilon (social fraternity). As a senior, I worked part-time as a grader for accounting instructors.

BRIEF PERSONAL HISTORY

When I was associated with DeKalb High School, I had frequent opportunity to meet and talk with sales representatives of various companies that supply schools with textbooks and equipment. Although I enjoyed teaching and administration, I became interested in selling because I felt it provided broader opportunities for me.

It turned out to be a wise choice—I found that I thoroughly enjoyed selling. Meeting new people constantly and providing counsel and services to the educational community was immensely rewarding. It still is. I have not lost my basic love for education, but I feel strongly that my influence is much greater in my present capacity.

In my two years as field sales supervisor at Horton-Miller, I have had an excellent opportunity to exercise what I believe is my real forte: motivating sales personnel and managing a sales organization. To me, the principles of sales management are the same, whether the product is a book, a desk, or a computer system.

REFERENCES

*Mr. A. J. Sholes, Director of Marketing
Horton-Miller Book Company
2001 Aurora Boulevard
Northbrook, Illinois 60062

Dr. James C. Hightower, Principal
DeKalb High School
DeKalb, Illinois 60015

Dr. Mary C. Hornstein
Professor of Business Education
University of Wisconsin
Madison, Wisconsin 53706

*Mr. Sholes is aware of my interest in changing positions. The opportunity to become a regional manager at Horton-Miller in the near future does not appear to be favorable because of a recent restructure in the field organization.

Situation

Dianne Seaton started as a private secretary at Livermore Manufacturing Company five years ago, and eventually moved up to administrative assistant to the executive vice president. Although she likes the work and is competent, for years she has wanted to be a teacher. Indeed, she earned her teaching credentials in college (history), but when she could not find a teaching position, she took a secretarial course in a business school and quickly landed a secretarial job.

In spite of her success in her present work, Seaton's desire to teach remains strong. During the past two years, she has been taking university extension courses in education, thinking that one day she would enter the teaching profession. She has just seen an advertisement in *The Wall Street Journal* for a supervisor of office training and decides to apply.

Analysis of the Résumé

1. *The heading contains all the necessary information (note that everything is centered). The home address rather than the business address is given.*

2. *Because Seaton knows the exact title of the position, she names it as position applied for.*

3. *Seaton describes her experience first; her five years as a secretary and administrative assistant will be exceptionally valuable in the position being applied for. Teaching and tutoring experience are listed because they may also be a big plus, helping to compensate for the applicant's lack of on-the-job training experience.*

The Résumé

DIANNE SEATON
517 Park Avenue
Omaha, Nebraska 68105
(402) 862-1175

Position applied for: Supervisor of Office Training

JOB EXPERIENCE

1980–present	Administrative assistant to the executive vice president, Livermore Manufacturing Company, 7400 West Center Road, Omaha, Nebraska <u>Duties:</u> Supervise general office activities (including one secretary and one clerk-typist) and assist the executive vice president with such matters as writing letters and reports, doing research, planning conferences and meetings, and representing the executive in various functions, particularly when he is away from the office (very frequent).
1977–1979	Secretary to the manufacturing manager, Livermore Manufacturing Company. <u>Duties:</u> General secretarial activities, such as receiving visitors, managing the appointment calendar, taking and transcribing dictation, writing routine letters and reports, assisting in the preparation of analytical and statistical reports, and handling other

responsibilities assigned by the manager. <u>Reason for Leaving</u>: Promoted to higher position in the company.

OTHER EXPERIENCE

1982–1983   Taught evening courses twice a week in word processing, typewriting, and business communication, Creighton University, Omaha.

1974–1975   Part-time assistant in the history department of the University of South Dakota, where I graded student exams and reports and did some tutoring of freshman students.

4. The writer briefly outlines her education— university, business college, high school, and extension courses. Supplying the name of the high school is optional, but it does give the applicant an opportunity to list two business courses completed.

Note that under university education, Seaton mentions honors and activities. An employer is almost always interested in these. In the interest of space, she does not list her high school honors and activities, although if they would enhance her qualifications for the position applied for, it might be a good idea to do so.

5. Although Seaton's special interests do not relate specifically to the position applied for, they do portray a picture of involvement, which provides some clue to her personality.

6. The applicant lists references from three educational institutions only. Note that she tells why she has not listed the two executives at Livermore Manufacturing Company. This will

EDUCATION

University   A.B. Degree, University of South Dakota, 1979. Major: History, Minor: Education. Honors and Activities: Dean's list three years (B+ average); vice president of Kappa Delta Phi (history fraternity); member of Choral Ensemble; received Award of Merit in History in senior year.

Business College   Diploma in secretarial administration, Yankton (SD) Business College, 1980. Courses included shorthand (two semesters), typewriting (two semesters), accounting, business mathematics, business communications, and secretarial procedures.

High School   Vermillion (SD) High School; graduated in 1976. (College preparatory course. Electives included one year of typewriting and one year of business English.)

Current Studies   During the past two years, I have taken extension courses at Creighton University in educational media, adult education methods, and personnel administration.

SPECIAL INTERESTS

My primary avocational interests include music (since junior high school I have always been associated with one or more school and community choral groups, often as soloist) and working with brain-damaged children at hospitals and social service agencies. I am also a sports enthusiast (especially water skiing and scuba diving), play better-than-average tennis, and am learning handball.

REFERENCES

Professor H. A. Douthit
Department of History
University of South Dakota
Vermillion, South Dakota 57069

be understood by the people who receive her résumé. Later, if she seems to have a good chance of getting the job, she can tell her present and former boss of her plans so that the new employer may contact them for information.

Mrs. Janette Cellars
Yankton Business College
Yankton, South Dakota 57078

Mr. Jason Carew, Principal
Vermillion High School
Vermillion, South Dakota 57609

<u>Note:</u> References from the two executives with whom I have been associated at Livermore Manufacturing Company will be submitted upon request. Neither is aware that I am interested in a career change at this time.

30-3   JOB RÉSUMÉ— HIGH-LEVEL POSITION

Situation

Frances Rosen, an executive in a large Baltimore corporation, learns from a friend that the director of public relations in a large firm in the same city is retiring. She is not sure what the company's plans are in filling the position, but she decides to make application.

Analysis of the Résumé

1. *The heading is simple but contains the necessary elements. Note that Rosen does not supply a telephone number. Since she works during the day, she cannot be reached at home during business hours, and she doesn't wish to be telephoned at her office.*

2. *Since her professional experience is impressive and highly relevant to the position she seeks, she describes it first. Note that she is specific in outlining the duties in each position.*

The Résumé

L. FRANCES ROSEN
1703 Salisbury Road
Baltimore, MD 21201

Position desired: Director of Public Relations

PROFESSIONAL EXPERIENCE

1975–present   Manager, Corporate Communications, Regent Chemical Corporation, Baltimore. <u>Duties:</u> Responsible for employee magazine and other publications, communications with stockholders, general publicity, and media relations.

1968–1975   Assistant Director of Public Relations, Marchand Manufacturing Company, Arlington, Virginia. <u>Duties:</u> Handled PR correspondence, news releases, preparation of reports to stockholders, institutional promotion (including advertising and special brochures). Also responsible for instituting and directing a school and community relations program, which included the development of educational materials, speaking before various groups, and representing the company at most civic affairs. <u>Reasons for leaving</u>: Professional and financial advancement afforded by a larger organization.

3. *In 1968 Rosen changed jobs. It is standard practice to indicate the reasons for leaving a job, especially if it is not self-evident that a promotion was involved. However, there is no rule that such information is required.*

1965–1968   Editor and publisher of <u>Periscope</u> (employee magazine), Marchand Manufacturing Company. <u>Duties</u>: Directed a staff of five in producing the magazine and distributing it to employees and others. Also, upon request, assisted various department heads in preparing new-product information releases.

1963–1965   Administrative assistant to the director of publicity, Marchand Manufacturing Company. <u>Duties</u>: Secretarial and office management; composing drafts of news releases and other publicity; and writing routine letters and reports for the director's signature.

4. *The activities listed indicate that Rosen is deeply involved in her profession and has other community interests as well. This information is apt to score high marks for her.*

PROFESSIONAL ACTIVITIES

Member of the Baltimore Advertising Club (Secretary-Treasurer, 1962), National Public Relations Association, Baltimore Women Executives Club, and the Board of Directors, Baltimore Symphony Orchestra. Frequent speaker at public relations conventions and contributor of articles on public relations and management communications to various trade publications.

5. *Rosen has used a slightly different set-up for the "education" section, and this is fine. The enumerations are helpful. Note that she has included honors and achievements in item 3. She could have provided a separate head, but there is nothing wrong with this arrangement.*

EDUCATION

1. A.B. degree, University of Virginia, Charlottesville, 1963, with a major in journalism.

2. I have taken graduate courses (evenings) in journalism, public relations, and management communications at the University of Baltimore and Georgetown University.

3. While at the University of Virginia, I was editor in chief of <u>Daily Cavalier</u> for one year and a member of Gamma Theta Pi (a journalism sorority of which I was president in my senior year). I was selected the outstanding student in the School of Journalism upon graduation.

6. *A statement of personal philosophy obviously seemed important to Rosen. In her experience, she may have learned that PR people are considered merely publicists who sit in an ivory tower. She leaves no doubt about her own views of the PR function.*

PERSONAL PHILOSOPHY

I am deeply committed to the concept that public relations is essentially education—that is, educating people in favor of one's organization—and embraces seven basic groups: the local community, employees, customers, suppliers, stockholders, the financial community, and the general public. While I believe that those engaged in public relations have the main responsibility for developing and

7. *Rosen indicates that she will supply references on request, including people in her present organization. However, until she knows that she really wants the job and has a good chance of getting it, it's best to handle the matter as she did.*

enhancing a positive image in the eyes of the public, I feel strongly that their end objective should be company growth in terms of sales and profits.

REFERENCES

References, including Regent Chemical Corporation executives, will be supplied on request.

30-4 JOB RÉSUMÉ— LITTLE RELATED JOB EXPERIENCE

Situation

When Leonard Lambeth finished college, with a major in advertising, he took a job in the university's athletic department, where he organized and directed miscellaneous sports, such as fishing, boat handling, hunting, and backpacking. Although Lambeth enjoyed the work, it paid very little, and he admitted to himself that he kept the job simply because he was reluctant to leave that comfortable environment and face the real world. But after three years he became restless and decided to resign and get started on a career in his chosen field. His professor of journalism, a personal friend, told him about an opening for an assistant advertising manager of *Southern Outdoorsman*, in Charleston. He decides to apply for the position.

Analysis of the Résumé

1. *Lambeth boxes the heading of the résumé to make it stand out*

2. *Because Lambeth plans to return to his parents' home on August 19, he supplies both the Loris and Columbia addresses.*

The Résumé

Qualifications of

LEONARD B. LAMBETH

*As Assistant Advertising Manager
Southern Outdoorsman*

Present address:

391 Daly Street
Columbia, SC 29205
(803) 271-4660

Address after August 19:

414 Maple Drive
Loris, S.C. 29569
(803) 542-1151

3. *Lambeth makes no mention of high school education. This is optional here, although this information may be asked for on the application form.*

4. *He lists courses taken in his major as well as any related business courses. Note that he includes three electives that he believes may be of interest.*

EDUCATION

B.S. degree, University of South Carolina, Columbia, 1982
Major field of study: Advertising

Courses in Advertising

Advertising Theory and Practice
Copywriting and Layout
Advertising Art
Advertising Media
Publishing and Printing Techniques
Advertising Department Management
Advertising Research

Related Courses

Principles of Marketing
Sales Principles and Management
Marketing Statistics
Business Communications
Business Psychology

Special Electives: Newswriting, Photography, Typewriting

5. *He then lists honors and extracurricular activities, choosing those that he thinks are most relevant and important.*

Honors and Extracurricular Activities

President, Angler's Club (1981); member of university golf team (1980–1982); student member of National Advertising Council, Columbia Chapter (1981–1982); advertising manager of The Gamecock (1982); and occasional staff writer for student newspaper (1981–1982).

6. *Lambeth has made about as much as possible of his work experience. Although most of the jobs referred to are not high-level, they do relate directly or indirectly to his career objective.*

RECENT
EXPERIENCE

1982–present	Instructor, athletic department, University of South Carolina. Duties: Organized and directed miscellaneous outdoor sports, including fishing, boat handling, hunting, and archery.

OTHER EXPERIENCE

1. Sold advertising space (part-time and summers) for a small local magazine (The Grand Strand), Myrtle Beach, S.C., 1976–1977.

2. Clerked at the Sportman's Place, Loris, S.C., in the summers of 1978, 1979, and 1981.

3. Worked at the Horry County Beacon, a weekly newspaper, in the summer of 1980 (feature writing, copy editing, proofreading, and make-up).

4. Earned money at various times repairing fishing rods (ferrules, grip, guides, and windings).

7. *He includes personal data and mentions his plans to marry. This is a matter of personal preference, but it is not inappropriate to do so.*

PERSONAL DATA

Height: 5 feet, 11 inches
Weight: 165 lbs.
Health: Excellent
Marital status: Single, but engaged to be married in December of this year.

8. *The references provided appear to be excellent choices.*

REFERENCES (by permission)

1. Dr. Sophia C. Levinthal
   Professor of Journalism
   University of South Carolina

2. Mr. Patrick L. Patton
   Athletic Director
   University of South Carolina

3. Mr. C. Raymond Dykstra
   Publisher
   Horry County <u>Beacon</u>
   Atlantic Beach, S.C. 29577

4. Mr. Harry M. Petrie (owner)
   The Sportsman's Place
   Loris, S.C. 29569

THE APPLICATION LETTER

If you have prepared a really good résumé, the hard work is done. Now you merely transmit the résumé by means of a personal letter. The main objective of both documents is to obtain an interview; few people are hired sight unseen, no matter how impressive the written description of their qualifications is. So your objective has been achieved if you get a letter or telephone call inviting you to come for an interview; it means that you looked good enough on paper to be seriously considered for the position.

People have different ideas about letters of application. Some letters are two or more pages long and loaded with self-promoting statements. Others consist of only a line or two, saying in effect, "Here's my résumé." We think something in between is best. Do not simply repeat what is in your résumé.

A good application letter, in our opinion, contains the following elements:

1. *How you learned about the vacancy (unless you're applying blind).*

2. *A brief statement as to why you are interested in the job and why you believe you qualify for it.*

3. *A request for a personal interview.*

4. *Information about where you can be reached.*

Caution: *Do not use your company letterhead, hotel stationery, or so on. Use plain white paper of high quality, with a matching envelope. The following application letters are to accompany the four résumés illustrated earlier.*

Situation

Russell Buchanan decides to write to the national sales manager of Kauffman Institutional Equipment Inc., whose name he obtained by telephoning the company in Milwaukee.

Analysis of the Letter

1. *Buchanan makes contact by referring to the AASA convention (Hewlett will know what this is), then applies for the job.*

2. *He then refers to his summary of qualifications, pointing out the important fact that he knows the education field from both the inside and outside.*

3. *In the third paragraph, Buchanan gives a good reason for wanting to be associated with Kauffman. Assuming he is completely honest, it is a very effective statement; nearly every company likes to think it is the best in its industry.*

4. *The reference to Sholes is wise. Even if Hewlett doesn't get in touch with Sholes, he will be impressed by Buchanan's confidence that his record at Horton-Miller will be praised by the top marketing person.*

5. *In the final paragraph, Buchanan asks for an interview and gives specific instructions on how he can be reached.*

The Letter

Dear Mr. Hewlett:

At the recent convention of the AASA in Detroit, I learned that Kauffman Institutional Equipment Inc. has an opening for a regional sales manager. Please consider me a candidate for the job.

A summary of my qualifications is enclosed. You will see that I have had several years' experience in education (teaching and administration) and in sales and sales administration, so I feel that I know the educational community from both the inside and the outside.

Ever since I first purchased Kauffman classroom equipment and later became acquainted with a number of your representatives, I have considered the Kauffman name synonymous with quality and style. It is with such an organization that I am eager to associate myself. Although I'm not an expert on your entire line, I'm quite familiar with much of it and, frankly, I think so highly of your products that I would consider it an honor to represent your company.

A. J. Sholes, the director of marketing at Horton-Miller Book Company, is aware that I am making application (you will see his name on my list of references) and has said that he would welcome a call from you if you wish to know more about me.

In the meantime, I would be glad to come to Milwaukee to see you whenever it is convenient. You may write to me either at my home or at Horton-Miller. If you wish to telephone me, you may call (312) 255-6000, which is the home office in Northbrook. The people there always know where to reach me.

Cordially yours,

30-6

APPLICATION LETTER FOR JOB RÉSUMÉ 30-2, page 242

Situation

Following is the application letter written by Dianne Seaton to accompany the résumé she prepared for the position of supervisor of office training. (The ad in *The Wall Street Journal* gave only a box number.)

Analysis of the Letter

1. *Seaton refers immediately to the ad in* The Wall Street Journal *and the specific job title.*

2. *Seaton then mentions the enclosed résumé, highlighting the experience and education that she believes are tailor-made for the position.*

3. *She explains briefly her original plans, but is quick to point out that it was actually fortunate that she chose the career she did. Notice that she does not hesitate to say that she thoroughly enjoys administrative office work and has a talent for it.*

4. *This leads to the admission of a preference for teaching, at which time she emphasizes her expertise in and liking for secretarial/office work, which make an excellent combination for the position advertised. She reveals her age—not necessary, but not inappropriate—and her desire for a new challenge.*

5. *Finally, Seaton volunteers to visit the company for an interview when it is convenient.*

The Letter

Ladies and Gentlemen:

This is my application for the position advertised in The Wall Street Journal (May 16) – supervisor of office training.

The résumé enclosed reveals five years of responsible secretarial and administrative office experience, a broad education that includes an academic degree, specialized training in secretarial science and related subjects, and teaching experience in classes designed expressly for working people.

You will see that my original plans were to teach history, but jobs in this area just didn't exist at the time I graduated; thus I chose a secretarial occupation where there were many opportunities. I am very glad I did. Not only do I enjoy being a part of the business world, I have learned that I have an unusual talent for administrative office work.

Yet the desire to teach remains. You will see that I have been teaching evening courses in word processing and related subjects during the past two years. I find teaching immensely exciting and rewarding—even more satisfying than my regular job.

I truly believe that responsible business experience, expertise in secretarial skills and procedures, and a sincere love of teaching make an ideal combination for the position you advertised. At age 28 I feel ready for a new challenge, and I hope you will offer that challenge to me.

Your ad indicated that the position is open in a large electronics firm in the Midwest. I would be pleased to visit the company at any time that would be convenient for you. May I hear from you?

Sincerely yours,

30-7

Situation

Frances Rosen decides to write the executive vice president of Farraday Plastics Manufacturing Company. This is the person to whom the director of public relations reports, according to her informant who told her about the imminent retirement of the current director.

Analysis of the Letter

1. *Rosen does not give the precise source of her information about the possible vacancy, since the individual who gave it to her did not want to be identified. Therefore, the phrase "It has come to my attention . . ." is appropriate.*

2. *She calls attention to her résumé, highlighting the things that are most relevant to the job applied for.*

3. *Rosen refers to the section of the résumé in which she presents her concept of the PR function. Indeed, the reason she wrote her philosophy on the résumé was to refer to it in the letter of application.*

4. *She explains that she wants to leave her present job only because it lacks the challenge she wants. This is good for two reasons: (a) Klaff will know that she is not just another disgruntled employee, and (b) it indicates that she has higher aspirations.*

5. *She asks for an interview and offers to adjust her schedule to fit Klaff's preference.*

The Letter

Dear Mr. Klaff:

It has come to my attention that your current director of public relations is on the verge of retirement, and that that position may be open shortly. If this is true, would you please consider this as my application for it.

The enclosed résumé indicates my broad experience in the area of public relations and management communications. It seems to me that this experience, together with my education (which continues), has given me ideal preparation to assume the role of the director of public relations in a firm such as yours. All of my professional experience has been in manufacturing organizations. My current employer, Regent Chemical Corporation, manufactures products closely allied to your own, so I am quite familiar with the kinds of issues and problems that your public relations people have to deal with.

I'd like to call your attention to page 2 of my résumé, on which I describe my concept of public relations. I am convinced that this function can make enormous contributions to growth and profits, and I am most eager to prove it to you.

Let me say that I have been very happy with my work at Regent Chemical Corporation. However, I see no opportunity in the near future to direct a full-scale public relations program (the present director is quite young and highly competent), and I am eager to become established with a large company where I can assume this broader responsibility.

May I have the privilege of an interview? If you will let me know when it is convenient for you to see me, I will arrange my calendar accordingly. You may telephone me on my private line (622-4418) or write to me at the address given.

Sincerely yours,

Situation

Leonard Lambeth accompanies his résumé with a letter of application. Professor Levinthal, who recommended that he apply for the job, supplied the name of the person to whom to write.

Analysis of the Letter

1. *Lambeth mentions Dr. Levinthal as the person who recommended that he apply for the job. This is an excellent way to establish rapport with the recipient.*

2. *In the second paragraph, he mentions what he has been doing since graduation, emphasizing his eagerness to get started in his chosen career—advertising.*

3. *Next, he calls attention to his education and, at the same time, his knowledge of and enthusiasm for outdoor sports. The reference to speaking the language of the outdoorsman is a very good idea.*

4. *Finally, Lambeth requests an interview and mentions his immediate availability. The last sentence adds a personal touch that is also a strong selling point: familiarity with the product.*

The Letter

Dear Mr. Reinheimer:

The position of assistant advertising manager of Southern Out-doorsman was called to my attention by Dr. Sophia Levinthal, professor of journalism at the University of South Carolina. It is upon her recommendation that I am sending you my application.

When I graduated from the university in 1982, I accepted a job in the athletic department as an instructor of various outdoor sports. After three years, I decided that I would never be content until I became launched on a career in the field in which I was trained—advertising.

As you will see in the enclosed résumé, I was an advertising major at the University of South Carolina, a program that I thoroughly enjoyed and did well in. The résumé will also reveal my knowledge of and enthusiasm for all outdoor sports—all those that interest your readers. Believe me, Mr. Reinheimer, I can speak their language.

I hope you will give me the opportunity to talk with you in person. I can come to Charleston at any time and am available to begin work at a moment's notice. Incidentally, I'm a regular reader of Southern Outdoorsman (including the ads), and I am confident that I can quickly become an effective member of your advertising staff.

Cordially yours,

OTHER EMPLOYMENT COMMUNICATIONS

You may have occasion to write six other types of employment communications: requesting permission to use a person's name as reference, follow-ups on job applications, accepting a job offer, declining a job offer, letters of recommendation, and letters of resignation. These are all covered in this section.

LETTERS PERTAINING TO REFERENCES

As mentioned earlier, always ask permission before you list a person's name as a reference on job applications. In some cases, you can do this by telephone, but in others you will find a letter necessary. Here are guidelines for permission letters:

---

1. *Describe your job-hunting plans.*
2. *Ask for permission to list the reader's name as a reference.*
3. *Express your appreciation for the favor.*
4. *Add any personal message you think is appropriate.*

When you have landed a job, you should write each of your references a letter of appreciation. Although you may not really know whether any of the references you supplied were contacted, the chances are good that they did receive an inquiry and said what you hoped they would. Here are some guidelines for such letters:

---

1. *Mention the position you obtained and your excitement about it.*
2. *Thank the reference for help, even though none may have been given.*
3. *Include any personal remarks that you think appropriate to the occasion.*

31-1

REQUESTING PERMISSION TO USE A PERSON AS A REFERENCE

Situation

Before Leonard Lambeth completed his job résumé (see page 246), he wrote to various people for permission to use their name as a reference. One was the publisher of the Horry County *Beacon*, for whom Lambeth worked one summer while attending college.

Analysis of the Letter

1. *Lambeth immediately asks for permission to use the recipient's name as a job reference. He then proceeds to bring Dykstra up to date on his activities since 1980. (He could have done the updating first, then asked for permission.)*

2. *He describes the job he is applying for and why he thinks he is qualified for it.*

3. *He refers to his work on the* Beacon *in the summer of 1980 and says he thinks the experience might be important to the prospective employer. He mentions the postcard enclosed.*

4. *Lambeth ends the letter on a personal note.*

The Letter

Dear Mr. Dykstra:

May I use your name as a reference for a job that I am interested in?

Let me bring you up to date. After I received my degree from the University of South Carolina in 1982 (my major was advertising), I accepted a job in the athletic department of the university as an instructor in outdoor sports. Now after three years I'm eager to get started in the advertising field.

The job I'm applying for is assistant advertising manager of Southern Outdoorsman in Charleston. I believe I have a good chance at it. I know I have the academic credentials, and, as you've heard so often, consider myself an "authority" on outdoor sports.

I think my experience on the Beacon (summer of 1980) could be very important, and I'd appreciate your support in case someone wants to make inquiry about me. A postcard is enclosed for your response.

Thanks—and leave some of the king mackerel for me!

Sincerely,

31-2 THANKING A REFERENCE

Situation

Leonard Lambeth (see previous letter) receives word from *Southern Outdoorsman* that he has been accepted, and he writes each of his references to relay the good news. One of the persons listed on his résumé is Dr. Sophia Levinthal, professor of journalism at the University of South Carolina.

Analysis of the Letter

1. *Lambeth announces the good news immediately and supplies other details.*

2. *Lambeth thanks Professor Levinthal for her help. He does not mention her letter of recommendation since he does not know whether she was asked to supply one, but the reference to his training will, if she wrote no letter, make the "thank you" meaningful.*

FOLLOW-UP LETTERS

The Letter

Dear Professor Levinthal:

I think you'll be pleased to know that I have been hired as assistant advertising manager of <u>Southern Outdoorsman</u>. I report to work July 21. This gives me a little time, and I hope to drop in to see you before I leave for Charleston.

At any rate, I want to thank you for your help. The job looks very challenging, but because of the thorough training I received at USC, together with your own informal coaching, I'm confident I can handle it.

Best wishes,

There are two instances when you may wish to write a follow-up letter on your application for employment:

1. When you have not heard within a reasonable time from the firm to which you applied.

2. When you want to call attention to something about your experience, education, activities, and so on, that was omitted from your résumé. (Often this is simply a ploy to increase your chances of being hired, which says, in effect, "I still want that job and think I am the right person for it. Don't forget me.")

Here are three guidelines for writing follow-up letters:

1. *Be brief.*
2. *Be tactful and courteous—don't pressure.*
3. *Reemphasize your interest in the position.*

31-3 FOLLOW-UP FOR REASON OF ELAPSED TIME

Situation

Russell Buchanan (see Job Résumé 30-1, page 240) receives an acknowledgment of his application for the job of regional sales manager, with the assurance that he will hear from the national sales manager "shortly." Two weeks go by and nothing happens. Buchanan decides to write a follow-up letter.

Analysis of the Letter

1. *Buchanan tactfully asks whether the position he applied for is still open (not "has been filled").*

2. *He expresses continued interest in the job, but asks for definite information soon so that he "can make appropriate plans" (meaning look for another opportunity).*

3. *The letter ends with a "thank you."*

The Letter

Dear Mr. Hewlett:

May I ask whether the position I applied for April 11 (regional sales manager) is still open?

I'm still greatly interested in the job and hope I'm still in the running for it. However, I would like to know right away so that I can make appropriate plans.

Thank you.

Very cordially yours,

31-4   FOLLOW-UP TO PRESENT ADDITIONAL INFORMATION

Situation

A few days after Frances Rosen (see Job Résumé 30-3, page 244) applies to Farraday Plastics Manufacturing Company, she decides to send a reprint of her recent article in the *Journal of Public Relations*. Although she could have attached it to her résumé, she decided to hold it and use it now as a follow-up device.

Analysis of the Letter

The purpose of the letter is merely to evoke further interest from Farraday in Rosen's qualifications. The objective is accomplished in as few words as possible. Nothing further needs to be said.

The Letter

Dear Mr. Klaff:

Right after I sent you my résumé, it occurred to me that you might like to see a copy of my article, "The Role of Public Relations in Corporate Planning," which appeared in the September issue of the Journal of Public Relations. It is enclosed.

Sincerely yours,

ACCEPTING A JOB OFFER

After the interview, you may receive a letter from the employer telling you that you have been selected for the position you applied for and asking you to report to work on a certain date. If the reporting date is, say, a couple of weeks hence, it's usually wise to write a letter accepting the job and saying you will report on the date suggested. This is a good idea, even if you are not asked to accept the job in writing, for it leaves no doubt that you're going to show up and expect the job to be held for you.

Guidelines for writing job-acceptance letters are as follows:

1. *Express your enthusiasm for the news.*
2. *Confirm the date you are to report to work with assurance that you will be there.*
3. *Indicate your anticipation in getting started.*

31-5 ACCEPTING A JOB OFFER

Situation

A week after Leonard Lambeth (see Job Résumé 30-4, page 246) is interviewed, he receives a letter from Mr. Reinheimer telling him the job is his and asking him to report to work in three weeks. Lambeth accepts the job by letter.

Analysis of the Letter

1. *Lambeth reveals his enthusiasm at the good news and accepts the position offered.*
2. *He then confirms the place, date, and time of reporting.*
3. *In the final paragraph, he shows his eagerness to get started.*

The Letter

Dear Mr. Reinheimer:

Your letter brought wonderful news. I am delighted to accept the position of assistant advertising manager of <u>Southern Outdoorsman.</u>

As you suggested, I will report to the medical department at 9 a.m. on July 21 and then proceed directly to your office.

I thoroughly enjoyed meeting you and the others on your staff, and I really look forward to joining you.

Sincerely yours,

REJECTING A JOB OFFER

It sometimes happens that after people have received a letter in which they are offered a position they applied for, they have changed their minds. Maybe the present boss learned about their plans to leave and came across with a promotion, or after they left the interview, they unexpectedly received a better offer from another firm, or they were not favorably impressed with what they saw when they were interviewed, or there may be other reasons. When you decide not to accept a job offer, it is common courtesy to tactfully decline in writing.

Letters rejecting job offers are often difficult to write. Follow these guidelines:

1. *Express your appreciation for the offer.*
2. *Give the reason why you must decline. (Here you must be very careful. Obviously, you don't want to say, "I don't think I'd like working for you," even if that's your real reason. Nor will you say, "I've found something that pays a lot more." We'll supply examples of what your message might look like.)*
3. *End on a pleasant note, such as saying something favorable about the company or the people you met at the interview.*

31-6 REJECTING A JOB OFFER— BETTER OPPORTUNITY

Situation

Linda Parish applies to a large insurance company for the position of systems analyst. She receives notice that she has been selected for the job. In the meantime, however, a new position is offered in the publishing company where she is presently employed. It is not only a better job (including salary), but she is certain that she likes publishing better than she would like insurance. She declines the offer.

Analysis of the Letter

1. *Parish expresses appreciation for the offer.*

2. *She then proceeds to describe the promotion she has just received, emphasizing the opportunity it offers. Note that there is no mention of a bigger salary or her preference for publishing over insurance. Nothing would be gained by it.*

3. *She ends with a "thank you" and a warm sign-off.*

The Letter

Dear Mrs. Weiman:

I appreciate your letter offering me the position of systems analyst which I recently applied for.

Shortly after I arrived back at my office from my visit with you, I was told by our administrative vice president that I was being promoted to the position of manager of computer services. It is an excellent opportunity (which came as a complete surprise), and one that I feel I cannot pass up. Therefore, I must decline your generous offer.

Thank you for all the courtesies extended me. I enjoyed my brief visit with you.

Yours very cordially,

31-7

REJECTING A JOB OFFER— NO INTEREST IN THE POSITION

Situation

Kenneth Bianca, purchasing manager for a small manufacturer of electronic parts in a suburb of Seattle, receives an inquiry about his availability as purchasing director for a large business machines manufacturer in St. Louis. Bianca is interviewed and eventually offered the job. However, he does not like the structure of the company or the job description, so he decides to decline the offer.

Analysis of the Letter

1. *Bianca expresses appreciation for the offer.*

2. *In the second paragraph, he declines the offer; his liking for his present job and lifestyle are his reasons. No purpose would be served by pointing out that he doesn't like Calumet's structure or the job.*

3. *Bianca then expresses thanks and extends regards to all the people he met.*

The Letter

Dear Louis:

I am flattered by your offer of the position of purchasing director of Calumet Inc. It is very generous.

After giving the matter much thought and discussing it with my family, I have come to the conclusion that I should stay where I am. Certainly, the opportunity to work with such a prestigious firm as Calumet is most attractive. On the other hand, I do enjoy my work here at Electronics Unlimited immensely, and I guess you might say we are "addicted" to the Seattle area and the lifestyle it affords.

Thank you for your confidence in me and for the opportunity to meet with you, Jim, Alice, and Quincy in St. Louis. My best regards to all.

Cordially yours,

LETTERS OF RESIGNATION

When you resign from a position, there is no rule that says you must write a letter of resignation. Certainly, if you're leaving in a rage and can think of no way to conceal it, then don't write. Just tell your boss you're leaving and why (if asked). It's just not wise to leave on record an angry message with your name on it; it may very well haunt you later.

But if you want to write a letter of resignation—whether it's a genuinely friendly separation or one that has negative overtones—that's up to you. If you have regrets about leaving the company, the letter gives you the opportunity to express appreciation for the breaks you received, your high opinion of the people, and so on—a good gesture that certainly can't hurt you. On the other hand, you may have been bypassed for a promotion you expected, and you may want to register your disappointment in writing simply for the record. In this case, we recommend that you express your feelings in a straightforward manner, but avoid namecalling and vituperation.

31-8

LETTER OF RESIGNATION—DISLIKE FOR TRAVEL

Situation

Craig Sherman has been a traveling sales representative for an appliance manufacturer for nearly eighteen months. Although he enjoys meeting with dealers and likes the company he works for, he objects to being away from home several weeks at a time. He has discussed the problem with the sales manager, Gerald Bergstrom, several times, but of course the job requirements cannot be altered, and there are no inside positions that appeal to him. He decides to resign in writing.

Analysis of the Letter

1. In the first paragraph, Craig mentions his decision to resign, indicating that it will not be a surprise to his boss. Note the phrase, "at your convenience but not later than June 12." This means that Craig is willing to leave at once if Bergstrom has a replacement.

2. In the second paragraph, he first emphasizes his liking for the company and its people, then indicates that this fact does not compensate for the hardships of traveling.

3. Craig then reveals his thinking about future plans, which lets Bergstrom know that he (Craig) is not planning to join a competitor.

4. Finally, he expresses appreciation for courtesies extended.

5. Craig is confident that Bergstrom thinks well of him. Therefore, the "P.S." is a good opportunity to ask for permission to use Bergstrom's name as a reference.

The Letter

Dear Jerry:

I am sure it will come as no surprise to you that I wish to resign my position as a sales representative, effective at your convenience, but not later than June 12.

You are fully aware of my problem, Jerry. Although I like the company and the people I work with, being on the road for weeks at a time does not appeal to me. I think the situation would be entirely different if I were single or even married with no children. But with two youngsters (2 and 4 years old), traveling represents a real hardship on me and especially on my wife Gretchen. After each trip it gets increasingly harder for me to tear myself away from my family to go back on the road.

I really have no plans at the moment. I need to take some time to think about what I want to do. I may try to get back into coaching, and I'm also considering buying into a local sporting goods store. Whatever I wind up doing, it will have to be something that will permit me to stay anchored in one place.

Thank you for everything you have done for me. I really don't know how I could have received better treatment from a company or a manager.

Sincerely,

P.S.   In case I need a reference, may I use your name? I would very much appreciate it.

31-9

LETTER OF RESIGNATION— NO OPPORTUNITY FOR GROWTH

Situation

Helen Leavitt has been administrative assistant to Raymond Durward for three years. She quickly proved to be an excellent assistant, and frequent salary increases attest to her boss's high opinion of her. However, Durward is one of those people who will not delegate responsibility, and Leavitt is eager to assume the duties of a bona fide administrative assistant. She has discussed the matter several times with Durward, but only got noncommittal responses, such as "I'm happy with what you're doing—why change things?" Finally, she decides to resign and writes Durward, giving the reasons for her action.

Analysis of the Letter

1. *Leavitt announces her resignation immediately, suggesting an effective date (typically, this is two or three weeks in advance of leaving).*

2. *In the second paragraph, she explains precisely why she is not satisfied with her present position. Although her remarks are not bitter, she shows a firm determination "to grow professionally as well as financially."*

3. *She next mentions her conversations with placement counselors and the encouragement they gave her. (Leavitt is not required to reveal this information, of course, but we think that such a confession adds strength to her resolve.)*

4. *Finally, she thanks Durward for his help and personal kindnesses.*

The Letter

Dear Mr. Durward:

Please consider this as my resignation from my position as your administrative assistant, effective August 10.

Although I have enjoyed working with you and have learned a great deal, I would really like to operate in a wider management sphere, and since you have not been willing to provide this opportunity, I feel that I should seek a position that allows greater freedom to make decisions and to function more independently. As you know, my job has not changed in the three years I have been with you. Although you have been very fair in terms of compensation, I feel the need to grow professionally as well as financially.

I have discussed my management aspirations with two placement counselors in Portland, and both stressed the accelerated demand for women management trainees in various areas. So I think I'll have no difficulty finding what I want.

Thank you for all your help and your many personal kindnesses.

Sincerely,

31-10

LETTER OF RESIGNATION—BYPASSED FOR PROMOTION

Analysis of the Letter

1. *Michaels submits his resignation "at once," which is clearly his privilege in this unhappy situation, and tells why the letter is being sent to Spanswick.*

2. *He then describes the circumstances that led him to believe that he was slated for promotion when the financial vice president's job became vacant.*

3. *In the third paragraph, Michaels pays tribute to Spanswick, but in the same breath makes it known that he does not "buy" Spanswick's reason for bypassing him and the other two managers. The tone is blunt, but we think this is entirely justifiable here.*

4. *Finally, he alludes to the pleasant experiences at Mariposa Industries, but expresses the conviction that Spanswick will understand his decision.*

Note: Spanswick may have had good reasons for not naming Michaels to the vacated position. If so, they should have been revealed long before H-hour so that Michaels would have had an opportunity to overcome his deficiencies. The reason given by Spanswick is spurious, and under similar circumstances many people would, upon hearing it, simply clear their desks and walk out. Michaels wants his resentment on record, and there's nothing wrong with that.

Situation

Lewis Michaels is one of three department managers (all on an equal level) reporting to the financial vice president, C. J. Spanswick. During the five years he has been with the company, Michaels has had several job offers at a better salary, but each time Spanswick has urged him to stay on. "You're doing a great job, Lew," Spanswick would say, hinting that he would have the first shot at Spanswick's job if it became vacant. But when Spanswick moves up to treasurer of the corporation, the vacancy is filled by an individual outside the company. The explanation given by Spanswick to the three department managers is: "You're all three indispensable in the jobs you have now—it's much easier to replace me than any of you." Michaels decides to resign, giving specific reasons for doing so.

The Letter

Dear C. J.:

Please consider this as my resignation effective at once. I am writing to you rather than to the new financial vice president because I want you to know exactly how I feel.

You will recall that during the five years I have been on your staff, I have had offers from several companies, all of which promised better compensation and greater responsibilities. On each occasion, I discussed the situation with you and you gave me reason to believe that I would replace you, if and when you moved up. I confess that you did not actually say, "You're the next financial vice president, Lew," but that is the distinct impression I got from our conversations.

Your promotion to treasurer of the corporation came as no surprise; certainly, no one is better qualified than you for that position. The genuine surprise was that, instead of choosing one of your three department managers to replace you, you selected an individual from outside the company. I'm sorry that I cannot accept your reasoning—that we're indispensable in our present jobs; this would mean that a person can be penalized for doing <u>too</u> good a job. Clearly, this would mean that I can have no hopes for promotion here.

I leave Mariposa Industries with many pleasant memories; the experience has been rewarding in many ways. Under the circumstances, however, I'm certain you will fully understand the reason for my decision.

Cordially yours,

263

31-11

LETTER OF RESIGNATION— BETTER JOB OFFER

Situation

Frances Rosen (see Letter 30-7 on page 251) has been named director of public relations at Farraday Plastics Manufacturing Company. Before accepting the position, she discusses it with her boss at Regent Chemical Corporation for whom she has a high regard. She receives his encouragement and congratulations and decides to write a personal letter shortly before her departure to express appreciation for courtesies and friendship.

Analysis of the Letter

1. *Because Rosen has been genuinely happy with her work at Regent Chemical, this is not so much a letter of resignation as an expression of appreciation.*

2. *She recounts her reasons for being in the boss's debt and expresses the hope that they will continue to be friends.*

3. *A copy notation is going to the president of Regent Chemical, which is a courtesy gesture on behalf of her boss.*

The Letter

Dear Whit:

Before taking my leave next Tuesday, I want to acknowledge with deep thanks your many kindnesses to me during the years I worked with you.

It's not everyone who has a boss who is consistently cooperative, generous, and understanding, and I feel that I've been blessed. Not only have I enjoyed working with you; I have learned how a really good public relations department should be run. It's really because of the training I received from you that I feel qualified to undertake my new assignment.

My best wishes to you always. Don't be surprised to get some telephone calls from me, asking for advice and perhaps a sympathetic broad shoulder. If I can return any of the many favors you gave me, all you have to do is pick up the telephone and dial 333-5649.

Sincerely,

cc: A. J. Merriam

31-12

LETTER OF RESIGNATION—PERSONAL CONFLICT

Situation

Walter Prevatte is an internal auditor for Bridewell Enterprises, where he has worked for three years. Although he has progressed financially at a satisfactory rate and therefore assumes that he is valued by his boss, J. Richard Allender, Prevatte gets no satisfaction from his work. Allender is demanding, demeaning, cold, and often verbally abusive—one of those executives who "knows it all" and refuses to give credit to subordinates for brains or ideas.

Prevatte decides to resign. In his letter of resignation, however, he believes it best not to reveal the real reason (Allender). Although it would feel good to get some things off his chest, he thinks he would lose rather than gain by doing so. So he decides to announce the decision to resign without revealing animosity toward anyone.

Analysis of the Letter

1. The writer indicates that this decision was reached only after much thought. This is not necessarily untrue, even though the reference to "soul-searching" could be to the agonies inherent in the job.

2. The writer does not, however, commit himself to a definite course of action; he is merely "thinking about applying to graduate school." Thus, if he immediately applies for another internal auditing position and Allender is contacted for a recommendation, Prevatte can always say that he changed his mind.

3. An effective departure date is suggested, but the offer is made to extend the date by two weeks, or, if more convenient, to depart earlier than June 30. This should tell Allender that Prevatte really wants to be cooperative.

The Letter

Dear Richard:

After considerable thought and soul-searching, I have decided to resign my position as internal auditor at Bridewell Enterprises. I assure you it was not an easy decision to make.

Perhaps you have heard me mention on occasion that I would like to have my own accounting business. Ever since I graduated from Rutgers, this has been my long-range goal. I am thinking of applying to a graduate business school to earn an MBA in accounting and eventually to sit for the CPA exam.

I suggest an effective date of June 30. If, however, you would like more time to find a replacement, I am willing to extend that date by two weeks. On the other hand, if you feel that an earlier departure would be more convenient to you, I will certainly understand.

I value the experience I have received at Bridewell Enterprises. I'm confident that it will be very useful to me in my accounting career.

Sincerely yours,

PART 11

SOCIAL CORRESPONDENCE

Social correspondence includes formal and informal invitations, formal and informal acceptances and regrets, and expressions of appreciation for hospitality and special favors (often called "bread-and-butter" letters). Although such communications would seem to be appropriate only for books on etiquette, the fact is that many are business related.

Several formal and informal messages are illustrated in this part. Guidelines for their preparation are given in the analysis of each communication.

SECTION 32

FORMAL INVITATIONS AND RESPONSES

Business firms and other organizations often issue formal invitations to special events—a reception to honor a new president, a dinner to recognize outstanding achievements or anniversaries of employees, an open house to celebrate the organization's anniversary, a banquet to honor some dignitary, a reception to announce a merger of two companies and introduce key personnel to one another, and so on. Such invitations are often printed or engraved on stationery similar to that of a formal wedding announcement. Some ask for a response (R.S.V.P.) which, if no response card is included with the invitation, generally requires a formal note of acceptance or regrets.

Situation

Rothmoor University has appointed a new president who will take office in late summer. A formal invitation is sent to the alumni of the university and other important people to attend a reception in the president-elect's honor.

Analysis of the Invitation

1. *The invitation is printed in black on high-quality white paper of postcard weight. A popular size is 4¼ by 4½ inches, although a number of different sizes may be used.*

2. *The placement of the message varies, but note that each line is centered.*

3. *The envelope is usually hand-addressed, and there is often a card of the same quality as the invitation, enclosed with the following message:*

   "I will _____ will not _____ attend the reception for President-elect Cleverdon on Thursday, June 2. Name_____"

4. *A stamped, self-addressed envelope is enclosed for mailing the card.*

5. *If no reply card is provided and it is not clear to whom the acceptance or regret is to be sent, this information will appear as follows: "R.S.V.P. Dean of Faculty"*

The Invitation

THE BOARD OF TRUSTEES AND THE FACULTY

of

ROTHMOOR UNIVERSITY

invite you to attend a reception

in honor of

DR. MARTHA SILLS CLEVERDON

President-elect

to be held in American Women Patriots Hall

on the Campus

Thursday evening, June 2

at half after eight o'clock

R.S.V.P.
Dean of Faculty

32-2

FORMAL INVITATION TO AN ANNUAL BANQUET

Situation

The Lakeport Business Council in Support of the Arts invites members and special guests to its annual banquet meeting by a formal printed invitation.

Analysis of the Invitation

1. *The stationery and the setup are similar to the invitation on page 269.*

2. *The notation "Black Tie" means formal wear (tuxedos for men and evening gowns for women).*

3. *Note that the response can be made by telephone, and the person's name and number appear under "R.S.V.P."*

The Invitation

THE LAKEPORT BUSINESS COUNCIL IN SUPPORT OF THE ARTS

cordially invites you to its

Annual Meeting and Banquet

at the Lakeport Country Club

on Saturday, May 8, at half after six o'clock

featuring

Anton Michetti, Director of the Pine State Symphony

speaking on "What Is Good Music?"

and a special performance by the

Abelard String Quartet

R.S.V.P.   Black Tie
Pamela Webster
258-4417

32-3 ACCEPTING A FORMAL INVITATION

Situation

Cynthia Dolan, vice president of a pharmaceutical house, receives a formal invitation from the National Medical Research Foundation to a reception in honor of Dr. Ormond Shipley, who has received the foundation's annual award for outstanding medical research. Although the invitation included an R.S.V.P., there is no card enclosed for the response. Dolan accepts the invitation.

Analysis of the Acceptance

The response is handwritten on a blank, high-quality card or a social note sheet either monogrammed or blank. If the sheet contains her full name, Dolan can begin the acceptance as follows:

"I accept with pleasure your kind invitation to a reception . . ."

Then she signs her name below the message.

The Acceptance

Cynthia Dolan
accepts with pleasure
the kind invitation of
The National Medical Research Foundation
to a reception in honor of
Dr Ormond Shipley
on Wednesday, the fifth of December
at five-thirty o'clock
The Century Club

ACCEPTING A FORMAL INVITATION WITH A QUALIFICATION

Situation

Janette Reichel, an executive, and her husband Kenneth receive a formal invitation from the parents of Janette's administrative assistant to a party to announce their daughter's engagement. The social hour begins at four o'clock, followed by dinner at seven o'clock. The Reichels will attend the social hour, but because of a previous engagement, cannot remain for dinner.

Analysis of the Acceptance

The message may be handwritten on a plain white card or note sheet. Note that the acceptance precedes the regrets.

The Acceptance

Janette and Kenneth Reichel
are pleased to accept the kind invitation of
Mr and Mrs. Overstreet
to the party on Sunday, May fifteenth, at four o'clock.
Because of a previous engagement
we sincerely regret that we will be unable
to remain for dinner following the social hour

32-5 EXPRESSING REGRETS TO A FORMAL INVITATION

Situation

JoAnne and Wilford Roos receive a formal invitation to a dinner-dance, but must decline because they will be out of the country on the date of the affair.

Analysis of the Regrets

Again, the regrets are handwritten on formal stationery. Note there is no need to indicate the nature of the occasion or the location.

The Regrets

Wilford and JoAnne Roos
sincerely regret
that because they will be in Mexico City all of September
they are unable to accept
Mr. and Mrs. Guilford's
kind invitation for the twelfth of September

SECTION 33

INFORMAL INVITATIONS
AND RESPONSES

Arrangements for informal parties, dinners, and other get-togethers are, more often than not, made by telephone or by face-to-face meetings in the office. Depending on the occasion, some people prefer to send written invitations, either on social stationery or a special executive letterhead.

Generally, responses to written invitations are also handwritten.

INFORMAL INVITATION TO DINNER

Situation

Edward Agajanian, executive vice president of a corporation, and his wife Peggy are having a farewell dinner in their home for Ted and Virginia Novak (Novak is a subordinate of Agajanian) prior to the Novaks' departure for a foreign assignment. Ten couples, friends of the Novaks, are being invited.

Analysis of the Invitation

1. *Some executives have personal stationery that can be used for messages such as this, with either the business or home address (or both). Usually it is smaller than standard letter-head size—either Monarch (7¼ by 10¼ inches) or Baronial (5½ by 8½ inches). The stock is sometimes tinted—light tan, gray, and so on.*

2. *The message may be typewritten since it is a social-business event as opposed to a purely social one. For the same reason, the letter appropriately comes from Edward Agajanian, rather than from Peggy.*

3. *At a farewell dinner, anniversary event, or similar occasion, it is usually wise to indicate whether a gift is expected.*

4. *To reduce the business flavor of such a message, the inside address may appear below the letter.*

The Invitation

EDWARD G. AGAJANIAN
Old Mill Creek Road
Princeton, New Jersey 08540

Dear Ruth and Cliff:

Peggy and I would like it very much if you would be our guests at dinner on August 9 at seven o'clock. It's an informal farewell party for Ted and Virginia Novak who, as you know, will be leaving in a few weeks for Hong Kong, where Ted will be the managing director of our new office there. We're inviting ten couples, all of whom are special friends of the Novaks.

I know that Ted and Virginia would be delighted to have you in the group, as would we. By the way, it's not a surprise and no gifts are expected.

Will you call me or Peggy if you <u>can't</u> come? Otherwise, we'll be expecting you. My office number is 997-2174 and our home number is 457-6120.

Yours,

Mr. and Mrs. C. H. Renfro
120 Cedar Drive East
Briarcliff Manor, New York 10510

ACCEPTING AN INFORMAL INVITATION

Situation

During the week of April 11, Dr. Russell Chancellor and his wife Maureen will attend a medical convention in Seattle. Old friends of the couple who live in Seattle have written a note inviting them to dinner at a downtown restaurant, followed by attendance at a performance of the Seattle Symphony.

Analysis of the Letter

1. The letter is written by hand on either plain social stationery or a personal letterhead.

2. Note that Maureen tells Grace and Milt where she and Russ will be staying in Seattle. This is always a good idea in case there is any change in plans.

Note: The letter may be written by either of the Chancellors.

The Letter

Dear Grace and Milt,

How nice of you to invite Russ and me to dinner on April 14 when we are in Seattle and to attend a performance by the Seattle Symphony. We're delighted to accept.

It will be wonderful seeing both of you again. We're stopping at the Sheraton, and I'll give you a ring when we are settled in. Seattle will be a new experience for me, and I'm really looking forward to it.

Affectionately,
Maureen

33-3 EXPRESSING REGRETS TO AN INFORMAL INVITATION

Situation

Agatha and Culver Wisniewski receive an informal invitation from friends for a weekend of skiing. They are unable to accept.

Analysis of the Letter

This letter can come from either Agatha or Culver Wisniewski. It should be handwritten either on plain social stationery or a "Mr. and Mrs." letterhead. Note its informality.

The Letter

Dear Cindy and Ed —

Culver and I wish so much that we could accept your invitation to join you in Steamboat Springs the weekend of February 16. Unfortuneately, we cannot. Ed's family is having a big reunion that weekend in Salt Lake City, which is really a must for both of us.

We'll be thinking of you and the rest of the gang. Both of us have happy memories of our numerous stays at Wynward's Chalet and hope you'll ask us again one day. Have fun!

Fondly,
Agatha

SECTION 34

"BREAD-AND-BUTTER" LETTERS

All of us learn at a very early age to say "thank you" to people who do us a favor. Ninety-nine times out a hundred, we can express our appreciation in person or by a telephone call.

There are certain special occasions, however, when a "bread-and-butter" letter is required. Two examples are given in this section.

34-1

EXPRESSING THANKS FOR A PERSONAL FAVOR

Situation

Lou Aldridge, an assistant purchasing manager, is discussing his summer vacation plans with Len Rogoff, the sales representative for a long-time supplier. "This year," Lou tells his friend, "Beth and I are going to take the boys on a trip through New England—you know, a little camping and fishing, sightseeing, and the like." "That sounds great," Len says, "Millie and I have a small lakefront cottage near Bridgton, Maine. You're welcome to use it if you're headed in that direction." Lou quickly accepts the invitation, and upon returning home writes Len a letter of thanks.

Analysis of the Letter

The letter can be written on plain paper or on the company letterhead (we prefer the former), and it may be handwritten or typewritten, depending on how personal Aldridge wants to make it. In any event, he is appropriately warm, grateful, and whimsical.

The Letter

Dear Len:

Here's the key to "Rogoff's Retreat," along with my deepest thanks for allowing us to stay there. We spent a couple of days and three nights there—easily one of the best memories of our trip.

The boys became fairly expert in maneuvering that 3½ horsepower motor boat around the lake and even caught a few pickerel of respectable size. Cathy and I mostly swam, sunned, and lolled on that breezy screened-in porch, catching up on our reading, crossword puzzles, and napping. It was a great interlude for all of us. Even Fitz, the dog, was reluctant to leave—too much fun yapping at the ducks that dropped in on us every day.

It was very generous of you and Millie to lend us "Rogoff's Retreat," and we're mighty grateful.

Best regards,

P.S. I think I fixed that drip in the outdoor shower you spoke about. I fully intended to mow the lawn, but the machine simply coughed a few times, proving (to no one's surprise) that dad doesn't know a lot about motors.

34-2 EXPRESSING THANKS FOR GENEROUS HOSPITALITY

Situation

Peter Hostler is a buyer of men's clothing for a department store in Dayton. On a recent buying trip to New York (accompanied by his wife Lisa), the couple is given royal treatment by Bernard Jacobi, a sales representative for a men's apparel manufacturer. Upon returning home, Hostler writes a letter of appreciation.

Analysis of the Letter

1. *In the first paragraph, Hostler mentions the memorable afternoon and evening.*

2. *He then points out each of the treats they received, showing that none was forgotten.*

3. *The letter ends on a business-social note and with a hearty "thank you."*

The Letter

Dear Bernie:

Lisa and I are still talking about the great afternoon and evening you gave us in New York. It is an occasion that will be long remembered.

Although you probably take New York in stride, everything we saw and did was a grand adventure: the boat trip around Manhattan Island, cocktails at the top of the World Trade Center, dinner at The Four Seasons, the Broadway revival of our favorite musical, "Camelot," and finally the famous cheesecake at Lindy's.

The buying trip was very successful, and my boss was immensely pleased with my selections. Never again will I believe the old adage, "You can't mix business with pleasure." You provided the pleasure—and, incidentally, some of the business. Thank you!

Sincerely,

INDEX

ABOUT THE AUTHOR

Roy W. Poe was a publishing executive for over twenty years, specializing in business books for one of the country's largest publishers. He has also been a government training supervisor, an associate dean of a collegiate school of business, a president of a small college, and has taught communications in secondary schools, colleges, university extension classes, and management development programs. A business education consultant, Mr. Poe also is the author of *The McGraw-Hill Guide to Effective Business Reports*, in addition to several business textbooks.